Evidence and the Politics of Reform

Evidence and the Politics of Reform

Lessons from Indonesia's Social Welfare Development

SUDARNO SUMARTO

OXFORD
UNIVERSITY PRESS

OXFORD
UNIVERSITY PRESS

Oxford University Press is a department of the University of Oxford.
It furthers the University's objective of excellence in research, scholarship,
and education by publishing worldwide. Oxford is a registered trade mark of
Oxford University Press in the UK and in certain other countries.

Published in the United States of America by Oxford University Press
198 Madison Avenue, New York, NY 10016, United States of America.

Library of Congress Cataloging-in-Publication Data
Names: Sumarto, Sudarno, 1960- author
Title: Evidence and the politics of reform / Sudarno Sumarto.
Description: New York, NY : Oxford University Press, [2026] |
Includes bibliographical references and index.
Identifiers: LCCN 2026005367 (print) | LCCN 2026005368 (ebook) |
ISBN 9780197831687 hardback | ISBN 9780197831694 epub | ISBN 9780197831717
Subjects: LCSH: Public welfare—Indonesia | Indonesia—Social policy |
Indonesia—Social conditions
Classification: LCC HV403 .S925 2026 (print) | LCC HV403 (ebook)
LC record available at https://lccn.loc.gov/2026005367
LC ebook record available at https://lccn.loc.gov/2026005368

DOI: 10.1093/9780197831717.001.0001

Printed by Marquis Book Printing, Canada

The manufacturer's authorized representative in the EU for product safety is
Oxford University Press España S.A. of El Parque Empresarial San Fernando de Henares,
Avenida de Castilla, 2 - 28830 Madrid (www.oup.es/en or product.safety@oup.com).
OUP España S.A. also acts as importer into Spain of products made by the manufacturer.

MIX
Paper | Supporting responsible forestry
FSC® C103567
FSC
www.fsc.org

For my parents, Yitmo Sumarto and Hana Rumini — with gratitude for your love and sacrifices.

Contents

List of Figures

List of Tables

Preface

My journey in the field of public policy began in 1987 when I joined the Center for Policy and Implementation Studies (CPIS), a think tank under President Suharto's (1968–1998) economic team after completing my bachelor's degree in Economics. CPIS played a pivotal role in providing evidence-based recommendations that supported the economic successes of Suharto's 'New Order' regime. While Suharto's government is often remembered for its authoritarianism, it also pioneered evidence-based policies that significantly reduced inflation, improved education, achieved rice self-sufficiency, and lowered poverty rates. After working at CPIS for approximately three years, I received a scholarship to pursue my PhD in Economics at a university in the United States. Upon my graduation in 1996, I returned to CPIS to continue its mission in informing policy with evidence until the 1997–1998 Asian Financial Crisis.

In the wake of the economic crisis, I joined the World Bank to help establish the Social Monitoring and Early Response Unit (SMERU). Created during Indonesia's most severe economic downturn in its modern history, SMERU initially focused on assessing the social impact of the 14% economic contraction in 1998 and identifying appropriate policy responses. In 2001, the unit evolved into The SMERU Research Institute, an independent, non-profit think tank, structured with standard administrative, research, and financial divisions. I served as its director from 2001 to 2009, during which SMERU broadened its mission beyond post-crisis recovery to addressing long-term issues such as poverty mapping, decentralization, labor policy, and social protection. Through rigorous empirical research and active engagement with government institutions and international donors, such as the AusAID, World Bank, and the Ford Foundation, SMERU became a key contributor to national and local policymaking, influencing legislation, program design, and service delivery in sectors like education, health, and welfare.

In 2010, having worked in social policy research for 15 years, I was invited by Vice President Boediono (2009–2014) to join the TNP2K under his office. The TNP2K itself was a government think tank, which initially focused on improving social assistance targeting and the delivery of poverty alleviation programs. With support from the Australian Department of Foreign Affairs and Trade, the TNP2K could hire professional staff members, produce robust evidence to support sound policymaking, collaborate with international institutions to enrich global social policy discourse, and later broaden its focus to support reform in other areas of welfare policy.

The path to reform in Indonesia—and other places as a matter of fact—has been neither simple nor linear. As an economist with over two decades of experience in policymaking in Indonesia, I have come to understand that crafting effective policies involves more than selecting theoretically optimal solutions. It requires the art of balancing rigorous research, strategic political maneuvering, and an acute understanding of institutional and human dynamics.

Beyond just a collection of cases or a personal memoir, I invite the book's readers to reconsider the role of evidence in shaping policy. It challenges conventional wisdom about evidence-based policy making by highlighting Indonesia's experiences. Through these chapters, I argue that trust, political acumen, and adaptability are as crucial as academic insight in producing evidence and translating it into workable policy. By examining Indonesia's social welfare development, this book contributes to a broader understanding of how complex reforms unfold in dynamic political landscapes. It offers valuable lessons for policy makers, scholars, and anyone interested in the art and science of policy reform in a rapidly changing world. Though my stories are geographically bounded, I believe that the lessons that come out of these stories will resonate beyond Indonesia.

Thank you for accepting my invitation. This manuscript was completed in May 2025 and slightly revised ahead of its publication in April 2026.

Sudarno Sumarto
May 2025, Cambridge MA

Acknowledgments

Writing this book has been one of the most rewarding journeys of my life—one that would not have been possible without the support, wisdom, and encouragement of many remarkable individuals. I am deeply grateful to everyone who has walked alongside me, offering their time and insight, and having faith in this work. Although space limits prevent me from naming everyone who contributed, I would like to take a moment to acknowledge a few individuals whose support proved especially influential throughout this journey.

First and foremost, my deepest gratitude goes to my wife, Wiwik Widowati, whose patience, strength, and unwavering love have carried both our family and me through this journey. While I was away in Cambridge, she held everything together in Semarang with incredible grace and resilience. Those final two months we spent together in Cambridge, as I completed this manuscript, were especially valuable. To our children—Jesita Wida Ajani, pursuing her dreams at Oxford; and Hanna Wida Kiana and Adrien Wida Devachandra, each building their own futures in Jakarta—thank you for being a steady source of support and inspiration. Your love and understanding have reminded me of what matters most.

My journey into policymaking was profoundly shaped by the opportunity to serve under Vice President Boediono at TNP2K. I am deeply grateful for the privilege of working with him and the entire TNP2K team, especially Bambang Widianto, Suahasil Nazara, Elan Satriawan, and Suprayoga Hadi. I would also like to thank Andie Megantara and Nunung Nuryantono at the Coordinating Ministry for Human Development and Cultural Affairs. These are the individuals I have had the honor of working with over the years, and I thank them for their commitment to evidence-based decision-making in public policy, even in the face of challenges.

I am deeply grateful to Lant Pritchett, whose early encouragement and belief in the value of this story and its relevance beyond Indonesia—and my ability to tell it—helped transform a nascent idea into a fully realized book. I am equally thankful to Scott Guggenheim, Elan Satriawan, Rema

Hanna, and Benjamin Olken for their invaluable support throughout the development of this book. I am especially indebted to Scott and Rema for their thoughtful and constructive feedback, which significantly enriched both the structure and content of several chapters.

I would also like to express my heartfelt thanks to Zahra Amalia Syarifah for her dedication, insight, and unwavering support throughout the entire course of this project. From early research and interviews to shaping and refining the manuscript, her thoughtful contributions were integral at every stage. Her commitment to the work—and to the story it seeks to tell—was vital to bringing this book to completion. I would also like to express my sincere gratitude to Ardi Adji, Adama Bah, Herman Palani, Taufik Hidayat, Hendratno Tuhiman, Goldy Dharmawan, Priadi Asmanto, Gracia Hadiwidjaja, Siti Nurfitriah Farah Dewi, Wisnu Setiadi Nugroho, and Jovanni Enralin Silalahi for their valuable support in providing essential data and for their contributions to the implementation of key aspects of our research project that were fundamental to this book.

Bridging research into policy—the central story of this book—has required close collaboration with many government stakeholders. I would like to express my sincere appreciation to Badan Perencanaan Pembangunan Nasional (Bappenas), particularly Vivy Yulaswati, Maliki, and Pungky Sumadi; Badan Pusat Statistik (BPS), especially Kecuk Suharyanto, Nurma Midayanti, Ateng Hartono, and Rusman Heriawan; the Ministry of Education, especially Suharti; the Ministry of Trade, particularly Mari Elka Pangestu; and the Ministry of Finance, especially Sri Mulyani Indrawati and Chatib Basri. Their invaluable support and engagement have been instrumental in generating robust evidence and advancing our research as a key input into policy formulation and adoption.

I am deeply thankful to Hal Hill for his intellectual partnership and for his trust and belief in my work. His insight and steady encouragement strengthened this project and gave me the confidence to pursue its most challenging questions. I am grateful to Daniel Suryadarma for his insightful feedback on the education chapter and conclusion, and to Asep Suryahadi for his comments on the introduction and for reminding me to properly cite our own previous work to avoid any risk of plagiarism.

My work has benefited immensely from collaborations with coauthors over the years. My sincere thanks to Abhijit Banerjee, Asep Suryahadi, Christopher Manning, Elan Satriawan, Emmanuel Skoufias, Indunil De Silva, Jan Priebe, Jordan Kyle, Julia Tobias, Menno Pradhan, Muhamad

Ikhsan, Samuel Bazzi, and Teguh Dartanto. Each of you has contributed to my thinking in crucial ways, and your work is reflected throughout this book.

I would like to express my sincere gratitude to my colleagues at the Harvard Center for International Development for making my sabbatical both productive and deeply rewarding. It has been a privilege to be part of such a dynamic academic community—participating in world-class seminars, engaging with scholars from around the world, and sharing my own research through CID seminars and the classes I taught at the Kennedy School, where students' intellectual curiosity and thoughtful questions helped shape many of the ideas presented in these pages. I am especially thankful to Mary May for her invaluable editorial support. I'm also deeply grateful to Asim I. Khwaja, Fatema Z. Sumar, Alexa Weiss, Katy Doyle, Valerie Krempus, and Eve Margolis for their warm welcome and steadfast encouragement during my time at HKS. I would also like to extend my heartfelt thanks to my fellow CID colleagues, as well as other Harvard fellows—Erick Baumgartner, Philipp Barteska, Vishnu Venugopalan, Natalia Rodrigues, and Arief Pratama—for their friendship and for the many enjoyable moments we shared around Harvard Square after office hours, which made the process of writing this book all the more meaningful.

I would like to acknowledge the RISE Indonesia team, particularly Shintia Revina, Luhur Bima, Risa Wardatun Nihayah, Emilie Berkhout, Asri Yusrina, and Romatio Wulandari. Your rigorous research laid the foundation for the chapter on education and helped inform broader themes throughout the book.

The SMERU Research Institute has long been central to the discourse on social protection and poverty in Indonesia. A special thanks to Anthony Iswara for his insightful perspectives and excellent comments on the lessons learned chapter. I also would like to thank Liza Hadiz, Sulton Mawardi, Muhammad Syukri, Syaikhu Usman, and Sirojuddin Arief—for their feedback during the development of this book, and to Nuning Akhmadi, Widjayanti Suharyo, and the researchers at SMERU Research Institute for their invaluable contributions to the many research projects conducted at SMERU, which greatly enriched the story of the book. Special appreciation also goes to Heru Sutapa for his work on indexing this book and preparing the glossary.

Following closely, I extend my sincere thanks to my colleagues at J-PAL Southeast Asia. I've been fortunate to work with an exceptional team—Hector Salazar, Lina Marlina, Nadia Rayhanna, Masyhur, Poppy Widyasari,

Bertha Fania Maula, and Frieda Siregar—whose dedication and day-to-day commitment to impactful policy research has been invaluable. Their efforts—especially in advancing evidence-based work in the area of social protection—deeply shaped the empirical foundation of this book and the broader narrative of policy change in Indonesia.

I am also extremely thankful to James Cook at Oxford University Press for believing in this project from the outset and to my editor Jodie Keefe and Robyn Drain for their expert editorial guidance, sharp eye for detail, and thoughtful suggestions. I am equally grateful to Varsha Velmurugan, Production Editor and Project Manager, and Carol Neiman, Copy Editor at Integra Software Services, for their dedication and invaluable support throughout the production of this book.

Thanks also to the anonymous reviewers whose useful comments improved both the accessibility and the relevance of the text for a broader audience.

I am also grateful for the valuable feedback received on specific chapters—from Hasbullah Thabrany and Dyah Larasati (health), Vivi Alatas (targeting and poverty), Ranjan Shrestha (rice transfer), Hannah Duncan (village governance), Jan Priebe (poverty measurement), and John Maxwell and Christopher Stewart (introduction). Your insights helped refine key arguments and improve the book's narrative flow.

This book has also benefited enormously from the generosity of the donor community, particularly DFAT- as well as researchers, practitioners, and community members across Indonesia who shared their experiences, data, and reflections—often candidly and at considerable professional and personal commitment. While I am unable to name them individually, I remain deeply grateful for their trust and openness; their insights form the backbone of this work.

And finally, to you—the reader. Thank you for your interest, your time, and your willingness to engage with these ideas. I hope this book contributes to the broader conversation around effective public policy in Indonesia and beyond. This work is as much yours as it is mine.

Introduction

Indonesia has been an exemplar for successful welfare reform. However, the story of *how* it went from a country with virtually no social protection to one with a comprehensive set of social assistance programs is not well known. Following its democratic transition in 1998, Indonesia's system for social protection saw a dramatic expansion in both its scope and reach. Indeed, dramatic regime changes are often accompanied by high aspirations for more pro-poor policies. However, all too often, the high hopes fade away as elites reconsolidate, and recalcitrant bureaucrats stymie popular reforms. In Indonesia, the elites *did* reconsolidate after 1998, but at the same time popular aspirations for more inclusive policies did, in fact, translate into universal healthcare provision, cash transfers to the poor, greater access to pensions, unemployment insurance, and other programs that were not on the table prior to the fall of Suharto's New Order regime.

Indonesia sits at the edge of the Asian continent and is the world's largest archipelagic state. With over 280 million people, it is the world's fourth most populous country. Java, the world's most populous island, is home to more than half of the country's population and is the country's economic powerhouse, contributing around 57% of Indonesia's Gross Domestic Product (GDP) in 2024. With road networks that facilitate commerce and governance throughout the island, Java has been Indonesia's most developed island since the Dutch colonial era and continues to be so today.

Indonesia's economic activity today is driven by both the private sector and the government. As the only G20 member state in Southeast Asia, it is the largest economy in the region. In 2023, its nominal GDP stood at USD 1.371 trillion, while its GDP at purchasing power parity (PPP)[1] was USD 4.34 trillion, ranking 16th and 8th globally, respectively. Meanwhile, its per capita GDP in PPP is USD 15,415, while nominal per capita GDP is USD 4,876.

[1] Purchasing power parity compares the price of a market basket of goods and services across different countries to determine fair exchange rates and to make more accurate cross-country comparisons of economic well-being, GDP, and productivity. It is based on the idea that identical goods should cost the same everywhere after accounting for the exchange rate.

Evidence and the Politics of Reform. Sudarno Sumarto, Oxford University Press.
 DOI: 10.1093/9780197831717.003.0001

The country's economic structure has shifted over time. In the 1950s and 1960s, agriculture dominated. However, industrialization and urbanization picked up in the late 1960s through the 1980s—especially in cities across Java. Falling oil prices in the late 1980s then prompted diversification into manufactured exports, which resulted in dramatic economic growth as the GDP rose at an average rate of nearly 7% between 1986 and 1996 before taking a severe hit during the 1997-1998 Asian financial crisis. By then, GDP had contracted by as much as 13%; inflation reached 78%, and GDP grew by only 0.8% in 1999. Recovery began in the early 2000s as the country transitioned to democracy, with prudent banking regulations, improved monetary and fiscal policies, and flexible exchange rates. Yet, regional inequality remains an issue, especially in rural areas and provinces outside of Java. This inequality is reflected in the country's Gini ratio, which averaged at 35.46 between 2020 and 2021. This figure is substantially higher than the 30.9 at the peak of the Asian financial crisis in 1998 and reflects the unevenness of development throughout the country, set against economic growth and political reform, in the past two and a half decades. At the same time, poverty has fallen from 24.20% in 1998 to 8.47% in 2025. All of these highlight the role that both Indonesia's economic growth and social protection system play in reducing poverty, despite its limitations in addressing the country's distributional issues.

By 2022, Indonesia's tax-to-GDP ratio was only 12.1%. In contrast, the figure is 34.0% for Organisation for Economic Co-operation and Development (OECD) countries. Indonesia's low tax-to-GDP ratio reflects the challenges it is facing in collecting and mobilizing tax for government expenditures. This includes administering a social protection system. At the same time, within the past two and a half decades Indonesia has managed to invest in a welfare infrastructure able to support broad-based social protection programs. Starting from targeted transfers for people in poverty after the financial crisis in 1998, this system has evolved into a comprehensive system including a conditional cash transfer program that couples social transfer with investment in human resources, a rice transfer that reaches nearly 30% of the country's population, a social registry that lists around 40% of the country's population for benefit-targeting purposes, and even a universal healthcare scheme covering the country's more than 275 million people. All of these are among the world's state-of-the-art poverty alleviation instruments backed with research evidence—or what many scholars call *evidence-based policymaking*.

How did this happen? Is there a link between these developments and the country's political reform? Did Indonesia's democratic transition bring about greater redistribution in the form of social programs? It is tempting to say that Indonesia's reforms were brought about by successful evidence-based policymaking. And in fact, the way Indonesia adopted global best practices and planned reforms based on research evidence does seem to indicate that is indeed what happened. At this point, if you think that the Indonesian case might just be a matter of luck, where the country is blessed with visionary leaders who are willing to take research evidence into account in policymaking, you might want to stop reading. After all, many of us stopped believing in fairytales a long time ago, and this might just seem to be another. However, after more than 25 years of working in policy research, I can tell you with certainty that "evidence-based policymaking" is very intentional.

This book offers a firsthand account of how Indonesia, a major nation in the Global South, has leveraged evidence-based policymaking to build a comprehensive social protection system. Countries in the Global South are often perceived as having limited state capacity, but Indonesia's experience demonstrates that capacity can be developed over time. More importantly, evidence-based policymaking did not rely solely on foreign expertise, as local researchers and policymakers took the lead in shaping the policy agenda. Indonesia's social protection programs are designed with policy instruments rooted in research, such as a welfare-ranked targeting system and electronic benefit-delivery mechanisms. While challenges remain, data from continuous monitoring and evaluation help key decision makers enhance program efficiency and impact. This robust framework also enabled Indonesia to deploy a range of social safety net programs during the COVID-19 economic crisis, preventing a sharp rise in poverty. As a result, Indonesia has emerged as a model for successful welfare reform. This book presents a concrete, real-world example of evidence-based policymaking from the Global South, illustrating how local expertise, in collaboration with international scholars, can drive meaningful and sustainable reform.

Many books and articles on evidence-based policymaking focus on how it works, often highlighting its successes. While these accounts are valuable, they can create an illusion that well-designed policies, once backed by evidence, naturally lead to effective implementation. This book is more than just a collection of stories behind successful reforms; it seeks to demystify that notion by not only showcasing achievements but also exposing the setbacks, missteps, and political struggles that shape the policymaking process. Evidence does not speak for itself—it must be negotiated, adapted, and sometimes even contested. By looking beyond the polished success stories, the book offers a more nuanced understanding of how evidence-based policymaking unfolds on the ground.

Second, this book provides a firsthand, institutional perspective on the conditions that enabled the successful implementation of evidence-based policymaking within Indonesia's evolving political and economic landscape. Policy decisions are never made in a vacuum. They are shaped by the dynamics of political competition, shifting incentives, and the ever-changing rules of the game. In Indonesia, these rules have continually evolved in response to economic, social, and political crises, creating both challenges and opportunities for reform. Amid this turbulence, an "epistemic community" of researchers, policymakers, and technocrats emerged, building sustained relationships with those in power. By aligning evidence with the priorities of politicians and bureaucrats, this community carved out a space to influence decision making, demonstrating that evidence-based policymaking is not just about having the right data but also about navigating the political landscape effectively. Now, let me turn to this epistemic community.

In truth, much of policy reform is political—even when we are talking about evidence-based policymaking. Although scholars and researchers may produce evidence for the "best" way to devise a social protection program, in the end, these reforms do not exist in a vacuum. Each party will have their own "best" policy outcome—be it politicians with one that maximizes their electoral outcomes, bureaucrats with one that aligns well with the existing workflow and regulations, or researchers with one that maximizes some scientific metric—but at the end of the day, the "best" policy is a result of the negotiations between all these parties. While "evidence-based policymaking" has been in vogue as of late, Indonesia's scholars have had a long engagement with key government decision makers for years, with varying degrees of success in influencing policy outcomes.

Indonesia's epistemic community, which planted the seeds for today's evidence-based policymaking, was developed during a period of centralized political leadership in the country's past. Even though today, Suharto's government is often remembered for its authoritarianism, his New Order government should also be remembered as a regime that embraced economic development. At that time, many of his economic policies were based on evidence generated by relatively independent think tanks under his ministries. This was a radical change from the previous regime's closed economic policies. After the chaos and economic collapse in President Sukarno's last years that ended in the 1965 coup, Suharto's New Order government thought that a more open economic arrangement would generate rapid growth.

By the end of his rule, President Sukarno (1945–1967) left the country in economic shambles and political turmoil. Between 1964 and 1965, Indonesia experienced hyperinflation that exceeded 600%, an increase in the poverty rate, and stagnating production output. The political climate worsened with the violent anti-communist purge of 1965, during which an estimated 500,000 to a million people lost their lives. This purge effectively ended leftist politics in Indonesia to this day. Amid this unrest, Sukarno mandated Suharto to get the situation under control, which marked the start of Suharto's 32-year period of centralized and strongly controlled governance.

Under his rule, Suharto took a rationalist approach to policymaking. From the outset, Suharto recognized that the Sukarno administration's anti-capitalist attitudes were a part of the problem.[2] Hence, the policy of reintegrating Indonesia into the world economy began almost immediately after Suharto's government took office and was a cornerstone of the New Order government throughout its rule. In consequence, the New Order government gradually reduced trade and investment barriers—particularly after the oil boom era had ended in the early 1980s—out of necessity rather than conviction.

On the foreign front, Indonesia's new anti-communist government quickly abandoned the Sukarno government's anti-Western policies. Indonesia rejoined the United Nations, from which it had withdrawn in January 1965. Meanwhile, on the economic front, the new political leadership sought economic assistance from Western countries and Japan. Indonesia also rejoined the International Monetary Fund (IMF) and the World Bank after Sukarno had withdrawn from both in August 1965 as part of his efforts to cut links with the capitalist world. Suharto believed that restoring links with these organizations was essential to assist Indonesia's economic recovery.

Following the economic turmoil left by Sukarno, particularly runaway inflation from excessive deficit spending, Suharto sought advice from

[2] Hollinger, 1996: 25.

economists at the University of Indonesia. His trust in them grew after attending their lectures on Indonesia's economic challenges during the 1966 Second Army Seminar. These economists had also been teaching senior army officers at the Army Staff and Command School (Seskoad), giving Suharto his foundational economic knowledge. Over time, the relationship between the military and academics deepened through regular courses across military branches, with the army most engaged due to its dual military and socio-political role under Suharto's government. These collaborations helped form the military–civilian alliance that cemented Suharto's New Order regime.

Following the economic instability left by Sukarno, in September 1966 Suharto appointed a team of five economists from the University of Indonesia, led by his Major-General, to advise his government on economic and financial matters. This marked the rise of the "economic technocrats" or "Berkeley Mafia," as several members had studied economics at the University of California, Berkeley.[3] Tasked with stabilizing the economy, they developed a Program for Stabilization and Rehabilitation, which became formalized as official policy through presidential decree. The plan focused on balancing the budget, improving the balance of payments, rebuilding infrastructure, and boosting food production and agriculture. By the late 1960s, their efforts had stabilized prices and set the stage for rapid economic growth. The plan enjoyed the full support and confidence of Suharto and the strong support of the Inter-Governmental Group on Indonesia (IGGI), an international aid consortium chaired by the Netherlands. This patron–client relationship was ideal for a president who legitimated his leadership through a commitment to bringing growth to the country. Some of these economists' contributions included reducing the rate of inflation, building schools to combat illiteracy, attaining rice self-sufficiency, and reducing poverty at the fastest rate of any country since World War II. Over the next three decades, Indonesia transformed from an agriculture-dependent economy into a newly industrializing economy with a booming manufacturing sector.

Indonesia's rapid economic growth was underpinned by high rates of domestic capital investment. These capital investment rates were sustained by rising rates of gross domestic savings. Gross domestic investment consisted of public, domestic private, and foreign direct investment.

[3] Wie, 2002.

Additionally, during the oil boom years of the 1970s, huge resource rent taxes enabled the Indonesian government to undertake large investments. These investments were particularly in physical infrastructure and social development, primarily health and education. After the end of the oil boom in the early 1980s, private investment, which included foreign direct investment, played an increasingly important role.

The country's rapid growth came to a halt during the 1997–1998 Asian financial crisis, which began in Thailand and spread across the region. The crisis devastated Indonesia's economy, causing the Indonesian rupiah to lose 80% of its value and driving inflation above 50%. Economic contraction led to widespread layoffs, especially in urban sectors, and a resurgence of poverty. Compounding the crisis was a severe El Niño drought that hurt agriculture, caused widespread forest fires, and led to falling oil prices, which reduced export and government revenues. This marked a sharp reversal of Indonesia's economic progress under the New Order.

The 1997–1998 Asian financial crisis was a pivotal moment in the history of the Indonesian welfare system. Prior to the crisis, Indonesia had few broad-based social welfare programs. It lacked both the economic framework and the political infrastructure necessary to implement extensive, wide-reaching transfer programs. The emphasis of social spending was primarily on social services, with "social insurance" being provided by families and communities. As in many oil-producing countries, the government primarily used fuel subsidies—initially to combat inflation, and later as a form of social subsidies to keep poverty at bay. However, fuel subsidies are both extremely costly and inefficient as a means of social transfer, with the largest share of the benefits going to the more well-off, car-owning middle and upper classes rather than to the poor[4]. Even so, periodic efforts to roll back these subsidies were met with widespread public backlash.

The financial crisis reached Indonesia in mid-1997, and by the first half of 1998 it had already developed into a full-blown economic and political crisis: two of its impacts were a sudden increase in the poverty rate from 17.3% in 1996 to 23.4% in 1999,[5] and a real economic contraction of 13.7%.[6] This was a sharp turnaround from the sustained poverty reduction and high

[4] In 2004, the Indonesian government only spent around 14% of its kerosene subsidies and only around 6% of other fuel subsidies on the poor and the rest on non-poor households (World Bank, 2004) and in 2005, Indonesia spent IDR 95.6 trillion in fossil fuel subsidies when its spending on social assistance was only IDR 24.9 trillion (Ministry of Finance, 2006).

[5] Suryahadi, Hadiwidjaja, and Sumarto, 2012.

[6] See Cameron, 1999.

growth of the previous three decades, when growth averaged over 7% annually. In the labor market, the crisis had a more pronounced effect on real wages, which decreased by approximately one-third from August 1997 to August 1998, compared to its effect on unemployment. During this period, the unemployment rate increased marginally, from 4.7% to 5.5%, while the underemployment rate rose from 35.8% to 39.1%. A year later, real wages began to recover gradually in most sectors; however, the unemployment rate continued to rise, reaching 6.4% in 1999.[7] The impact of the crisis on the labor market resulted in a wider domino effect. Children dropped out of school, either because their parents could no longer afford school fees or because child labor was suddenly needed to sustain the family. Access to health treatments was disrupted, exacerbating Indonesia's already mounting issues of maternal mortality, malnutrition, and stunted growth. Poor families began skipping meals, and in some parts of the country starvation, unknown for decades in Indonesia, reappeared.

Unable any longer to deal with the crisis, on October 13, 1997, the government turned to the IMF for financial assistance. In return for a standby loan of $43 billion, the Indonesian government pledged to implement a comprehensive reform program, including sound macroeconomic policies, financial sector restructuring, and structural reforms.[8] The IMF package was to be implemented over a three-year period and to be tightly monitored by the Indonesian government, assisted by experts from the IMF, the World Bank, and the Asian Development Bank. However, unlike Thailand and South Korea—the other two most-affected Asian countries that had, from the outset, vigorously implemented the agreed-on reform programs in return for IMF assistance—Suharto's government did not seem to be fully committed to implementing the promised reforms. Hence, when the rupiah failed to strengthen and the economy continued its fall, in January 1998 Suharto reluctantly signed a second agreement with the IMF. This time the agreement encompassed a more detailed 50-point reform program, which included provisions for a social safety net for those most severely affected by the economic crisis. At the same time, the country could no longer afford to sustain fuel subsidies, whose removal became part of the package negotiated between the IMF and President Suharto. This combination of mass unemployment, a currency devaluation that reached as high as 1700%, and

[7] Manning, 2000 and Suryahadi, Sumarto, and Pritchett, 2003.
[8] Ministry of Finance, 2016.

the rise in consumer prices as fuel subsidies were reduced, triggered social unrest in cities across the country, with deadly protests that forced President Suharto to step down.

Suharto's resignation in May 1998 meant that the budget approved for the fiscal year (running from April 1998 to March 1999) was no longer operative. Thus, in July 1998, the new government produced a budget which allocated funds for a "safety net," or the JPS (*Jaring Pengaman Sosial*) programs. The magnitude of the budget for the JPS programs was not the result of costing out programs, nor was it grounded in any historical baseline; rather, it was based on macroeconomic, political, and multinational institutions' budget supports, as well as other financial forces around which programs could be designed. However, prior to the crisis most of Indonesia's population had not depended significantly on government safety net programs. The government lacked both the economic infrastructure and the political mechanisms needed to implement extensive transfer programs across an archipelago with a population of 205 million at that time. Consequently, creating crisis programs in Indonesia in 1998 was not just about broadening an existing network but also about creating an entirely new one.

The Indonesian government's JPS fell into five areas, which were food security, employment creation, education, health, and community empowerment, with geographic and household/individuals-based approaches to targeting. The rice subsidies program, which was the largest of the JPS schemes, covered 12.8 million families across the country, or around 25% of the country's then-population.[9]

When the 1997–1998 Asian financial crisis brought an end to Suharto's regime, the technocrats that he had placed at strategic positions in proximity with key decision makers stayed. This also included the economists. During the crisis, Indonesia had at its disposal trained economists strategically located in positions of power within the government. With a power vacuum in the absence of Suharto-centric governance, social unrest due to global economic meltdown, general distrust of the government, and support for a technocratic approach to crisis recovery from international agencies such as IMF and the World Bank, the technocrats had an upper hand in influencing policy outcomes. In terms of social-protection program provisions, this included both the design of the intervention and its evaluation. This dynamic during and after the crisis animated Indonesia's policymaking

[9] Suryahadi, Sumarto, and Pritchett, 2003.

landscape from then on. More than two decades since the onset of the crisis in 1997, researchers, scholars, and international donor agencies have remained a part of Indonesia's epistemic community, along with bureaucrats, politicians, and decision makers in the government in charge of a range of social and economic policies. I was a part of this community then, and I still am now.

My journey in the field of public policy began after I earned a bachelor's degree in economics and joined the Center for Policy and Implementation Studies (CPIS), a think tank under President Suharto's economic team. CPIS played an important role in providing evidence-based recommendations that contributed to the economic successes of the New Order era. CPIS provided me the opportunity to pursue further education in the United States. Upon completing my studies, I returned to Indonesia in 1996 and worked with international development agencies, including the Asian Development Bank and the World Bank's Indonesia office. Following the Asian financial crisis, my focus shifted to full-time research on Indonesia's post-crisis economic recovery, particularly regarding safety net programs.

During my tenure as a World Bank consultant, I collaborated with Lant Pritchett, Scott Guggenheim, and Andrea Silverman to form a team tasked with monitoring the impact of the crisis and proposing mitigation strategies. Many team members were former CPIS researchers, and the group eventually became known as the Social Monitoring and Early Response Unit (SMERU). This initiative received funding from the Asia-Europe Meeting (ASEM) trust fund, Australian Aid (AusAID)—now integrated into Australia's Department of Foreign Affairs and Trade (DFAT)—the Ford Foundation, and the United Kingdom's erstwhile Department for International Development (DFID). SMERU laid the groundwork for what is now the SMERU Research Institute. I led SMERU for approximately nine years before taking a one-year sabbatical at Stanford University. Upon my return to Indonesia in 2010, Vice President Boediono invited me to advise the National Team for the Acceleration of Poverty Reduction (TNP2K), which he led. Today, SMERU is recognized as one of the most productive research institutes in Indonesia in terms of academic publications, fostering a vibrant, evidence-based discourse on poverty and social protection.

After 1998, crises continued to set the background for the dynamic between researchers and government actors, who continue to be in close proximity to one another. No longer able to afford the fuel subsidies, the new government over the next few years decided to roll out broad-based social safety net programs to restore social stability and minimize the impact of economic reforms on Indonesia's riot-prone population—including the decision to roll back the highly popular fuel subsidies through a number of reform episodes. These social safety net programs ranged from rice transfers, scholarships, and healthcare subsidies for the poor to village block grants and public works at the community level that fostered simple productive infrastructures and compensation of villagers for their labor. Bypassing much expert international advice that argued for tight targeting to the poorest, in 2004 Indonesia opted for broad-based targeting instead. This occasion not only demonstrated Indonesian technocrats' creative agency in the face of powerful foreign donors but also marked a key moment in Indonesia's quest to build the infrastructure of broad-based welfare provisions.

In 2010, President Susilo Bambang Yudhoyono signed a presidential decree to establish. The National Team for the Acceleration of Poverty Reduction (Tim National Percepatan Penanggulangan Kemiskinan, TNP2K). TNP2K was mandated to coordinate poverty alleviation efforts across the government, which included establishing an instrument for social program targeting, designing and overseeing new social assistance and poverty reduction programs as well as consolidating and improving the efficiency of existing programs. TNP2K's members comprised key ministries and government agencies in charge of welfare issues, which included the Ministry of Social Affairs, Ministry of Health, Ministry of Education and Culture, Ministry of National Development Planning, and Statistics Indonesia, and was headed by Vice President Boediono. Moreover, TNP2K was to be supported with a Policy Working Group, which acted as a think tank for the government of Indonesia. Having lobbied the Australian government for support, Boediono secured nearly $50 million to fund TNP2K activities. This included hiring experts at a competitive rate and facilitated the formal inclusion of technocrats into the country's highest policymaking circles.

I have been part of TNP2K's Policy Working Group since 2010. During this time, I served as a policy adviser responsible for providing inputs to the government on social policy alongside the head of the group. In addition to this role, I conducted policy research with both the internal TNP2K research team and external research partners. Within TNP2K, I worked closely with bureaucrats in a number of ministries and government agencies to identify problems, design research and policy evaluation, and draft regulations. This dynamic has demonstrated how knowledge generation and application cannot be separated from processes on the ground. When I left TNP2K in 2024,

Indonesia's poverty rate was 9.03%—the lowest it had been since Statistics Indonesia began calculating the country's poverty rate in 1976.

There are two key factors that lent TNP2K a unique ability to strategically bring research evidence into policymaking and formalize the link between technocrats and decision makers. First, the funding of TNP2K not only allowed us to hire experts but also to engage with scholars and development agencies to bring rigorous research to policymaking. Over the years we have worked not only with scholars at local universities but also the world's best universities and research institutions in collaborating with government bureaucrats and policymakers to solve real problems on the ground. In a sense, our position bridges abstract theories to real-world problems, and the reality in turn informs the theories. Second, being a part of the government meant that technocrats could gain the trust of decision makers and bureaucrats when we brought research evidence to the table. Backed by evidence, TNP2K could gain scientific legitimacy while at the same time, backed by regulations, TNP2K could gain political legitimacy. These connections are what makes the Indonesian model work. In a sense, this close relationship between technocrats and decision makers in the government was nothing new, as it had been the case with Suharto's administration in the past. If anything, it was just an extension of that model but with more formal structures around it. However, the close relationship between technocrats and the government was different this time around, given the newly democratizing country's political landscape.

Having been under colonial rule for hundreds of years, a "guided democracy" after its independence, and then a centralized, tightly controlled government, Indonesia and its story post-1998 is one of learning of what it means to govern a diverse nation of more than 250 million people in a democracy. In the face of rising tension in regions outside of Java—the country's population center—a law on decentralization was signed in 2004. The decentralization law led to the devolution of power from the central government to regional governments in most areas of governance except a few, such as foreign policy, defense, law and order, and monetary and fiscal policy, and was enacted in the early 2000s.[10] Intended to improve the ability of local governments to respond to local conditions, Indonesia's decentralization project allowed local governments to adopt locally appropriate regulations, experiment with policies that would advance development and welfare,

[10] See also Brodjonegoro, 2009; Seymour and Turner, 2002.

and manage their budgets in ways best suited to local needs. This logic of development from the periphery contrasts with the centralistic model that Indonesia had been accustomed to in the past. It meant that local governments were no longer extensions of the central government, but rather partners in development. Beyond this decentralization dynamic, Indonesia's multi-party landscape and democracy meant that the country's political discourse became noisier than in the past. While the efficacy of these parties in representing the voices of their constituents, or the role of the press in providing checks and balances to the government is a topic for another discussion, their presence marked a shift in Indonesia's welfare policymaking landscape. It is amid this changing political landscape that Indonesia's epistemic community operates.

Democracy also brings with it term limits for elected officials, which makes long-term commitment to specific development goals more challenging. At the same time, in a democratic competition, politicians have an incentive to be associated with social transfers because their visibility and perceived success are key to winning elections.[11] This political context is a double-edged sword for researchers. On the one hand, when new politicians are elected to office, program reforms can be pushed because the politicians can rebrand existing programs and associate themselves with them. This was the case with the Raskin (*Beras Miskin*) rice subsidies that were rebranded into Rastra (*Beras Sejahtera*), in-kind rice transfers, when Joko Widodo came into office in 2014. On the other hand, a long-term goal or vision may be difficult to adhere to, as politicians have a shorter time horizon than under authoritarianism when there are no term limits. For instance, while initially the Joko Widodo administration (2014–2024) continued many policies to create an integrated social protection system that was started under the Susilo Bambang Yudhoyono regime (2004–2014), the new administration's failure to update a beneficiary targeting database posed challenges in reducing program targeting errors.

With the political dynamism that exists under democracy, influencing policy outcomes is a whole different game for many economists who had been once favored and backed by the authoritarian regime. While there are concerns over program longevity, I want to advance what is perhaps a controversial thought. When reformers are talking about change, the bureaucracy's resistance to change is often seen as a hindrance to progress.

[11] De La O, 2015.

Sometimes it can be frustrating to work around these institutional blockers. However, the bureaucracy can also be a force that moderates sudden policy changes when new leaders come into office, precisely because of its persistence and continuity. This carries important lessons for new government reformers. For policy reformers, the key to success is to identify champions within the bureaucracy and to understand what incentivizes them to want to seek out reforms. Civil servants have an immense understanding of the laws and regulations that may pose constraints for reformers, where problems lie, and areas in need of reform. Knowing key people within the bureaucracy can help anticipate where problems might arise and find work-arounds for blockages.

At the same time, Indonesia's epistemic community is extremely small for a middle-income country of 275 million. This community is also very centralized, as it is bunched in Jakarta and nestled so close to the government in power. Thus, it is no wonder that the policy recommendations that come out of this community reflect this pattern. Whether it is consciously or unconsciously done, the types of social assistance chosen tend to be highly centralized systems that a handful of technocrats can manage, rather than locally initiated or managed programs. This reflects not only an underdeveloped and centralized knowledge sector but also weakly integrated systems of public administration—particularly in the localities. Despite Indonesia's transition to democracy and efforts to decentralize power, inequality remains a persistent challenge—one that the centralized model has failed to address. While cracks have begun to show in this system, they have not led to meaningful devolution of power. Instead, they have exposed the limits of a model that struggles to adapt to Indonesia's diverse and decentralized realities.

President Prabowo Subianto's administration, which began in 2025, exemplifies this tension. One of his flagship policies—the launch of a universal free school meal program—offered an opportunity to engage local communities in service delivery. Yet, rather than mobilizing local networks, the government relied on the military and a select group of vendors to manage the program nationwide. This choice reflects a broader pattern: despite Indonesia's democratic progress, policy implementation remains dominated by centralized actors. Indonesia's reforms, in many ways, remain unfinished. The question, then, is whether the country's epistemic community will continue reinforcing this top-down model—or whether a more inclusive, locally responsive approach to policymaking can emerge. The persistence of this centralized policymaking is not merely an issue of institutional inertia; it is also shaped by the way research informs decision making in Indonesia. At the same time, while technical expertise plays a role in shaping policy, reforms ultimately also depend on the political and bureaucratic actors who interpret and implement them.

There is a tendency among researchers to give most of the credit to technical capacity in producing valid evidence. However, the success of policy reform efforts and implementation on the ground rests upon decision makers and bureaucrats in the government. Although researchers may have an idea of what policy course is "the best," their technical expertise must be set against a broader economic, social, and political context that involves multiple stakeholders in the government. In this regard, trust between key decision makers and bureaucrats in the government, which is contingent upon interactions over time, is critical. There is always good research done on Indonesia. However, Indonesian policymakers and the public are often skeptical of them. They have often though of research evidence as part of a foreign conspiracy to undermine the Indonesian government's legitimacy. While Suharto's centralized government served as a key supporter of the technocrats, essentially handpicking them to design policies and commanding bureaucrats to implement these policies, under democracy, gaining trust is a different game. Researchers need to engage with many political actors that may not have the same goal—including decision makers, politicians, research or program donors, and bureaucrats in the government. For a reform to take place, these actors need to negotiate and align their interests. Scientific evidence is merely one "language" that researchers speak in their effort to align these often-competing interests and enact reforms.

Adding complexity to this matter, while researchers can work to produce valid evidence and foster relationships with key actors in the government, at the end of the day, political openings can present opportunities or can close the door for reforms to occur. Shocks like the 1997–1998 Asian financial crisis, or the cycle of elections when the political power balance might shift—or when politicians, for any reason, actively seek out support from technocrats to enact policy changes—are political openings that reformers can exploit. While it is true that many things are beyond the researcher's influence, there are some things that researchers can engage with to create a policy environment more conducive to change.

Beyond partnering with the government and international entities, researchers also play a key role in public outreach, producing publications, and conducting qualitative research that could turn technical evidence into a source of accessible information for journalists, the broader public, and media opinion leaders who now can obtain views different from the standard government lines.

Today, Indonesia is a middle-income country of more than 275 million people with aspirations to become a high-income country by 2045. Within two and a half decades since 1998, it has managed to build a social assistance program that regularly covers at least 25% of its citizens on a monthly basis. It has also shifted away from indiscriminate fuel and food subsidy programs toward better-targeted cash transfers. Targeting for these programs relies upon a national dataset, which aids in identifying and reaching out to people in need. It has also succeeded in rolling out universal health insurance and an emergency safety net whose coverage reached 50% of the population during the COVID-19 pandemic. As concerns over the country's soon-to-be aging population mount, by the 2020s the government has already begun thinking of moving toward a "life-cycle" approach to the country's social protection systems. Given the limited social provisions prior to 1998, it is not an overstatement to say that such welfare coverage was unthinkable in the past.

Indeed, Indonesia has achieved a lot since then. Under President Suharto's "New Order" rule (1967–1998), Indonesia was a highly centralized, quasi-military government. At that time, social provisions like pension and insurance were only available to Suharto's key support groups: the military and civil servants, along with a small share of private sector workers. In place of broad-based social provisions, the government ran multiple in-kind subsidies, which ranged from fuel and seeds to fertilizer subsidies. At the same time, it was also well known that the government was marred by corruption. With the idea of broad-based social provisions being so far-fetched at that time, it is nothing short of miraculous that Indonesia established a relatively comprehensive social protection system in just two and a half decades. At the same time, Indonesia's social reforms are an ongoing project with new challenges emerging and existing problems growing, both posing challenges to anyone aiming to govern the country or reform its social welfare system.

While the idea of evidence-based policymaking has been sold as a means to bring about effective governance and reforms, it is not a magic bullet that one just shoots to fix everything. Instead of being a product of a visionary leader, evidence-based policymaking is a product of political openings and an epistemic community that is in place to influence decision makers. This community comprises researchers, scholars, bureaucrats, politicians, development agencies, social and labor activists, and donors, who are all in close engagement with one another. While we usually see researchers and scholars as knowledge producers, in this community they produce knowledge in collaboration with bureaucrats and politicians as key actors in policy and decision making. Development agencies and donors in this dynamic play a part in providing support across various aspects of evidence-based policymaking, ranging from knowledge production, capacity building, and policy implementation to documentation and information curation. As government actors and foreign actors are involved in this dynamic, the discourse in this epistemic community is naturally political in nature. This includes the very beginning of research, when the agenda is being set, to the very end of the research cycle when decision makers determine which evidence makes it into formal policy. At the same time, while the dynamics in this community are highly political, it does not mean that researchers and scholars should sacrifice rigor. In fact, what I have learned over the years is that scientific rigor and accountability are what enables scholars and researchers to survive changes in political tides.

Although my book tells Indonesia's story, its themes may resonate more broadly than one might expect. Indonesia's social and economic development trajectory over the past 30 to 50 years mirrors that of many middle-income countries. Like Brazil and Mexico, Indonesia has undergone structural transformation, shifting from an agriculture-based economy to one driven by manufacturing and services, though concerns over premature de-industrialization persist. Rapid urbanization has fueled economic dynamism, expanding the middle class and driving domestic consumption. Similar to Malaysia and Chile, Indonesia initially relied on resource-based exports before diversifying, although commodity dependence remains a challenge. Investments in education and healthcare have significantly improved access, but persistent inequality gaps mirror those seen in India and South Africa. Meanwhile, income inequality and a large informal sector continue to hinder inclusive growth, much like in the Philippines and Peru. Governance and institutional challenges, such as corruption and policy inconsistency, echo the experiences of Turkey and Argentina. Yet, as in Brazil, Mexico, and Thailand, the expansion of social protection programs, such as Indonesia's universal healthcare and the Family Hope Program, has played a critical role in reducing poverty and vulnerability. These parallels underscore the shared opportunities and challenges among middle-income countries as they navigate economic and social development.

Indonesia's response to the post-Suharto and post-crisis era set in motion the development of one of the world's largest social protection systems in terms of coverage. The shift to democracy fundamentally altered the policy landscape. Technocrats who once operated under the government's patronage now had to adapt to a new political reality, where policymaking was shaped by negotiation, competing interests, and institutional constraints. It is within this evolving socio-political context that Indonesia's epistemic community, with its network of researchers, policymakers, and reform advocates, has worked to advance evidence-based policymaking with varying degrees of success. This book is about that epistemic community, one that I have been a part of and one I hope to see flourish in the hands of a new generation of scholars, researchers, bureaucrats, and decision makers. Through these pages, I share lessons from my experience, offering insights for those seeking to make evidence-based policymaking work, not just in Indonesia but in other corners of the world.

We naturally prefer to see examples of successes in evidence-based policymaking. However, I believe that its failures are just as important. They too provide valuable lessons. Besides, revisiting these failures reminds us to remain humble and measured in our craft. This book contains stories of successes for basing social welfare policy reform on evidence. However, I am also sharing stories of the failures that I encountered along the way.

Chapters in this book are written in a way that they can be read both continuously or as stand-alone works. The ordering of the chapters is not chronological, but earlier chapters provide background to later chapters. Thus, readers who are interested in specific topics can choose to engage with specific chapters. However, to get the full story, I certainly recommend reading the book from front-to-back and returning to specific chapters as needed.

In the *first chapter*, I talk about the evolution of the Indonesian social protection system. It will provide context for the other chapters in this book. I talk about how Indonesia's social welfare policies developed under different governing regimes. The *second chapter* examines Indonesia's landmark effort to revoke regressive fuel subsidies in the 2000s—a reform initially hailed as a triumph for avoiding social unrest through compensatory cash transfers and schemes that later evolved into permanent social protection programs. This bold move freed billions of dollars from the national budget, redirecting funds toward education, health, disaster management, and other pro-poor investments. Notably, this period also saw the establishment of Indonesia's social registry system, a critical innovation that improved targeting, transparency, and evaluation of social assistance programs, marking a turning point in the government's approach to welfare. However, the chapter underscores the fragility of such reforms: despite early success, fuel subsidies stealthily re-emerged and were fully reinstated under President Joko Widodo in 2020, justified as part of the COVID-19 pandemic response. By weaving together narratives of progress and regression, the chapter highlights both the transformative potential of reform and the challenges of sustaining it.

The *third chapter* discusses Indonesia's Unified Database. When TNP2K was established, close monitoring and evaluation of national poverty alleviation programs became the norm. This was when efficiency, targeting error, and program impacts became key metrics to assess the success of welfare policies in Indonesia. These new metrics came to replace budget spending, which previously served as the key assessment metric and revealed little about the nature of program efficiency and efficacy. Thus, one of TNP2K's first tasks was to establish the Unified Database, which is the national targeting system that contains a list of the names and addresses of potential social assistance beneficiaries. Covering and ranking millions of families based on their welfare level, it was one of the most advanced targeting instruments in the developing world. However, promoting its use across the government has been a challenge, as distrust among government units hindered effective utilization of the database. Moreover, data governance and administration has been a contentious matter since it involves personally identifiable welfare information of nearly half of the country's citizens. While we tend to see the state as one homogeneous actor, this chapter reveals how political dynamics between bureaucrats in the government shape the way poverty is "seen" and administered by the state.

The *fourth chapter* focuses on lessons learned from efforts to reform Indonesia's rice transfers policy. Indonesia's poverty line reflects both food and non-food spending. The poorer one is, the larger the share of one's expenditure is spent on food. Among the poorest 10% families in Indonesia, more than 20% of expenditure is spent on rice.[12] This stands in contrast

[12] Calculated using March 2021 National Socioeconomic Survey (SUSENAS).

to the richest 10% families in Indonesia, who do not spend more than 1% of their expenditure on rice. What this means is that fluctuation in food prices, with rice as a staple food, may push one below the poverty line. Hence, maintaining the price stability and availability of rice can help ensure general well-being. However, transferring rice directly to the citizens turned out to have many problems. Rice stored in government warehouses can get wet or be eaten by weevils and rats. Moreover, unscrupulous middlemen can sell the rice privately and report it as having been properly delivered. At the same time, as flawed as these systems were, they were also politically popular because for certain families, some rice was always going to be better than no rice at all. Acknowledging the importance of rice for the poor and then finding a better way to make sure it reached them involved a lot of experimentation and evaluation. This chapter tells a story of Indonesia's transition from rice subsidies to in-kind transfers and, finally, to vouchers. This case exemplifies successful evidence-based policymaking that engaged scholars from the world's leading research institutions.

The *fifth chapter* discusses education. Poverty alleviation does not just revolve around short-term transfers. Policies that promote social mobility, such as education, are just as important if a society is going to break the chain of intergenerational poverty. Under President Suharto's governance, Indonesia's main educational challenge was related to access to schooling. Hence, the president mandated the construction of more than 61,000 primary schools between 1973 and 1979. With the enrollment rate no longer the most pressing issue, Indonesia's main problem after its democratic transition became that of poor educational input and processes. Therefore, the government legislated a law in 2003 which mandated that 20% of national budget be allocated for education, financing various reforms to Indonesia's education system. Yet, Indonesia's increased educational spending contrasts with its flat learning profiles, which puzzles both the government and researchers. This chapter is a story of the importance of re-adjusting policies to avoid policy drift: even when a policy has worked in the past, new problems call for new solutions.

Moreover, this fifth chapter is also a story of attempting reform in a fragmented political system. With democracy and political decentralization, much authority over educational policy moves away from the Ministry of Education and Culture and into local governments. This poses challenges of reform scalability beyond localities and policy sustainability given the political dynamics at both the national and regional levels. Additionally, teacher hiring falls under the purview of the Ministry of Home Affairs, which poses a problem in matching teacher demand and supply that compounds with teacher quality issues.

In the *sixth chapter*, I discuss Indonesia's healthcare system reform. This chapter is a story of how legal battles for social reforms are just as crucial as their technicalities on the ground. Moreover, it is also a story of how universalistic policies may have a limited impact in the face of structural inequities in the provision of basic services.

Indonesia's decentralization created a whole different game for policy reformers and researchers seeking to get policy buy-in. Therefore, I dedicate the *seventh chapter* to discussing Indonesia's decentralization policy with a focus on the Village Fund (*Dana Desa*) transfers. With around 43% of Indonesia's population living in rural areas according to the 2020 population census, the Indonesian government devolved some of its budgeting authorities to village-level governments in order to hasten rural development through the Village Fund transfers. Between 2015 and 2020, the Indonesian government transferred more than IDR 257 trillion to village governments, making it one of the world's largest inter-governmental transfers directed to the lowest level of government. While it is exclusively plotted for development, village governments are free to spend this money however they see fit, and the central government has no say in spending decisions. The Village Fund was created with regional autonomy in mind and with the thought that local governments know best about their localities' needs. However, it is also a story of how the government relented to political pressures despite evidence that reform was needed, as the program's incentives were misplaced and fostered political patronage instead of locally led development.

In the *eighth chapter*, I talk about how Indonesia's social protection system weathered the COVID-19 pandemic. To soften the pandemic's socioeconomic blow, the Indonesian government quickly mobilized its welfare system to act as a social safety net. The extensive breadth and coverage of the welfare programs rolled out by the government in 2020 played a key role in mitigating Indonesia's economic contraction to −2.07%, which is well below the global average of −3.5%. Despite the Indonesian social welfare system's extensive role in providing a social safety net for the population, the response was not exactly smooth sailing. Two major issues that diminished the safety net's efficacy were outdated social registry data that hampered beneficiary targeting and a highly bureaucratic system that posed a challenge in adjusting welfare programs to respond to the crisis. Moreover, although deemed successful in minimizing the impact of the crisis on the Indonesian economy, a strategy that relies on high spending on stimulus and aid when tax revenue is low is untenable in the long run. Indonesia's battle against the COVID-19 pandemic reveals weaknesses in Indonesia's social protection system, ranging from a poorly updated beneficiary list to limited flexibility for program scaling. The pandemic has revealed areas for improvement as Indonesia moves forward.

Beyond technical problems, there is also an issue with how the Indonesian social protection system is governed. With large reforms driven by the central government, and political decentralization that delegates a range of authority over governance and budgeting to local governments, there is an issue with highly motivated technical policymakers, ministries within the central government, and local governments that do not have the right incentives to maintain and respond to the systems that the central government has created. This raises the question of whether TNP2K, as the government body tasked to coordinate the poverty alleviation effort, has designed a social protection system that is either too hard for Indonesian political institutions to maintain or one that could only be maintained if a small number of central technocrats retain tight control over welfare policies.

After discussing welfare policy and poverty alleviation efforts throughout the book, I feel that it is fitting that we scrutinize Indonesia's poverty line in the book's *final chapter.* Indonesia's poverty line not only determines the number of people in poverty, but it also serves as a basis for the government to determine the poverty alleviation budget and much of the government's welfare policy design. Yet, methodologically speaking, Indonesia's poverty line has a weak relative nature instead of an absolute one. This means that poverty-alleviating policies chase a continuously moving target.

With the book talking much about the past, I then end it with a summary of my *lessons learned* and a short *afterword* in which I reflect on the Indonesian social protection system's present and its future path.

1

Two and a Half Decades of the Indonesian Social Protection System

The 1997–1998 Asian financial crisis marked a pivotal moment for Indonesia, not only politically, as the country transitioned to democracy, but also in terms of its welfare system. For the first time, the Indonesian government introduced targeted social transfers available to the public. The poverty rate, which reached nearly a quarter of the population, became a primary driver for the government to implement social welfare provisions. This ad-hoc welfare provision would then be transformed into the country's social protection system, which encompasses social-assistance transfers for those in poverty and the economically vulnerable, as well as contributory social insurance schemes for all of the country's citizens. Over the next two decades, Indonesia saw poverty numbers pushed down to just below 10% by the second half of the 2010s. The country's social protection system and robust economic growth are thought to have contributed to the country's poverty reduction. However, when the COVID-19 pandemic hit, and Indonesia entered a recession in 2021, the government's social protection system shouldered much of the work in keeping poverty rates low.

Despite the country's poverty-alleviation achievements, its poverty reduction target outlined in the country's medium-term development plan (RPJMN) has not been attained since the Susilo Bambang Yudhoyono–Jusuf Kalla administration (2004–2009) (see Figure 1.1). The closest Indonesia has been to attaining the target was in 2019, before the COVID-19 pandemic, when the government was just 0.91 percentage points away from its goal before the pandemic hit a year later. By the end of the Joko Widodo–Ma'ruf Amin administration in 2024, Indonesia was still 1.53 percentage points short of its target.

At the same time, poverty rates can also be seen "merely" as optics, given the fact that millions in the country still live very close to the poverty line and are vulnerable to falling into poverty with the smallest shock to their welfare level. Moreover, poverty rates do not capture welfare dynamics or

Evidence and the Politics of Reform. Sudarno Sumarto, Oxford University Press.
 DOI: 10.1093/9780197831717.003.0002

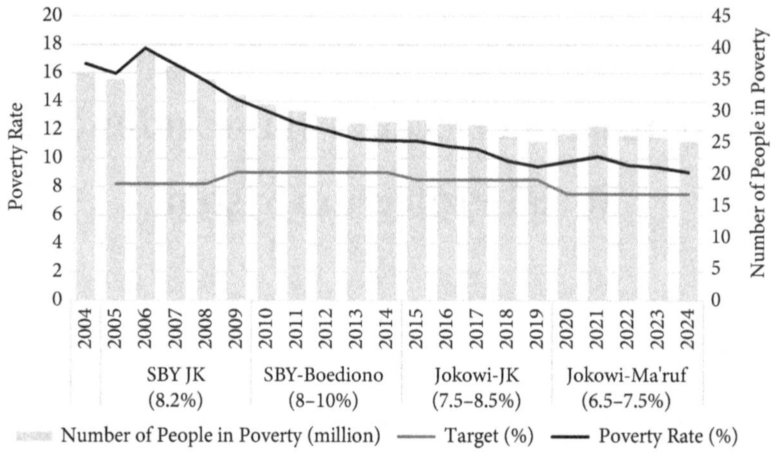

Figure 1.1 Poverty Rate at National Poverty Line and Government Targeted Poverty Rate (% of population)

how well-being levels change over time. By 2022, "only" less than 10% of the population lived under the poverty line. Yet, nearly a third of the country's population lived at just 1.5 times the poverty line (see Figure 1.2). This raises the question of whether Indonesia's social protection system is well-equipped to tackle broader welfare concerns, such as ensuring that there are no dramatic drops in well-being level or that people are lifted out of poverty sustainably, rather than just as long as they receive social assistance. Due to the social protection system's emergence from poor-relief schemes in the aftermath of the 1997–1998 financial crisis, it is not surprising that the Indonesian social protection system has a significant social-assistance component that is aimed at lifting people out of poverty. However, this reliance on poverty relief programs came at the expense of poorly developed economic empowerment programs, an underutilized social insurance scheme, and poor integration with active labor market policies—all of which play a role in sustainably lifting one's welfare level beyond government handouts.

The Indonesian social protection system is made up mainly of two types of programs that are designed to secure the population's well-being. The first type is composed of non-contributory social-assistance programs that range from food and nutritional assistance to conditional cash transfers and scholarships. Aimed at the poor and vulnerable populations, the Unified Database (UDB), housed under the Ministry of Social Affairs, serves as a program-targeting instrument. Aside from these regular transfers, there is

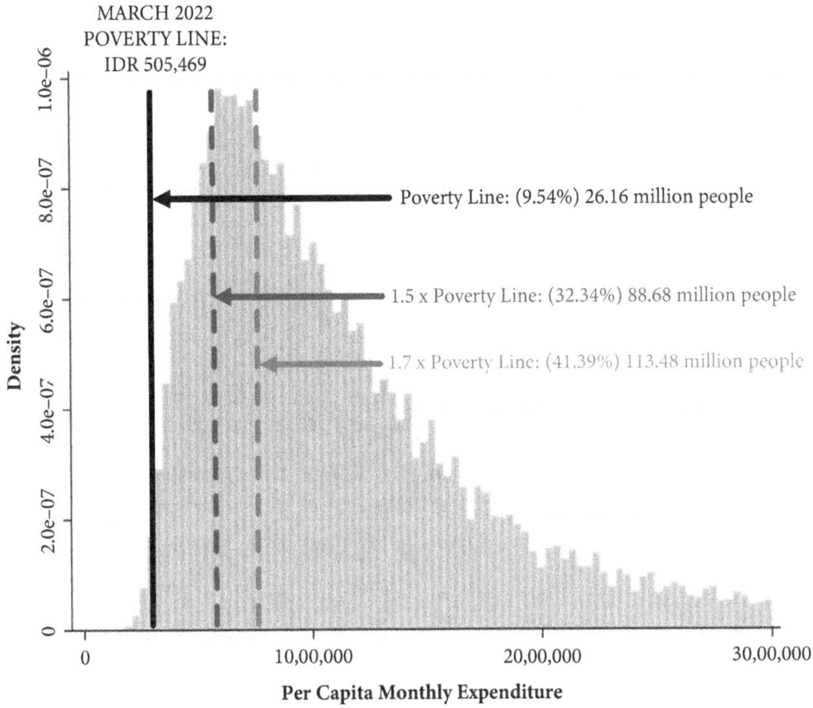

Figure 1.2 Poverty Headcount Ratio at National Poverty Line (% of population)
Source: Statistics Indonesia, Susenas, March 2022.

also a range of energy subsidies intended for those in poverty, such as gas cooking fuel, fuel, and electricity (Figure 1.3). Limited or one-off transfers, such as disaster-response assistance, are also available on a more limited scale. The second category of programs comprises contributory social insurance schemes that require beneficiaries to directly or indirectly pay into the system to access benefits. These include the national health insurance (*Jaminan Kesehatan Nasional*; JKN) scheme managed by the social security administrator for health (BPJS) and work-related insurance and pension schemes managed by the social security system for the employed (BPJS-*Ketenagakerjaan*). The latter covers pensions, work-accident insurance, death insurance, old age savings, and unemployment benefits. Beyond these programs, the government has also made attempts to integrate active labor market policies to improve one's opportunities in the labor market through the *Kartu Prakerja* (or the "Pre-Work Card") re-skilling scheme. Despite

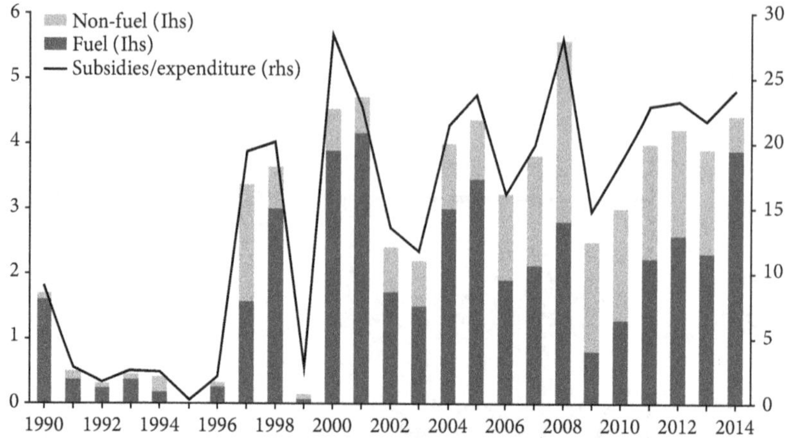

Figure 1.3 Fuel and Non-fuel Subsidies as a Share of Indonesian GDP and Government Expenditure, 1990–2014 (%)
Source: Howes and Davies, 2014.

this broad range of programs available in the Indonesian social protection system, the Indonesian government relies heavily on the social-assistance component of the social protection system, which also includes the subsidies, to secure the population's well-being. Yet the slowdown in poverty-rate reduction and significant share of people living in economic vulnerability raises the question of what direction Indonesia's social protection system ought to take as it moves forward.

Aside from questions of program mix and architecture, the sustainability of Indonesia's social protection system is a pressing matter. With the system largely comprising non-contributory social-assistance programs in terms of range and coverage, the government needs to shoulder much of the programs' costs. By 2023, the Indonesian government ran at least three nationwide regular social-transfers programs for those living in poverty and economic vulnerability (PIP, PKH, Program Sembako), reaching nearly 20 million families or around 30% of the country's population. These programs are also complemented with a range of energy subsidies, whose recipients exceed those receiving regular transfers due to weaker targeting mechanisms. On the other hand, schemes that require user contribution are more limited in scale. By 2023, around 250 million people, or 90% of the country's citizens, were enrolled in the JKN scheme. Despite its near-universal coverage, 44.51% of the JKN's members received government subsidies for their subscriptions, which raises concerns about its sustainability. Meanwhile, with a majority of the country's workers employed in the informal sector, BPJS-*Ketenagakerjaan*'s coverage is much more limited. By 2023, 54.88 million people were registered as BPJS-*Ketenagakerjaan* members, of which 64.33%, or only 34.30 million, were active members. This number is set against 146.62 million people in the country's total labor force. Efforts to expand contribution and coverage need to be undertaken if the government is to take the system's financial sustainability seriously.

Despite the large share of the population living in economic vulnerability, the government's capacity is constrained by limited resources, and there is a need to prioritize transfers to those deemed to be in the greatest need. Limited funds, however, not only cap program coverage but also put a strain on the quality of service delivery. Greater revenues are needed to finance welfare spending, such as by reforming the country's expensive and inefficient subsidies (see Chapter 2) as well as increasing the tax-to-GDP ratio. At the same time, the range and coverage of contributory programs that make up the country's social protection system needs to be increased so that the cost of welfare provisions can be shared between the government and its citizens. Contribution toward these provisions would also increase the citizens' stake in the programs' operations and incentivize them to actively demand that the government improve service delivery.

Although there is much to improve in existing social protection programs, reforming the country's social protection system is not simply a matter of changing the types of programs within the system or improving the existing schemes. This reform would need to entail more expansive changes that align the system with the country's broader economic policies and development strategy. Wherever Indonesia's social protection system is heading in the coming decade, it remains a work in progress. It has evolved from an ad-hoc, crisis-response, poor-relief scheme at the end of the 1990s to one of the developing world's most advanced targeting instruments in the latter half of the 2000s, as it sought to break free from weakly targeted programs and subsidies.

This chapter traces the evolution of Indonesia's social protection system since the country's transition into democracy in 1998, all the way through to the end of the Joko Widodo–Ma'ruf Amin administration in 2024. It tells the story of how welfare infrastructure was built over time as the government responded to crises and political pressures, along with the story of how past policy decisions constrained future choices as reformers sought to enact changes. While path dependency sets limits to the form of policies designed, political factors constrain the kinds of research evidence that is translated into or that helps shape public policy. This chapter is about change over time, and a cautionary tale on how good progress can break down if it is not well maintained. It is also about the past and how it shapes the present, as well as about the future that policymakers are shaping today.

Early Reforms During "Reformasi"

The 1997–1998 Asian financial crisis marked a turning point for Indonesia's welfare system. Before the crisis, the country had few broad-based social welfare programs, lacking both the economic infrastructure and political mechanisms needed for large-scale transfers. However, the crisis forced the government to build social safety net programs from the ground up, despite its limited capacity to deliver them at scale.[1] In the aftermath, Indonesia's transition to democracy not only reshaped its political landscape but also led to lasting changes in social protection. Some crisis-era safety net programs were retained as part of economic and social recovery efforts, and over time, the government moved beyond non-contributory poor-relief schemes to expand contributory social insurance for all citizens. This decade of rapid welfare expansion is often credited to democratization, which created new political incentives to strengthen social protection.[2]

Indeed, democracy changed the rules of the game for politicians in Indonesia by incentivizing them to be more responsive to citizens' demands for broader social welfare provisions. When she became president in 2001, Megawati Soekarnoputri had immediately set up a task force to design a national social security system. This system was slated to provide healthcare, pension, and work-related insurance programs for the population and followed the mandate of the fourth amendment of the country's constitution, which the House of Representatives passed in 2000. With a third of its seats held by Megawati's PDI-P party (*Partai Demokrasi Indonesia-Perjuangan*, "The Indonesian Democratic Party of Struggle"), the amendment was passed and included the provision that "the state shall establish a national social security system for all citizens." Seeking re-election support

[1] Suryahadi, Sumarto, and Pritchett, 2003.
[2] Aspinall, 2014; Jung, 2016.

from workers and the urban poor in the 2004 elections, Megawati and her party were then set to pass the National Social Security System bill. Given time pressures, the formulation and subsequent introduction of the bill in 2004 was done in a top-down manner by her government with little public consultation.[3] Despite the effort, Megawati lost the election to Susilo Bambang Yudhoyono, and the social security system did not become his administration's priority for the next seven years until the administration appointed an administrator for the insurance schemes.

Despite the slow progress on the Indonesian social security system in Yudhoyono's first term (2004–2009), the ratification of the National Social Security System Law strengthened citizens' claims to government welfare provisions. Moreover, progress on public welfare provisions advanced in other areas under Yudhoyono, as his government adopted a broad range of pro-poor welfare policies. With the retention of a range of social provisions for people in poverty that stemmed from the post-crisis social safety net, as well as a range of social insurance provisions for all Indonesian citizens by law, Indonesia had practically installed a welfare system within six years of its transition to democracy. These early welfare provisions—although limited in their scale and implementation—laid the groundwork for later reformers including scholars, researchers, politicians within the government, and international institutions. Behind the progressive direction taken by the Indonesian welfare system was far-reaching political change, which shaped the playing field for politicians in the country.

The period immediately after Indonesia's transition into democracy, dubbed the "Reformasi" era, saw the country adopting a range of social and political reforms. Two reforms, however, were key in shaping Indonesia's welfare politics. The first was the end of the authoritarian military-led political system, which came to be replaced with a democratic multi-party system. With the newly opened political space after Soeharto's fall, a whopping 48 parties competed in the 1999 legislative elections, and 21 of them won at least one seat in the House of Representatives. The large number of parties, however, made it difficult for a single party to hold a majority. Thus, Indonesian political parties have held onto power by sharing it through coalitions and allocating political appointments across the government to bind these alliances together. This power-sharing arrangement encourages politicians to make concessions to competing interests in order to protect their own

[3] Jung, 2016.

political interests and stability.[4] In this setting, key policy decisions are likely to be taken with intra-elite, alliance-building considerations in mind rather than the citizens' best interests.

The second key reform was the government decentralization that occurred in the 2000s. Due to the sudden and comprehensive devolution of power, scholars and political commentators have dubbed it a "big bang" decentralization approach.[5] This devolution of power has lent greater authority over political and fiscal decisions to local governments and is key in shaping central–local government relations in the country. This system of regional autonomy replaced the previous system of centralized government and development planning. This reform effectively made regional governments the central government's partners in development rather than the objects of national government development.

What these changes mean for welfare system development in Indonesia is twofold. First, political elite dynamics are—to a significant extent—likely to shape welfare policymaking and lead to a top-down approach in decision making. This dynamic can be seen in the social security reform in the first half of the 2000s. Meanwhile, decentralization means that local governments are not simply an extension of the central government's development policies, and they have a degree of authority in determining how regional budgets are to be spent. On the other hand, this could mean that regional governments could optimize spending on specific issues that matter for different localities instead of having to take a one-size-fits-all welfare policy. Thus it could, in theory, remediate some issues arising from the tendency for politicians in the central government to take a top-down approach to welfare policymaking. On the other hand, this opens a space for misalignment between central and local government welfare policies. For those seeking to reform the country's welfare policy, it means that policy advocacy requires taking into account intersecting political interests and identifying key decision makers within different levels of governance.

If, under Suharto's era, technocrats close to the central government could enjoy the ruler's patronage, under democracy they need to be policy entrepreneurs to secure policy buy-in. Aside from identifying the policy champions who would advance their reform agenda within the government, technocrats and reformers would also need to innovate to appeal to decision

[4] Blunt, Turner, and Lindroth, 2012.
[5] Alm, Martinez-Vazquez, and Indrawati, 2005.

makers. In this new playing field, research evidence emerges as a means to advance a policy agenda. With "scientific objectivity" as its main currency, it has emerged as a policy advocacy tool that can—to an extent—cut through politics.

Reforms in the Late "Reformasi" Era

Alongside the socio-political reforms during the Reformasi Era that shaped the welfare policymaking landscape, the 2000s were also marked by changes in state administration. In the name of accountability and transparency, between 2003 and 2004, the government legislated three related laws on state finance, state treasury, and auditing management. The new system replaced the old cash-based, single-entry system with a double-entry accounting system. It used a single treasury account, transparent management of the public treasury, expenditure and financial control with performance indicators and computerized reporting, and a tightly scheduled auditing system. One of its key implications is the way in which performance across the government can be measured through the ratio of budget spent. This governance paradigm was also the case with welfare programs, which are evaluated based on budgetary spending instead of their efficacy in improving recipients' well-being. However, aiming to make improvements in key economic indicators, Susilo Bambang Yudhoyono's administration began to adopt additional measures as indicators for a program's success.

The year that Yudhoyono took office in 2004 saw his administration facing its first test: for the first time ever, Indonesia became a net oil importer. Increased oil consumption and the National Oil Company's inability to meet demand pushed the government to finally make a difficult and expensive call, as Indonesia was now exposed to fluctuations in global oil prices. Making matters worse was the government's long-standing fuel subsidies policy, which had kept fuel prices artificially low. Initially used to control inflation, it soon became a means for the government to maintain the poverty rate for years, which effectively cemented fuel subsidies as the state's key welfare policy instrument. Yet, given its costs, the fuel subsidy policy also presented itself as a threat to the state's fiscal sustainability in the long run, forcing the administration to make another tough call—to revoke fuel subsidies, at least partly. Though facing public backlash due to the existing policy's popularity, it was a necessary step to be taken, as not only were the fuel subsidies encroaching upon the country's fiscal health but they were also a form of regressive welfare that benefited the well-off more than the needy (see Chapter 2). To truly be able to improve the population's well-being—and those in poverty in particular—fiscal space had to be freed up for programs that were more efficient and effective in alleviating poverty and economic vulnerability.

With the creation of the Crisis Social Safety Net in 1999, Indonesian welfare spending increased dramatically. However, following the financial crisis, growing fuel subsidies continued to curtail the Indonesian government's fiscal space for additional social spending. Since 2000, these subsidies have taken up as much as 25% of central government spending.[6] In the years following Indonesia's democratic transition, the government attempted to cut back the remaining subsidies with varying degrees of success.

The threat of fuel subsidies to the country's fiscal sustainability was not a new problem that had suddenly emerged under Yudhoyono's government. The challenge has been noted since Suharto's time but remained a ticking time bomb until the end of his rule. Throughout the Asian financial crisis recovery phase, the government had implemented a range of economic reforms, which included a reduction in the number of subsidized oil products from seven to just five in 1999. In the following year, kerosene, diesel, and gasoline prices for household consumption were raised despite public opposition that led to violent protests. However, by 2003 the increase was reversed as the government made an attempt to link the trend in domestic fuel prices with international prices. When Yudhoyono rose to the presidency in 2004, the issue imploded—global oil prices rose, just when the government began its new import strategy.

Although financial pressures created an urgency for fuel subsidy reforms, the memory of Suharto's corruption-ridden government made it difficult for these reforms to be separated from the public's dissatisfaction with the political system. Nearly all attempts by the Indonesian government to reform subsidies between 2000 and 2003 resulted in violent demonstrations. At that time, students and the public felt that the price increases were linked to powerful interest groups.[7] Making matters worse, despite the government's promise to use budget savings to help low-income households, subsidies for rice and education remained low, and many compensation programs never

[6] Howes and Davies, 2014.
[7] Bacon and Kojima, 2006; Beaton and Lontoh, 2010.

materialized.[8] Thus, when the Yudhoyono government opted to scale back subsidies and increase fuel prices, it sought to tread the waters more carefully than its predecessors by coupling fuel price hikes with temporary cash transfers for the poor.

Yudhoyono's government managed to increase retail fuel prices on at least three occasions in 2005, 2008, and 2013. To mitigate the impact of oil price hikes and to avoid public opposition, the government distributed cash transfers to the poor and near-poor. For instance in 2005, following his election, President Yudhoyono raised petrol prices by 150% in two stages, accompanied by a compensation package to dampen the hike's impact on the poor.[9] Another significant fuel price hike occurred in 2008, with a 33% increase in petrol price. This increase was also accompanied by a similar compensation package. However, the almost arbitrary nature of how a given family got to be recorded in the National Family Planning Coordinating Board (BKKBN) database and categorized as "pre-prosperous" or "prosperous"—and thus determined as eligible or ineligible for government transfers—exposed Yudhoyono's administration to criticism for a lack of transparency and poor targeting.

Realizing the delicate situation at hand, in 2005 Yudhoyono ordered BPS (Statistics Indonesia) to collect household socio-economic data for social-assistance targeting purposes. The database not only categorized households into "very poor," "poor," and "almost poor"—groups that allowed for more precise program targeting—but it also surveyed a greater number of households systematically. A more systematic approach to data collection aimed at minimizing the exclusion of households in poverty who should be prioritized for social-assistance transfers. Upon completion, the database was used to target beneficiaries for the fuel price increase compensation package in 2005 and 2008.

Although the targeting was imperfect, Indonesia's adoption of a beneficiary-targeting instrument marked a milestone in its welfare system development for at least three reasons. First, the adoption of a targeting instrument demonstrated the administration's effort to insulate welfare program administration from politics. To defend its programs from criticism, the Yudhoyono administration sought to obtain an air of legitimacy for these programs through de-politicized technical methods to determine benefit

[8] Beaton and Lontoh, 2010.
[9] Sen and Steer, 2005.

eligibility. While this was a political choice on Yudhoyono's end to gain approval for his programs, it was marked progress toward governance transparency. Second, the government made a significant investment in developing a complex targeting system, which built a foundation for more advanced targeting methods in the future. This foundation encompasses technical know-how regarding a specific data-collection method to consciously capture the poor and vulnerable population that is often marginalized and invisible to the state's eye, as well as being able to order and categorize this population for benefit-eligibility purposes. Finally, the introduction of technical methods in welfare program management also introduced new indicators for how well a program is administered. Instead of simply looking at the ratio of budget spent, the targeting instrument also introduced "inclusion/exclusion error" into the discourse of welfare program performance. While inclusion error refers to people who received program benefits but should not be eligible, exclusion error refers to people who are entitled to program benefits but were missed out. When compared to budgetary spending ratio, these indicators are better at capturing program efficacy.

The adoption of technocratic methods in program governance and technical languages in program evaluation became institutionalized as the administration established The National Team for the Acceleration of Poverty Reduction (*Tim Nasional Percepatan Penanggulangan Kemiskinan*, TNP2K) in 2010. Operating under the office of the vice president, the task of TNP2K was to coordinate poverty-alleviation efforts across the government. Among its first tasks was to develop a program-targeting instrument as well as to monitor and evaluate a range of poverty-alleviation programs. Working closely with Statistics Indonesia, TNP2K developed a household welfare ranking algorithm using the former's survey data, which allowed the government to prioritize social transfers to the neediest families with greater precision than the previously used welfare-categorized database. Alongside the newly developed targeting instrument was a practice of systematic program monitoring and evaluation to improve program delivery, as well as rigorous impact evaluation. In the latter, TNP2K offered technical support to government units or ministries who were tasked with administering various poverty-alleviation programs.

Beyond providing technical support to the government, the TNP2K is also engaged in what many call evidence-based policymaking. In collaboration with research institutes and universities around the world, TNP2K produces research evidence to support the government's decision making.

For instance, in partnership with The Abdul Latif Jameel Poverty Action Lab at the Massachusetts Institute of Technology between 2012 and 2013, TNP2K evaluated the impact of providing households with ID cards that could empower them to demand the full amount of rice subsidy program benefits they were entitled to and thus deter corruption in welfare program delivery.[10] The government of Indonesia then used insights from this research to scale up the ID card delivery. In June 2013, the government decided to scale up the ID card program to 15.5 million poor households, and by August of that year, 14.38 million cards had been distributed as Social Protection Cards.

It is also under TNP2K that the government's long-overdue commitment toward the country's social insurance system was renewed. After the fiscal pressure from the fuel subsidies was eased and a social protection system infrastructure was set up, Yudhoyono's administration could once more focus on ironing out the details of the country's social insurance system. In 2015, TNP2K launched a roadmap for the rollout of universal healthcare.

Yudhoyono's presidency was marked by a significant investment in social protection system infrastructure. These investments included the creation and broad use of targeting databases, the shift from regressive fuel subsidies to targeted transfers as the government's main welfare policy instrument that better reached the poor,[11] the institutionalized use of program indicators that better reflected their performance, and a broader acceptance of evidence-based policymaking in introducing welfare reforms. As a result of robust economic growth in this decade, along with a reformed social protection system, poverty rates were slashed by 4.72 percentage points throughout Yudhoyono's presidency. Although great strides were made in this period, the Indonesian government was faced with a new set of issues dubbed the "last mile" problem, namely the eradication of extreme poverty.[12]

The persistent and severe nature of poverty in the last mile implies that a business-as-usual approach may not be sufficient. One of the challenges in tackling this issue was the administration's limited ability to harmonize poverty-alleviation efforts between the central government and those of local governments. Power devolution through decentralization means that

[10] Banerjee et al., 2018.

[11] Hanna and Olken, 2018.

[12] *Extreme poverty* is a condition characterized by severe deprivation of basic human needs, including food, safe drinking water, sanitation facilities, health, shelter, education, and information. The World Bank calculated extreme poverty numbers using the USD 2.15 PPP poverty line.

power is no longer centralized at the national level, and neither are the dynamics of welfare reform. While the central government could create laws and regulations, as well as national frameworks for welfare policy implementation, localities are where the rubber meets the road. At this level, local governments and bureaucrats become the focal point in policy implementation. Beyond implementing central government policies, local governments can have their own initiatives, which may or may not align with the central government's strategy and may even compete for resources with central government efforts. Another question was whether the newly elected Joko Widodo's welfare policies could innovate and leverage the foundation that the Yudhoyono administration had built to tackle persistent poverty, or the "last mile" problem.

The Last Mile Problem

Joko Widodo's election to presidency in 2014 was a much-celebrated moment, which many observers dubbed a "new hope" for far-reaching reforms thanks to his humble civilian background, which was juxtaposed with the country's old political elites. Widodo's first term in office (2015–2019) saw a continuation of social policies from the Yudhoyono era. Emboldened by strong economic indicators and consistent decreases in the poverty rate, Widodo, at the start of his second term in 2020, set his gaze upon a new goal to eradicate extreme poverty by the end of his tenure in 2024. The majority of Widodo's two terms were characterized by political stability due to his PDI-P party's majority in the House of Representatives and consistently high public satisfaction with his presidency. Yet the lack of pressure that compelled his predecessor to take significant reforms raises the question of whether Widodo's complacency prevented him from doing more.

Inheriting a well-established social welfare infrastructure, Widodo had a strong start as he rolled out cards like the Social Protection Card program, launched in 2014, to cover a broader range of programs and further improve program targeting. The administration launched three cards for three preexisting programs: the Smart Indonesia Card, which marked eligibility for the Smart Indonesia scholarship for children in poor families; the Healthy Indonesia Card intended for subsidized JKN premium recipients; and the Prosperous Family Card intended for food assistance to eligible families.

Meanwhile, a new savings program was launched and accompanied by the Prosperous Family Savings Card. Moreover, Widodo's first term was also marked by an expansion in universal healthcare coverage, which by the end of his term had already reached 83.6% of the population.

Perhaps one of Widodo's most innovative legacies from his first term was when he decided to transform the long-running Rastra rice assistance program—from in-kind transfers to a digital voucher system to improve its delivery (see Chapter 4). Leveraging the long-established partnership between researchers in J-PAL and the Indonesian government, between 2017 and 2019, J-PAL partnered with TNP2K, the National Development Planning Agency (BAPPENAS), and the Australian Department of Foreign Affairs and Trade to roll out the reform in waves and measure its impact. The reform's positive impact led to its nationwide implementation when Widodo won his second term in 2020. Aside from the rice transfers, the government also applied the newly rolled-out digital benefit delivery system to other programs such as the Family Hope Program conditional cash transfer and the Smart Indonesia Program scholarship for students in poverty.

Widodo's second term, however, was when his administration was really tested. Just months after Widodo began his term at the start of 2020, the COVID-19 pandemic hit and drove the country into an economic recession. At that time, Widodo enjoyed legislative and popular support and could roll out an IDR 700 trillion emergency economic recovery package with no challenge from the legislative body. Within the recovery package, 38% was earmarked for social protection programs (see Chapter 8). This dramatically expanded budget meant that the government could expand existing social protection schemes like the rice transfers and electricity subsidies, launch new cash transfer programs, subsidize the national healthcare premium, and modify the newly launched *Kartu Prakerja* job re-skilling program amidst adverse labor market conditions. With a goal to cover as much of the population as possible, the government faced the need to quickly innovate in program-beneficiary identification and to rethink its benefit delivery mechanisms to address the movement restrictions that were in place.

The combination of the crisis and a dramatically expanded social spending budget finally prompted the administration to innovate by combining top-down targeting—using the government's existing database across the Ministry of Social Affairs, the BPJS, the BPJS-*Ketenagakerjaan*, and the National Electricity Company—with community targeting through consultation with village residents and governments, along with a self-targeting mechanism where people registered to receive social assistance according to their eligibility.

Despite the innovations that emerged during the crisis, it also marked a step back in evidence-based policymaking, as some reforms under Yudhoyono's administration were rolled back. At the start of the pandemic, Widodo's Social Affairs Minister was embroiled in a COVID-19 emergency transfers scandal and was replaced by another PDI-P cadre. Facing heightened public scrutiny, the new minister limited the access of other government bodies to the targeting database that had been used to target beneficiaries for a broad range of social welfare schemes. This decision effectively hampered the cross-government unit coordination in poverty alleviation that had been fostered under the Yudhoyono presidency. To make matters worse, the new minister stripped the database from its welfare ranking, which made it impossible to identify the neediest households. Thus, when Widodo set a target to alleviate extreme poverty by 2024, identifying people in extreme poverty was a challenge.

In the absence of a reliable targeting instrument, BAPPENAS stepped up to create a social registry that planned to record at least 80% of the country's population. However, by 2021 the database was still in its planning stage. With time pressures to attain the extreme-poverty alleviation goal by 2024, the Coordinating Ministry for Human Development and Culture initiated the creation of the Targeting Data for the Acceleration of the Elimination of Extreme Poverty (P3KE), which focused on the poorest of the poorest individuals in the country. Toward the end of Widodo's tenure, the Ministry of Social Affairs preferred to use the UDB to target the Family Hope Program conditional cash transfer and Program Sembako food assistance recipients, while other ministries and agencies matched their data with the P3KE. However, Indonesia needs to really think about where it is headed in the next decade. Poor coordination between welfare data providers and users in Widodo's second term highlighted several key welfare issues that plagued his administration, such as a lack of direction for coherent social protection policy and a vision for Indonesia's welfare system in the long run.

In the next decade, any government that takes office after Widodo leaves in 2024 will have to deal with several pressing issues. Firstly, the country's population is aging, and its pension system is still very limited in scale. By 2023, only 15.7% of its working population had some kind of pension coverage. What this means is that elderly well-being might be an emergent challenge in the coming years. At the same time, it will also mean that the JKN's financial burdens will increase, and its sustainability will be under threat. Second, with aspirations to become a high-income country, Indonesia's social welfare policy needs to be aligned with its broader economic development and growth strategies. This means that the social protection system needs to support investment in human capital through education as well as early life nutrition and healthcare, and it needs to be integrated with labor market policies. Third, global climate crises mean that disasters will be more frequent and severe, and those living in poverty are more likely to be more deeply impacted. What this highlights is the need for a social protection system that is dynamic and flexible enough to be able to tackle sudden shocks, as well as one that builds resilience in the face of new challenges. Rather than being fixated on poverty numbers, renewed commitment to the protection of citizens' well-being will require any incoming government to look at welfare issues more holistically and tackle these emerging issues head on.

At the forefront of Indonesia's emergent challenges is the persistent issue of inequality. A friend once described the country as possessing "two Indonesias": one that is relatively developed, well-connected, and well-served by basic services, and another that is not. This inequality often falls along urban and rural lines, with economic growth and access to social protection disproportionately benefiting urban areas, especially in Java. This disparity is evident in the pockets of extreme poverty, characterized by high poverty ratios and headcounts, that is prevalent in many rural regions. These areas underscore the problem of uneven development across the nation. While Indonesia's social protection system alone cannot completely address this issue, it must, at a minimum, ensure consistent service delivery quality nationwide. Ideally, it should also foster inclusive economic growth to bridge the gap between these two Indonesias.

More than two decades have passed since the fall of Suharto's New Order government, and Indonesia has established a fully-fledged social protection system that encompasses food, education, health, and energy transfers for the poorest. For the more well-off individuals employed in the formal sector, the government now provides pension and work-accident insurance schemes. However, the true resilience of Indonesia's social protection system will be tested in the coming decades. The question is whether time will reveal cracks in Indonesia's social protection system, or if reformers will take wisdom from the past and adapt the system to meet future needs.

2

Reforming Regressive Fuel Subsidies

Fuel subsidies have been a prominent feature of Indonesia's economic policy for decades. These subsidies were initially launched to combat inflation under President Suharto's administration (1967–1998). By keeping inflation in check, the government sought to maintain the people's purchasing power and keep poverty numbers low. Thus, the lack of social programs for the broader population under Suharto's rule meant that fuel subsidies served as the government's poverty alleviation strategy. Although a range of broad-based social protections programs that explicitly aimed to tackle poverty had emerged post-1998, fuel subsidies remained a regular ensemble in the government's public welfare repertoire. Yet, since subsidizing fuel is a costly policy—costing the government as much as or more than a quarter of the state's annual expenditure in 2004—the government had also considered revoking it on many occasions.

Despite the costs, fuel subsidies remained as a key economic and social instrument for the Indonesian government. As of 2025, the government still relies on fuel subsidies spending as a part of the country's social protections budget, highlighting the centrality of the policy in Indonesia's discussions on its social protection programs. At the same time, this pressure on the state budget has limited the government's ability to enact transformative social and economic reforms that are more effective than mere consumption subsidies. Yet, revoking the subsidies is no simple matter.

Fuel subsidies rollbacks played a role in weakening Suharto's grip on power, which culminated with his fall. As the rupiah depreciated in 1997, the cost of fuel subsidies that were tied to international oil prices and denominated in US dollars exploded in rupiah terms. Keeping domestic prices artificially low would have bankrupted the state budget. As a part of a bailout package from the International Monetary Fund (IMF), in November 1997, Indonesia signed its first Letter of Intent. One of the IMF's key conditions was the removal of "distortionary" subsidies, which included fuel and electricity, given their massive fiscal burden and economic inefficiency. Weeks of unrest followed the government's decision to cut fuel subsidies and

Evidence and the Politics of Reform. Sudarno Sumarto, Oxford University Press.
 DOI: 10.1093/9780197831717.003.0003

contributed to Suharto's resignation and the country's transition to democracy in 1998. What started out with increased fuel prices ended with the fall of a 30-year-long authoritarian regime, underscoring both the economic and highly political nature of fuel subsidy reform among Indonesian political elites, long after 1998.

For decades, Indonesia's fuel subsidies have allowed its citizens to enjoy fuel prices lower than the international average. These subsidies were given based on the difference between fuel retail price and a government-determined price. Beginning as a blanket policy to reduce poverty, fuel subsidy policy grew increasingly costly and untenable over time. Although fuel subsidies constricted the Indonesian government's fiscal space, fuel price adjustments were rarely done, since fuel subsidies were and remain a highly popular policy.

Fuel subsidies may appear to be pro-poor policies at first glance, but they actually favor wealthier households who consume significantly more fuel than poorer ones. This makes the subsidies regressive rather than progressive. Over the years, these subsidies have created a network of beneficiaries, posing challenges for government reform efforts. While the policy was intended to benefit the poor, the emerging middle class has become a rapidly expanding group that consumes more fuel (see Figure 2.1). The economic growth in Indonesia during the 2000s facilitated the expansion of this middle class, with increased prosperity driving higher rates of private vehicle ownership, including ownership of two or three cars. This issue is compounded by limited investment in public transportation, which has reinforced the public's dependence on private vehicles.[1] As a result the middle class, which benefits significantly from these subsidies, has a strong incentive to oppose fuel price hikes.

In 2010, the richest 10% of households in Indonesia consumed an average of 80 liters of fuel per month, 11 times the consumption of the poorest 10% households who only consumed an average of 7 liters of fuel per month.[2] This stark disparity highlighted the need to shift from regressive energy subsidies toward targeted social assistance programs to effectively address poverty. Yet, lifting fuel subsidies is not merely about economic efficiency. It is also a political matter, since its erasure impacts a large share of the population. Given the widespread popularity of fuel subsidies across social

[1] Hook and Replogle, 1996; Chelminski, 2018.
[2] Calculated using the National Socioeconomic Survey (SUSENAS).

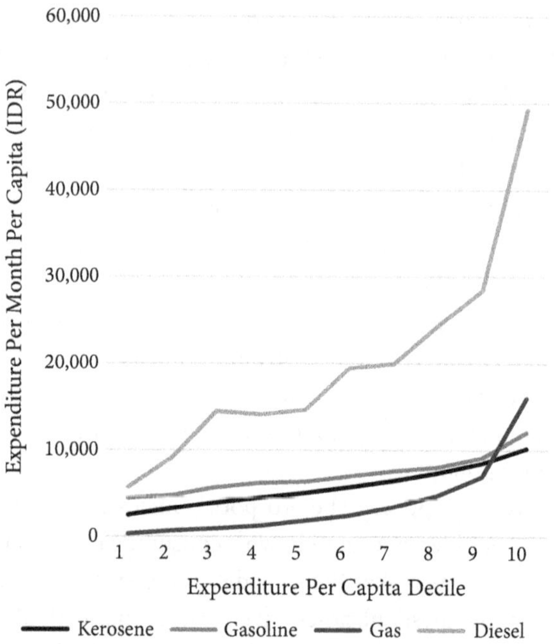

Figure 2.1 Fuel Consumption by Expenditure Decile (2003)

Note: Expenditure Decile 1 denotes the poorest 10% households, while Expenditure Decile 10 denotes the richest 10% households in Indonesia.

Source: SUSENAS (Indonesia Statistics, 2022).

classes, politicians face little incentive to advocate for their removal due to the risk of losing public support.

The political complexities of fuel subsidy reform run deep and may even undermine a country's democratic integrity. The concept of a "political resource curse" explains how oil abundance can strengthen authoritarian regimes. State oil companies often serve as profitable revenue streams that enhance political power, enabling governments to secure legitimacy or strengthen state control and thus extending their influence over the population.[3] Although Indonesia transitioned from authoritarianism to democracy in 1998, its government still maintains close ties with Pertamina, the state-owned oil company. This raises the concern that the government is politicizing fuel supply and prices to garner public support rather than allowing Pertamina to operate efficiently.

[3] Aslaksen, 2010; Dunning, 2008; Haber and Menaldo, 2011; Ross, 2012.

Further blurring the line between governance and business interests, Pertamina plays a dominant role across the oil supply chain. Pertamina's operations encompass production, refining, imports, and retail distribution. It held a monopoly on the retail market until 2004, when Regulation No. 36/2004 liberalized the downstream oil and gas sector. Despite increased competition, Pertamina's influence endures, bolstered by its connections to the government.

The entanglement between the state and Pertamina not only risks undermining Indonesia's democratic integrity but also poses a challenge to fuel subsidy reform. Despite these challenges, since 1998 Indonesia has made several fuel subsidy reform attempts with varying degrees of success. Within this period, spending on energy subsidies—which also includes fossil fuel—has fallen and been partially redirected toward targeted social assistance. In 2016, the country's budget for social welfare programs finally exceeded its budget for fuel subsidies.[4] Yet, this has less to do with the country's democratic transition and its desire to depoliticize fuel subsidies and more to do with fiscal pressures that forced the government to improve the efficiency of welfare provisions. Although fuel subsidies spending continues to fluctuate as global oil price rises and falls, Indonesia's trajectory marked a shift in how the government provides welfare to its citizens. Two decades after Indonesia's transition to democracy, social assistance programs replaced fuel subsidies as the country's main policy instrument to alleviate poverty.

Facing relatively little public backlash, Indonesia's experience with fuel subsidy reform in the 2010s is often cited as a successful example in attempts to roll back fuel subsidies. While significant strides were made in shifting from regressive subsidies to targeted social assistance, the intertwining of state interests with Pertamina highlights how deeply entrenched fuel subsidies are in Indonesia's political landscape. By the end of the 2010s through the early 2020s, the re-emergence of subsidies raised questions about the sustainability of these reforms. This chapter illustrates that lasting change depends not solely on economic necessity but also on strategic policymaking that accounts for public sentiment, political dynamics, and the role of social programs in easing resistance to reform.

[4] These programs entail the Smart Indonesia Program, Family Hope Program conditional cash transfer, Non-Cash Food Transfer, National Health Insurance subsidies, Direct Cash Transfer, KUBE small scale business assistance, Pre-Employment Card, and ad-hoc disaster relief social transfers, such as food assistance and cash transfers (Ministry of Finance, 2022).

Justifying Subsidy Removals

Governments enact subsidies generally either to influence consumers' behavior to achieve socially desirable outcomes[5]or, as in Indonesia's case, to provide some types of income protection.[6] In many low- and middle-income countries, the latter is usually a part of the government's welfare system—particularly in countries that do not have programs to target and reach the poor. In these countries, subsidies, including for the energy industry, are often used as a means to minimize income shocks. Yet, the lack of a targeting mechanism for subsidies often leads to wealthier households receiving most of its benefits. In 2004, the Indonesian government only spent around 14% of its kerosene subsidies and 6% of its other fuel subsidies on the poor, with the rest spent on non-poor households[7] (see Figure 2.2).

Aside from being regressive, subsidies also take up significant fiscal space. In many cases, governments spend higher amounts on subsidies than on other forms of social welfare programs. Subsidies strain national budgets and prevent governments from investing effectively in critical infrastructure

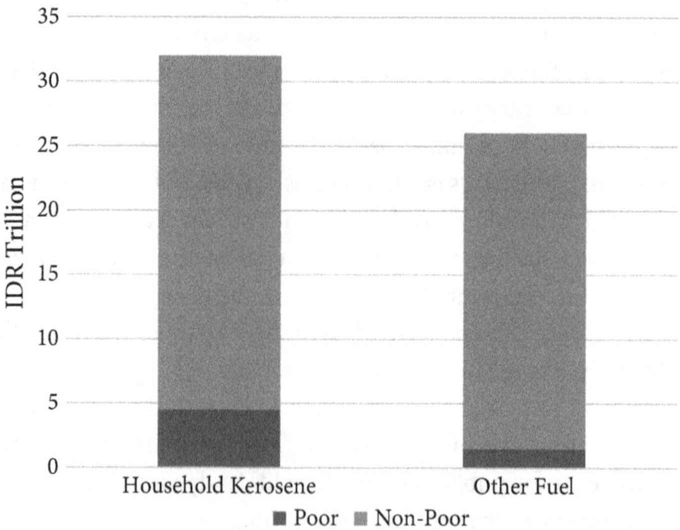

Figure 2.2 Budget Costs and Poverty Incidence for Fuel Subsidies (2004)

[5] Torani, Rausser, and Zilberman, 2016.
[6] Alderman, 2002; Yemtsov and Moubarak, 2018.
[7] World Bank, 2004.

and social services.[8] In 2005, Indonesia spent IDR 95.6 trillion in fossil fuel subsidies when its spending on social assistance was only IDR 24.9 trillion.[9]

Despite being a costly policy, past efforts to remove subsidies have faced backlash from the public, civil society, and trade unions.[10] Political opposition parties also opportunistically use price increases to foment protests that could challenge the incumbent's legitimacy.[11] These works provide an insight into the factors that can determine how the public would react to price increases, such as the justification for reform, the government's perceived legitimacy and credibility, the extent to which the burden is seen to be shared equitably, the policy's transparency, and successful communication about reform efforts. Even in times when fuel subsidies reform is an absolute necessity, how these factors play out remain key in the reform's success.

The 1997–1998 Asian financial crisis marked a turning point in the Indonesian energy policy, which concluded that the necessity to reform subsidies superseded its political unfavorability. As the crisis unfolded, President Suharto had no choice but to impose severe austerity measures, dramatically raising fuel prices by 2% for kerosene, 60% for diesel, and 71% for gasoline.[12] This triggered inflation, and with minimal support systems for the public the consequences were catastrophic. Massive protests erupted in cities across Indonesia, some turning violent, and eventually led to Suharto's resignation after a 30-year rule. This historical precedent has since made subsidy removal a politically sensitive issue for leaders considering reform. Fuel subsidies, originally aimed at poverty alleviation, evolved into a symbol of oil wealth redistribution, especially as limited re-investment in infrastructure or welfare deepened public dependency on subsidized fuel. The 1998 price hikes, therefore, not only underscored the government's struggles with social support but also illustrated the challenge of justifying such reforms to the public.

While fuel subsidies are usually a regressive policy that mainly benefits the wealthy, subsidy removal is likely to have the greatest negative impact on the poor. Unlike wealthier households, poorer households have little flexibility in their spending, so a rise in energy prices due to subsidy cuts may force them to cut essential consumption, risking their welfare or even pushing

8 Inchauste and Victor, 2017.
9 Ministry of Finance, 2006.
10 Bacon and Kojima, 2006; Siddig et al., 2014.
11 Chelminski, 2018.
12 Chelminski, 2018.

near-poor families into poverty. Such changes can have long-term, even intergenerational effects on nutrition, education, and overall well-being. Thus, in addition to the middle class, who increasingly consume subsidized fuel, lower-income households facing financial strain are also likely to oppose subsidy cuts. Because of fuel subsidy revocation's disproportionate impact on poorer households, any attempt to reform the policy must be paired with measures that cushion its effect on the poorest families.

Managing the Shock

With such an impact to household consumption, fuel subsidy reforms are likely to face resistance in the absence of compensation to those affected. Cash transfers have emerged as one of the most effective tools to reduce the immediate impact of fuel price increases following the reforms. In one IMF study of 25 subsidy reform cases, the authors found that when the subsidy removal was paired with cash transfers and a communication strategy, all reforms were successful. In absence of cash transfers, only 17% of the attempted reforms succeeded.[13] Yet, many governments still sought to implement fuel subsidy reform without pairing it with compensatory measures and were consequently met with protests. In 2018, France dropped its plans for a new energy tax, and by the end of 2019, Ecuador ended its attempts to eliminate fuel subsidies.[14] Meanwhile, early in 2022 Kazakhstan reversed its decision to end energy price controls after days of deadly protests.[15] The Kazakh government's policy reversal marked an end to a three-year-long effort to gradually revoke price controls. These cases show how implementation of fuel subsidy reform should be very carefully considered.

Although compensation through cash transfers might help allay pushback for reform, it may not necessarily be a feasible policy to implement. For instance, if compensatory cash transfers are to be effective, they must reach those that need it the most. It follows that there must be an accurate list of poor and vulnerable households for targeting purposes, which is something that a government may not always have at its disposal. As a result, much of the discourse on compensatory transfers is fixated on the

[13] Sdralevich, Sab, Zouhar, and Albertin, 2014; Rentschler and Bazilian, 2017.
[14] McAuley, 2018; Arnold, 2019.
[15] BBC News, 2022.

government's capacity to develop effective targeting tools, rather than factors like the importance of the implementation's timing. Overlooking such an issue risks underestimating its role in supporting a reform's success.[16]

Aside from the 1997–1998 Asian financial crisis, 2004 marked another historic shift in Indonesia's energy policy with two key events: the election of Susilo Bambang Yudhoyono and Indonesia's shift from being a net oil exporter to a net oil importer. The Yudhoyono administration soon realized that the government's subsidies on imported fuels had a disastrous impact on the country's budget. Moreover, the subsidies also posed an energy security issue, as it exposed the state's budget to major fluctuations in prices on the international market, tariff barriers, and potential geopolitical vulnerabilities in securing oil supply. At that time, energy subsidies consumed up to 24% of government expenditure and contributed to an ongoing energy crisis caused by insufficient supply and growing demand.[17]

In 2005 the Yudhoyono's administration decided to cut fuel subsidies, raising prices by a weighted average of 29% in February and by 114% in September.[18] While the fuel subsidies largely benefited middle to upper class households that could afford to have private vehicles, inflationary pressures, which saw consumer goods prices growing by 17.9% between February 2005 and February 2006, highlighted the indirect impacts of fuel subsidy reforms.[19] This inflation severely impacted the poor and pushed the near-poor into poverty. For the first time since the Asian financial crisis, Indonesia saw an uptick in its poverty rate. Between February 2005 and February 2006, an additional 3.8 million people slipped into poverty, representing an increase of 12%. Additionally, the corruption-ridden government body made it difficult for these reforms to be disassociated from the public's dissatisfaction with the government. With high public distrust, it was only to be expected that reforms would be met with protests across the country. Thus, to ease public backlash, compensation packages were rolled out to the poor.

At that time, the government launched a temporary cash transfer using fiscal savings created by the subsidy cutbacks to dampen the effect of the subsidy cut to the poor. The government provided nearly 19 million households with quarterly transfers of around USD 30, which was roughly one-eighth

[16] Vagliasindi, 2013; Bazzi, Sumarto, and Suryahadi, 2015.
[17] McCawley, 2014; Chelminski, 2018.
[18] Bazzi, Sumarto, and Suryahadi, 2015.
[19] Casier and Beaton, 2015.

of average quarterly household expenditures at baseline between October 2005 and September 2006.[20] These transfers were intended to compensate for the increased cost of living and were aimed at the country's poorest 30% of households. The transfers reached every village in the country and were provided to households via local post offices tasked with disbursing payments for each village. In addition to the cash transfers, the government also introduced a program called Schools Operational Assistance, which was designed to increase enrollment rates and expand the existing JAMKESMAS free healthcare program. Under time pressure, the government listed the transfers' beneficiaries within two months. To do so, the Indonesian government, through Indonesia Statistics, carried out a household survey aimed at identifying households entitled to the compensatory cash transfers. This household database is what would later be widely known as the Unified Database, which was the country's early attempt at a social registry.

Although this fuel price increase was met with opposition and protest from both the parliament and the public, Yudhoyono's administration managed to maintain the policy thanks to the introduction and expansion of various social assistance programs. These compensatory programs not only provided a buffer for economic shocks arising from fuel price increases, but also provided credibility for the government's commitment to social welfare.[21] When another wave of significant fuel price hikes occurred in 2008, this increase was also accompanied by a compensation package. On this occasion, data collected from the 2005 survey became a part of the framework for the government to, once more, conduct a survey and distribute unconditional cash transfers. However, this increase did not last, as it was reversed through three price reductions between December 2008 and February 2009. Although the hikes were reversed, the compensation package remained. This decision was partly motivated by the fall in global oil prices and the impending 2009 presidential elections, where President Yudhoyono sought a re-election.

Fuel prices were due to increase again in 2011 and, as before, the government planned to roll out compensatory cash transfers for the poor. Using detailed updates from the 2010 census, the government revised data from earlier household surveys to improve the accuracy of targeting. However, the Yudhoyono administration then abandoned the plan. Although the

[20] Bazzi, Sumarto, and Suryahadi, 2015.
[21] Perdana, 2014.

government backtracked on their plans to increase fuel prices in 2011, the data collected was used to target beneficiaries for other more permanent programs, such as the PKH conditional cash transfer, the Raskin food assistance, BSM educational aid, and the JAMKESMAS healthcare aid.[22]

The government made another attempt to raise fuel prices in 2012 with the agreement that any increase would require parliamentary approval, since it would be followed with substantial compensation packages.[23] However, the government failed to secure parliamentary approval until July 2013, when Yudhoyono's administration rolled out another price increase that averaged 40% of that year's revised budget.[24] This approval was needed, as the increase was accompanied by a compensation package that required budgetary changes. Although the administration recognized the need for further fuel price increases, significant hikes gave rise to the expectation of additional compensation and thus, in practice, required parliamentary approval that might be challenging to secure.

Beyond the Unified Database's use to allay pushback against energy reforms, in 2012 it was also used to determine households eligible to receive the Social Protection Card. The card was essentially Indonesia's first integrated benefit-targeting mechanism for the country's poorest families. At the time of card's launch in 2012, the government distributed 15.5 million cards for Indonesia's poorest 25% families registered in the Unified Database. Possession of the card signified an entitlement to permanent food, education, and health aid, in conjunction with more temporary cash transfers. When the government decided to increase fuel prices in 2013 and distribute temporary cash transfers to compensate the poor, the Unified Database and the Social Protection Card already existed as a targeting mechanism infrastructure that could be mobilized to identify program beneficiaries.

During Yudhoyono's tenure, Indonesia made progress in social welfare and garnered broader political support for subsidy reform. Despite the expansion of regular welfare program coverage and a reduced energy subsidy ratio compared to previous administrations, social welfare spending remained insufficient. Over Yudhoyono's two presidential terms, spending on social protection, health, and even education barely changed as a proportion of GDP.[25] In fact, during Yudhoyono's second term

[22] TNP2K, 2017.
[23] Howes and Davies, 2014.
[24] Nehru, 2013.
[25] Wisnu et al., 2017.

in 2009, spending on energy subsidies grew from 1.7% to 3.4% of GDP. This growth reflected a persistent budgetary imbalance that restricted the government's ability to expand investments in social welfare and infrastructure.

Fluctuations in global oil prices and currency exchange rates further complicated efforts to control subsidy spending. For instance, during the 2008 financial crisis, the Indonesian rupiah lost 28% of its value against the US dollar between October and November,[26] causing fuel subsidy costs to surge from IDR 83.8 trillion in 2007 to IDR 139 trillion just a year later. By the time President Joko "Jokowi" Widodo took office in 2014, he faced the difficult task of stabilizing Indonesia's fiscal position while attempting to push forward with lasting fuel subsidy reforms.

To Subsidize or Not to Subsidize

Beginning in 2014, bold subsidy reform was undertaken by the Jokowi administration. At that time, the government enacted a major fuel subsidy reform, emphasizing the need to reallocate public finances toward infrastructure investment, which was a flagship program during his presidential campaign. His administration's reform sought to allow domestic fuel prices to track the global oil market and to remove price controls. This change was further cemented by the legislation of a Presidential Regulation Number 191 of 2014 on The Provision, Distribution and Retail Selling Price of Oil Fuel. Table 2.1 summarizes key fuel pricing policies in Indonesia between 1997 and 2021.

Under the new fuel pricing policy, the government determined prices depending on the type of fuels: "special fuels," "special fuels for assignments," and "general fuels." Special fuels are oil products intended for certain consumers where the production volume and price are set and subsidized by the government. Fuel products under this category include kerosene and diesel. Meanwhile, special fuels for assignment are distributed in government-determined "assignment areas" and are not subsidized. Gasoline falls in this category. Finally, general fuel tends to be of higher quality, is aimed at the more well-off population, and is not subsidized. Any fuel products not falling into the first two categories are grouped under this category.

[26] Basri and Rahardja, 2011

Table 2.1 Indonesia's Key Fuel Pricing Reforms (1997–2022)

Date	Pricing reform
1997	Following the Asian financial crisis, government increased kerosene, diesel, and gasoline prices by 2%, 60%, and 71%, respectively.
2000	Kerosene, diesel, and gasoline prices were raised for households despite violent demonstrations.
2001	Kerosene, diesel, and gasoline prices were raised for industry.
2003	An attempt was made to link movements in domestic fuel prices and international prices.
2005	Prices increased by 29% in March and 114% in October. Industry was no longer eligible to access subsidized diesel.
2006	Prices increased for industrial users.
2007	Introduction of kerosene-to-LPG conversion program encouraged LPG use, and the kerosene subsidy was phased out.
2008	Prices increased in May by 33% for gasoline, 28% for diesel, and 25% for kerosene. Gasoline and diesel prices were lowered in December by 20% and 15%, respectively, as international oil prices eased.
2009	Prices lowered in January by 11% for gasoline and 7% for diesel, leaving gasoline prices the same as diesel prices (close to 2005 levels).
2013	One-off price increase averaged 40%.
2013	Base tariff increased by 15% over 2013 (households consuming more than 450 to 900 volt-amperes were not included).
January 2014	An attempt was made to raise prices of 12-kilogram cylinders, but the price increase was rolled back.
November 2014	Government initiated price increases of 31% for gasoline and 36% for diesel.
January 2015	Presidential Regulation No.191/2014 and MEMR Regulation No. 39/2014. Budgetary subsidy removed for premium gasoline, and Java, Madura, and Bali were excluded from the area of distribution; fixed subsidy level set at IDR 1000/liter for solar/biosolar diesel. Introduced a price band, ceiling and floor, for unsubsidized fuels.
July 2016	Energy and Mineral Resources Ministry Regulation No. 27/2016. Diesel subsidy reduced to IDR 500/liter.
November 2016	Energy and Mineral Resources Ministry Regulation No. 36/2016. Single price for fixed-price premium RON 88 gasoline and subsidized diesel established across Indonesia, including areas with less developed infrastructure.
April 2018	Government-enforced policy in MEMR Regulation No. 39/2014, on maximum retail price for non-subsidized fuel products. Retailers could not raise non-subsidized fuel prices without government approval.

continued

Table 2.1 *continued*

Date	Pricing reform
May 2018	Energy and Mineral Resources Ministry Decree No. 1851 K/15/MEM/2018. Fixed-price premium gasoline reintroduced in Java, Madura, and Bali.
September 2018	Energy and Mineral Resources Ministry Regulation No. 40/2018. Diesel subsidy raised to IDR 2000/liter.
October 2018	Premium gasoline price initially raised to IDR 7000/liter but was quickly restored to IDR 6450/liter.
May 2019	Price of premium gasoline adjusted to 6500 IDR/liter in Java, Madura, and Bali.
August 2019	2020 state budget reduces diesel subsidies back to IDR 1000/liter.
February 2020	Energy and Mineral Resources Ministry Decree No. 62 K/12/MEM/2020. Revised fuel pricing formula, removed the price floor for unsubsidized fuels.
July 2020	Energy and Mineral Resources Ministry to cut diesel subsidy by 50% to IDR 500/liter in the 2021 budget.
August 2021	Presidential Regulation No. 69/2021 to amend Presidential Regulation No. 191/2014 on The Supply, Distribution, and Retail Selling Price of Fuel Oil. This allows the Energy and Mineral Resources Minister to determine the retail selling price of special fuels and special fuels for assignment.
September 2022	Decree of the Minister of Energy and Mineral Resources No. 218.K/MG.01/MEM.M/2022 on Retail Selling Prices for Certain Types of Fuel Oil and Types of Fuel Oil for Special Assignments. The partly subsidized pertalite was increased by 30.7% from IDR 7650/liter to IDR 10.000/liter. Subsidized solar was increased by 32% from IDR 5150/liter to IDR 6.800/liter, and the unsubsidized Pertamax was increased by 16% from IDR 12.500/liter to IDR 14,500/liter.

Source: Chelminski, 2018; Xie and Harjono, 2020.

In November 2014, less than one month after Jokowi took office, gasoline prices were increased by 30% and diesel prices by 36% to lessen the gap between local and international oil prices. Later on, Jokowi's administration introduced a set of structural reforms. As global oil prices fell, by January 2015 the government announced the complete removal of the gasoline subsidy in the highly populated Java-Madura-Bali area, leaving only diesel and kerosene, which were intended for the poor, to be subsidized. However, gasoline sold outside the region was considered "special fuels for assignments" and thus still received a 2% subsidy. This subsidy served as compensation for higher distribution costs borne by Pertamina.[27] A fixed subsidy funded by the state budget was also implemented for diesel, set at IDR 1.000 (USD 8 cents) per liter below market prices to limit future fiscal exposure risk.

In 2016, the Indonesian government also introduced a new pricing formula that determined fuel price as a result of a given base price, constant, and margin.[28] This new pricing system aimed to limit volatility and equalize fuel prices across the country. Under this scheme, gasoline and diesel prices were to be adjusted regularly according to a published pricing formula. After initially adjusting fuel prices every month, by the end of 2015 the government decided that domestic fuel prices would be adjusted on a quarterly basis.[29] In the same year, the retail price of kerosene was fixed at IDR 2.500 (USD 20 cents) per liter across the country, and a fixed subsidy for diesel was set to IDR 500 per liter below market prices in July 2016 from IDR 1000 in the previous year. The introduction of this revised pricing and subsidy scheme coincided with a period of low global oil prices, meaning domestic price increases were limited. These measures, however, still resulted in the fall of fuel subsidy value from IDR 60.758 billion in 2015 to IDR 43.686 billion in 2016.[30]

In a renewed effort to even out fuel price disparities across the country, the government implemented the One Price policy in the beginning of 2017. Fuel retail prices have varied significantly in Indonesia due to disparities in distance and distribution infrastructure across the nation. In remote areas, fuel prices can be as much as three times higher than prices in the Java-Madura-Bali region, where energy infrastructure is more developed. The One Price policy aims at improving fuel affordability in Indonesia's remote and underdeveloped areas, or what the government calls the "assignment areas." The regulation stipulates that fuel prices in these areas should be the same as in the more developed regions of the country to achieve greater equity. However, in order to provide fuel to remote and underdeveloped regions, Pertamina needed to invest in new storage depots, fuel pumps, distribution agents, and airplanes to carry fuel to Indonesia's most remote areas.[31] Additionally, fuel distributors participating in the

[27] G20, 2019.
[28] Xie and Harjono, 2020.
[29] G20, 2019.
[30] G20, 2019.
[31] Xie and Harjono, 2020.

program are entitled to higher profit margins from Pertamina. The higher profit margins became an incentive for distributors to operate outside the Java-Madura-Bali region where distribution costs are much steeper.

These changes have resulted in an increase in Pertamina's operational costs by around IDR 900 billion a year.[32] While the policy has been progressively implemented, below-market pricing has resulted in substantial losses for Pertamina. Between 2014 and 2019, it is estimated that the underpricing of gasoline alone resulted in foregone revenue of IDR 54.5 trillion.[33] What this means is that artificial price controls were not reflected as fuel subsidies in the government budget, since this loss was borne by Pertamina. To resolve these losses, the government could "compensate" Pertamina as the executor of the "assignment." The government's ability to provide "loss compensation" is essentially the same as subsidy provision. However, if subsidies are regulated by parliamentary-approved state budgets, the provision of "loss compensation" hinges upon the government's decision to compensate for the losses. This strategy means that it is difficult to separate which falls under the domain of state administration or the government's responsibility, and which should be under the domain of the state-owned enterprise's business administration.

Although Jokowi's administration effectively circumvented the need for parliamentary approval through apparently more seamless price controls, this means that instead of dissipating, fuel subsidies have persisted, albeit in another form. If under Yudhoyono's administration fuel subsidy reforms were revoked by nominally setting fuel product prices, under Jokowi's administration the revocations were more subtle, through flexible price adjustments and policies targeting fuel distributors. The latter effectively shielded the cost of subsidies from political challenges in the parliament and blurred the line between state responsibility and Pertamina's business. Under Jokowi's administration, gasoline prices that were initially adjusted every month, and then every three months, were finally held steady between March 2016 and April 2018 despite a near doubled international oil price.[34] Despite rising international oil prices in 2018, and citing concerns over inflation and the need to maintain consumer spending, President Jokowi revised the course on the 2015 fuel subsidy reforms prior to the elections in April 2019.

[32] OECD, 2019.
[33] Laan and McCulloch, 2019.
[34] Xie and Harjono, 2020.

At that time, four policies were enacted. First, Jokowi ordered Pertamina to once more offer below-cost gasoline at fixed prices in Java-Madura-Bali region, despite high international oil prices and a depreciating Indonesian rupiah. Second, his administration increased the diesel subsidy to IDR 2.000/liter or about USD 15 cents. Third, it was decided that prices for gasoline and subsidized diesel would not be raised in 2018 and 2019. Finally, private fuel retailers were required to seek the government's approval to raise non-subsidized fuel prices. Only after Jokowi won the election were significant cuts to the diesel subsidy enacted. In August 2019, the administration halved diesel subsidies back to IDR 1000/liter in the 2020 state budget, and again to IDR 500/liter in the 2021 budget. These policies were further amended as of August 2021 through a new regulation that gave the government more leeway to set fuel prices and appoint state-owned enterprises to distribute fuel in assignment areas. In practice, this turned the government's explicit subsidies into implicit ones, and the costs were borne by Pertamina.

What the reforms under Jokowi's administration indicate is that despite numerous oil price shocks that had prompted reform since 1998, fuel subsidies remain an important political apparatus for any government in power—be it Suharto's authoritarian regime or the democratically elected Jokowi administration. However, the difference lies in how a functional social protection system under the latter was able to shift the conversation about poverty alleviation away from its focus on fuel subsidies.

Since the fall of Suharto, Indonesia had invested in building a social registry and social welfare infrastructure while pulling back on its fuel subsidy spending. However, when Russia invaded Ukraine in 2022 and fuel prices skyrocketed, the government opted to increase the price of the partly subsidized Pertalite by 30.7%, from IDR 7650/liter to IDR 10.000/liter; the subsidized solar by 32%, from IDR 5150/liter to IDR 6.800/liter; and the unsubsidized Pertamax by 16%, from IDR 12.500/liter to IDR 14,500/liter. To moderate pushback, the government launched cash transfers for the poor that amounted to IDR 600,000 per family, which was roughly the amount needed to avoid poverty numbers from rising. However, many eligible families were still excluded from the beneficiary list due to the poorly updated Unified Database. The government also launched an income support program amounting to the same value as the cash transfer for low-income formal sector workers. However, unlike during Yudhoyono's tenure, these programs did not add to the Indonesian social protection system infrastructure, as they only utilized the already existing welfare infrastructure with no long-term plans to keep any of them in place. This, along with the Jokowi administration's half-hearted effort to pull back subsidies, made fuel subsidy policies seem more like a response to crisis than a strategic move to ensure a just redistribution policy that is truly sustainable in the long run.

Toward Reform Sustainability and Progressive Redistribution

Indonesia's experience demonstrates that effective fuel subsidy reform requires a well-rounded approach that goes beyond merely cutting subsidies. Beyond revoking the subsidies, strategies for implementation, mitigation, and compensation schemes need to be considered—each contingent on factors such as politics, institutional capacity to implement reform strategies, and global fuel prices. By freeing fiscal space, subsidy reform could enable the government to reallocate funds toward sustainable welfare programs and to reduce its vulnerability to volatile fuel costs. However, the durability of these reforms remains uncertain.

Three key lessons emerge from Indonesia's approach to subsidy reform. *First*, successful reform depends heavily on well-crafted mitigation strategies. This entails both informing the public on why the reform is justified and compensating for those most affected by the new policies. In 2004, for instance, the Yudhoyono administration appealed to fairness by shifting from blanket subsidies to targeted transfers. Later, the Jokowi administration framed subsidy reduction as a way to redirect resources to infrastructure investments, fostering more equitable economic growth across the country.

The *second* is that for reforms to be effective, multi-sectoral effort is needed. Strategies to justify the reform, mitigate pushback, and compensate the losers require a coordinated effort across the government. Effective implementation of reform strategies, public outreach, and compensation packages require collaboration across government agencies. For example, the Ministry of Social Affairs, in partnership with Indonesia Statistics, administers cash transfers, while healthcare benefits fall under the Ministry of Health. This interagency coordination ensures consistent messaging and efficient distribution of compensatory support.

The *third* is that the reform's timing is crucial. Reforms should be enacted only when mitigation and compensatory measures are already in place. These measures help cushion the impact of price shocks and inflation, especially for poor and near-poor households. Moreover, timely distribution of this compensation needs to be taken into serious consideration. Timely disbursement of transfers is essential, as it allows households to maintain their spending levels. When transfers are delayed, households often reduce their expenditures significantly, by as much as 7.5 percentage points, thus risking further declines in welfare that could potentially push vulnerable groups deeper into poverty.[35]

Finally, subsidy reforms can free up fiscal space and, as in Indonesia's case, serve as an opportunity for progressive redistribution. In 2016, for the first time, social spending surpassed fuel subsidies, signaling a shift toward targeted welfare programs (see Figure 2.3). Years of gradual subsidy reductions have strengthened Indonesia's social welfare infrastructure. Not only could this infrastructure be mobilized to allay reform pushback, but later this infrastructure also can pave the way toward a fully fledged welfare system. This evolving infrastructure would include a social registry system, regulatory frameworks, and distribution channels that facilitate interagency collaboration.

In the two decades since Suharto's fall, Indonesia has expanded its social welfare system to cover most of its poorest 40% of households, with further expansion during the COVID-19 pandemic. Despite the persistence of fuel

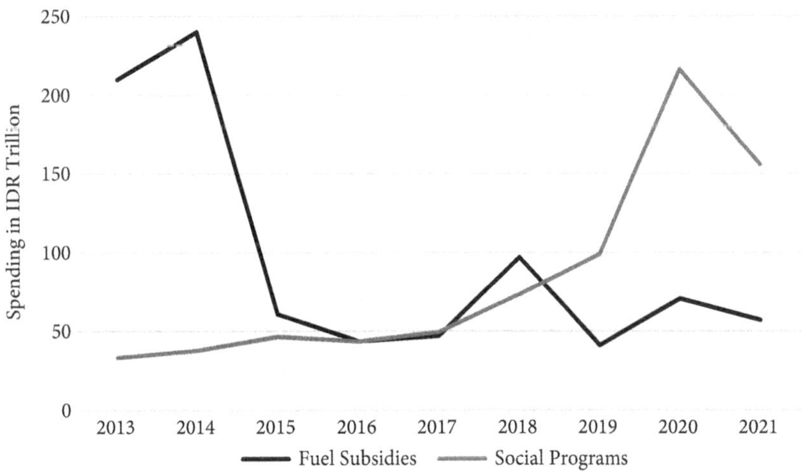

Figure 2.3 Fuel Subsidies and Social Program Expenditure (2013–2021)
Source: Ministry of Finance, 2022.

[35] Bazzi, Sumarto, and Suryahadi, 2015.

subsidies, social welfare programs have gradually become the government's main tool for addressing poverty. Under Jokowi's administration, Indonesia's social protection system has largely replaced subsidies as the primary welfare mechanism, although the durability of this shift remains uncertain, especially in times of global oil price volatility. Balancing direct social welfare support with the costs of subsidies will be an ongoing challenge.

Indonesia's story also underscores the potential pitfalls of state control over natural resources. Despite progress on subsidy reform, covert subsidies remain a risk, partly due to legislation that grants the government flexibility to adjust fuel prices without parliamentary oversight. This relationship between the state and Pertamina, Indonesia's state-owned oil company, raises questions about democratic accountability, as the government leverages Pertamina for political ends. History shows how state-controlled oil companies can be used to consolidate political power, as seen in cases like Venezuela, where state oil revenue funded authoritarian projects.[36]

The Indonesian government's influence over Pertamina does not just mean that the company is being subjected to government policy instrumentalization. It also means two things in terms of sustainability. First, Pertamina's sales of fuel below market prices prevents other private companies from competing. For instance Petronas, a Malaysian oil company that opened its first fuel pump in Indonesia in 2006, decided to close its Indonesian branches in 2012. Meanwhile, oil company French Total closed its doors by the end of 2020. While other companies remained as of 2025, such as British Shell and Dutch Vivo, the need to comply with government pricing and octane ratings remains a pressure for their businesses. This lack of competition for Pertamina, coupled with the certainty in demand from the government's subsidy policy, created little incentive for Pertamina to invest in research and development or to increase its efficiency and production capacity. To make matters worse, the government's demands that Pertamina bear the implicit subsidies burden has meant that the company might not be able to spare funds for research and development or to invest in productive infrastructure even if they wanted to.

Second, Indonesia's heavy reliance on fossil fuel subsidies has significant environmental implications, earning the country a C+ grade on the fossil fuel funding scorecard from the IISD. This independent think tank, focused on sustainable development governance, highlighted a 56% increase in

[36] Miller, 2005; Dunning, 2008; Aslaksen, 2010; Haber and Menaldo, 2011

Indonesia's support for fossil fuel consumption from 2014 to 2016 compared to prior years. These subsidies distort markets, hinder emissions reduction efforts, and create a competitive disadvantage for renewable energy development—directly opposing Indonesia's energy transition goals. The urgency for policy reform is clear: reducing fossil fuel subsidies is critical to prioritizing emissions reduction and advancing renewable energy projects. Yet, as demonstrated by the seemingly half-hearted reform effort over the years, reforming fossil fuel subsidies in Indonesia still presents a deeply entrenched challenge within the country's political economy.

Despite numerous subsidy scale-backs and attempted reforms, Indonesia's fuel subsidy remains, albeit hidden from plain sight. The government's inconsistent pricing adjustments under Jokowi's administration illustrate the political difficulty of permanently reducing fuel subsidies. This puts into question the success of previous so-called fuel subsidies reform in terms of its sustainability. Over the years, many factors have presented themselves as key challenges to reform, from the inflationary pressures of rising food prices that strain low-income households, to political concerns such as politicians' focus on electability and resistance to breaking entrenched subsidy traditions. With the inequitable distribution of subsidies that disproportionately benefit affluent households, these dynamics underscore the urgent need for equitable and sustainable policy reform. Indonesia's experience tells us a story of the trade-offs between populist pressures and economic efficiency, a lesson on the art of fuel subsidies reform, and a cautionary tale about state control over natural resources.

3
The Arts and Crafts of Program Targeting

Living below the poverty line is one justification for a right to receive government assistance. In practice, however, those who are living above the poverty line may still be living in precarity, as any shock, such as sudden death of a family breadwinner or a failed harvest, could send families below the poverty line. Even in the absence of welfare shocks, some people might find it harder than others to keep their heads above water, such as people with disabilities or women with children, who often find it hard to get well-paid employment with a stable income. This is where the government's social protection programs, especially social assistance, come into play to secure the citizens' well-being.

While ideally the government could provide transfers for all poor and vulnerable people, the government is usually faced with budgetary constraints in running social welfare programs. Funding for these programs often comes from tax revenue, so the government's ability and efficacy in levying taxes on the population plays a vital role in financing them. In less-developed countries like Indonesia, however, a substantial share of economic activity occurs in the informal sector, which includes casual labor, undocumented firms, and small farms. As much as 97% of the labor force in the entrepreneurship sector works in micro, small, and medium enterprises that are often informal in nature.[1] This implies that most individuals are outside the government's tax net. Even when individuals are engaged in the formal sector, 87.5% of Indonesia's formally employed workforce in 2016 had incomes below the tax exclusion thresholds. As a result, the cost of social programs must be shouldered by a small number of taxpayers. In this case, targeted transfers can help funnel limited resources to the right people instead of spreading them too thinly to actually benefit those in need.[2] If this policy option is taken, it means that some kind of criterion needs to be set up to determine who deserves to get program benefits. Identifying and reaching people deserving

[1] Ministry of Finance, 2020.
[2] Hanna and Olken, 2018.

Evidence and the Politics of Reform. Sudarno Sumarto, Oxford University Press.
 DOI: 10.1093/9780197831717.003.0004

of program benefits is an integral part of running Indonesia's social protection system and is often referred to as "targeting." In moving from weak targeting using geographical data in the late 1990s to a more sophisticated welfare-ranked "Unified Database (UDB)" that aids in targeting the poorest households in the country, Indonesia has embarked on a long and ambitious "visibility project."[3] This project entails accounting for the population to govern them more effectively.

In the context of Indonesia's poverty-alleviation effort, the visibility project makes the population subject to standardization with "welfare level" as a metric. To do so, government officials approached "well-being" or "poverty" as an exceptionally complex phenomenon, taking into account local social practices such as diets, housing arrangements, or lifestyles, and created standard categories where the population's welfare information and identifiers like name and address could be centrally recorded and monitored for government intervention. In other words, this visibility project allows the government to see its population in a specific and standardized manner, which turns them into subjects to be governed. Central to this visibility project is Statistics Indonesia, which was first established by the Dutch colonial government in 1920 to collect statistical data for taxation purposes; it then evolved into the country's main agency and collects a broad range of statistics today. Statistics Indonesia embodies decades-long experience and institutional practices that have allowed the country to develop the UDB as one of the developing world's most advanced targeting instruments. While Statistics Indonesia could determine the number of people in poverty in a certain area, identifying who were poor and where they could be reached were issues that the UDB sought to solve. Having the means to identify and locate people in poverty has allowed the government to more effectively devise poverty-alleviation interventions.

Indonesia's quest to set up a targeting instrument, however, has entailed not only the adoption of the latest statistical methods but also a change in norms. On the one hand, the UDB has allowed the state to see and govern the population. On the other hand, under a democracy it has also opened a door to scrutinizing their way of governance. The UDB is, therefore, as much about a state's optics as it is a looking glass. Since the introduction of the UDB for social program beneficiary targeting in 2011, close monitoring and evaluation of national poverty-alleviation programs became a key

[3] Scott, 1998.

metric by which to assess program efficacy. Prior to that, how close actual program spending was to its budgeted amount was a key measure for success. This measure, however, says little about the efficiency and accuracy of a program. Although the UDB itself could not guarantee perfect accuracy, its adoption has introduced a broader use of technical terms, such as "inclusion/exclusion" error, into the lexicon of both Indonesian policymakers and outside critics. While the former (inclusion) refers to people who should not receive program benefits but received them regardless, the latter (exclusion) refers to people who should receive intervention but were missing out. Inclusion errors often invoke social jealousy or suspicions that there is elite capture in a program's implementation. Meanwhile, exclusion errors raise concerns that government programs are poorly administered. This marks the entry of technical metrics into the political lexicon as a proxy for the government's performance.

At first sight, there seems to be little incentive for politicians in power to leave themselves vulnerable to criticism, however, as the UDB's development was supported by donors such as the World Bank and the Australian Department of Foreign Affairs and Trade, who demanded accountability. So there is a strong demand for the use of technical terminology across the government. In addition, with mass and social media's prevalence under democracy, public pressure has also pushed for government accountability. Employing statistical methods to rank citizens based on their welfare level and determine program eligibility, the UDB minimizes room for politicians to mobilize social programs simply for popular support. At the same time, adhering to this list means that program benefits can be concentrated to those who are actually in poverty instead of being dispersed to more well-off households.[4] Aside from increasing program accountability, the UDB also improves program efficacy in alleviating poverty. Moreover, the UDB has also served to improve administrative efficiency in various government programs. Instead of requiring ministries, government agencies, and local governments to collect their own data to create separate beneficiary lists for different programs, the UDB can serve as a list that covers a large enough share of the population for it to be used across the government. This feature also allows various parts of the government to coordinate their poverty-alleviation efforts by providing beneficiaries with benefits that are complementary in nature. For instance, a family in poverty can receive

[4] Banerjee et al., 2023.

scholarships for their children from the Ministry of Education, subsidized health insurance from the Ministry of Health, and food assistance from the Ministry of Social Affairs, all at the same time.

Despite the UDB's ability to improve program efficacy, accountability, and efficiency, advocating for the database's use across the government has been a challenge. Housed under the Ministry of Social Affairs since 2016, distrust between government units has hindered its effective utilization beyond its home ministry. While part of this distrust was due to increased scrutiny of the Ministry of Social Affairs over data management, another part was the ministry's attempt to protect sensitive public administration data. Indeed, data governance is a contentious matter. While some other ministries and government agencies can figure out whether their program beneficiaries are listed in the UDB, access to other parts of the data, such as receipt of other social programs or a household's welfare status, remains restricted. This makes program complementarity and coordinated planning easier said than done. Moreover, as the UDB involves personally identifiable welfare information of nearly one-half of the country's citizens, there are concerns that unscrupulous politicians with access to the data could mobilize the data for personal gain.

With little trust among state administrators, some ministries have preferred to construct their own database to determine program beneficiaries while others, such as the Ministry of National Development Planning (BAPPENAS) and the Ministry of Finance, launched initiatives to build a database that takes over the UDB's role. This distrust has been proven to be costly, as it sets back Indonesia's progress in addressing poverty, vulnerability, and inequality. When a change in leadership at the Ministry of Social Affairs occurred at the outset of the COVID-19 pandemic in 2020, a new policy on the use of UDB data was implemented by the incoming minister. This new policy limited access to the UDB by other government agencies and ministries, which led to delays in disbursing COVID-19 emergency social safety net benefits. While we often see the state as a homogeneous actor, political dynamics among bureaucrats in the government shape the way poverty is to be governed by the state.

With the database's central role in Indonesia's social-protection system infrastructure, its maintenance is of high priority. Nevertheless, anyone thinking that its management is "just" a technical matter that involves selecting the best algorithm to identify people in poverty will be sorely mistaken—it is as political as it is technical. In the short run, maintaining the database's validity and promoting its use across the government for program transparency should be prioritized; however, in the long run, data governance and administration needs to be carefully considered to foster trust among its users. Moreover, as poverty numbers continue to fall, the emerging question is not just about how to target the poor, but also about how this data could aid in providing effective social protections for the rest of the population.

Targeting Over Time

The Asian financial crisis of 1997–1998 marked a turning point for Indonesia's social protection system. To mitigate the crisis's impact on the poor, the government launched the social safety net programs (*Jaringan Pengaman Sosial*; JPS), despite having no large-scale welfare infrastructure in place. This required building social programs, distribution mechanisms, and targeting instruments from scratch. Before the crisis, Indonesia primarily used geographic targeting for social programs rather than identifying specific households or individuals. A key example was the 1993 Presidential Instruction on Underdeveloped Villages, which focused on regional investment in infrastructure and financial assistance. At the time, broad-based fuel subsidies and regional programs were the main welfare policies; however, the crisis—which tightened fiscal space while poverty surged—forced the government to adopt a more targeted approach to social assistance.

A major component of JPS was the rice subsidy program, aimed at those in poverty; however, only 52.7% of the poorest 20% of households benefited, while one-fifth of the top 20% also received assistance.[5] Despite increased welfare spending, these targeting inaccuracies limited program effectiveness. Nevertheless, this early attempt at benefit targeting laid the groundwork for Indonesia's future social protection system.

To identify JPS beneficiaries, the government used a geographic approach, supplemented by household surveys conducted by the BKKBN.[6] Beneficiaries of the rice subsidy program were classified as "pre-prosperous" or "prosperous I" families based on 23 variables, some of which were non-economic, such as religious obligations.[7] These criteria, along with a shortage of trained

[5] Sumarto, Suryahadi, and Widyanti, 2002.
[6] TNP2K, 2015.
[7] Isdijoso, Suryahadi, and Akhmadi, 2016.

Database	Data Keluarga Sejahtera	Pendataan Sosial Ekonomi - PSE 2005	Pendataan Perlindungan Sosial(PPLS 2008)	Unified Database / Data Terpadu Kesejahteraan Sosial (DTKS)	Unified Database / Data Terpadu Kesejahteraan Sosial (DTKS)	Data Pensasaran Percepatan Penghapusan Kemiskinan Ekstrem (P3KE)
Implementing Agency	National Family Planning Agency	Statistics Indonesia	Statistics Indonesia	Statistics Indonesia	Statistics Indonesia	National Family Planning Agency
Year Launched	1998	2005	2008	2011	2015	2021
Coverage (Number of Households)	N/A	19,1 Million	18,5 Million	25,2 Million	28 Million	71 Million
Preliminary Data	N/A	N/A	PSE 2005	National Census 2010	PPLSS11 + Program Beneficiary List	National Family Database
Community-Based Data Collection Mechanism	N/A	Input from the Village & Community Leader	Confirmation of the Village & Community Leader	Consultation with the poor & Community Leader	Focus Group Discussion with Village/Sub-Village	N/A
Data CollectionType	Pre-Existing Administrative Data	Primary Enumeration	Primary Enumeration	Primary Enumeration	Primary Enumeration	Primary Enumeration
Ranking Method	Cut-off Index	Weighted Score 14 variables	Proxy Means Test	Proxy Means Test	Proxy Means Test	Proxy Means Test
Program Targeted with the Database	Rice Subsidies	Direct Cash Transfer	Direct Cash Transfer	Direct Cash Tranfer, Family Hope Program, *Raskin* rice transfer	*Raskin* rice transfer, Smart Indonesia Program, Family Hope Program	Extreme Poverty Alleviation Effort

Figure 3.1 Indonesia's History in Developing a Database for Targeting
Source: Sumarto, 2024.

data collectors, contributed to poor targeting. Despite its flaws, the BKKBN data later evolved into Indonesia's UDB, which became a crucial tool for targeting social programs in the following decades (see Figure 3.1).

While the UDB's inception was linked to the Asian financial crisis and the creation of the country's first large-scale social safety net, its development was closely tied to Indonesia's oil subsidies reform. Since the early days of Indonesian independence in 1945, subsidies have been an important part of its economy,[8] however, when domestic oil production fell and consumption grew, in 2004 the Indonesian government chose to start importing fuel to avoid the less popular decision to revoke fuel subsidies. After years of economic boom, partly driven by lucrative oil exports, in that year Indonesia became a net oil-importing country. This shift, however, exposed Indonesia to global fuel-price dynamics. When global fuel prices rose and subsidies were no longer tenable, the government had little choice but to increase fuel prices.

When the Indonesian government increased fuel prices in 2005, compensation packages for the poor and near-poor were rolled out to avoid public backlash. This entailed an Unconditional Cash Transfer program.[9] Such a policy move would have been nearly impossible to justify if the government had not compensated the poor—particularly since the product that needed the largest price adjustment was kerosene, which was a common fuel for cooking among the poor. With over 60 million people intended for coverage, the Unconditional Cash Transfer program would be the largest such scheme in the developing world. Like the JPS safety net programs that were launched in 1998, the cash transfer program also needed some kind of database for targeting purposes. As before, identifying the poorest households in the country was an enormous challenge that had to be undertaken under immense pressure. Instead of using the same targeting method as the JPS, however, the Indonesian government sought to make targeting more precise. This was partly due to the government's need to maintain some accountability, as they needed to convince the legislative body to approve budgetary changes.

Statistics Indonesia was mandated with the task and developed the needed database by first interviewing village leaders and other local informants to develop a list of potentially poor and near-poor households. A survey of

[8] Beaton and Lontoh, 2010.
[9] Bazzi, Sumarto, and Suryahadi (2015).

these households, known as the PSE 2005, was then undertaken to ascertain key economic and social characteristics that could be used to determine the households' welfare levels. Statistics Indonesia identified 14 non-monetary variables from the survey, which ranged from flooring type, type of lighting used in the house, to the number of meals that family members have in a day. Each of these variables were then used to construct a household welfare index. Based on the index, the government recorded and classified 19.1 million families in the PSE 2005 database as "very poor," "poor," or "near-poor." Based on this categorization process, the government determined that 15.5 million families were eligible to receive the cash transfer. Nevertheless, despite improved targeting accuracy when compared to BKKBN's database, the PSE 2005's three welfare categories meant that data accuracy was limited. The three welfare categories were not adequate to determine the fine differences in a family's welfare level that could have determined benefit eligibility.

In 2008, Indonesia faced another sharp fuel-price hike, with petrol prices rising by 33%. To cushion the impact on low-income households, the government once again provided unconditional cash transfers, similar to the compensation package in 2005. To identify eligible recipients, Statistics Indonesia updated household data by conducting a new survey, the PPLS 2008. This survey built on the existing PSE 2005 database, gathering fresh socio-economic information to create a preliminary list of potential beneficiaries known as the "pre-list." To improve accuracy and ensure no poor households were overlooked, local village leaders and community members were consulted, just as they had been in 2005. In addition to newly surveyed households, the pre-list also incorporated data from the PSE 2005 and additional household records from 1,023 subdistricts across 97 regencies and cities in 15 provinces.[10] This comprehensive approach aimed to refine targeting and ensure that cash assistance reached those most in need.

In the 2005 socio-economic survey (PSE 2005), Statistics Indonesia categorized households into different welfare groups using an index; however, for the PPLS 2008 survey, they introduced a more refined approach—proxy means testing (PMT).[11] This method used household characteristics and socio-economic data collected in the survey to estimate each

[10] Statistics Indonesia, 2011; TNP2K, 2015.
[11] TNP2K, 2015.

household's welfare level through a statistical model. Based on these estimates, households in the pre-list were ranked according to their predicted economic status. Through this process, Statistics Indonesia compiled a final database of 17.5 million families in the PPLS 2008 dataset, thereby providing a more data-driven approach to targeting social assistance.

Starting in 2008, households in the database were no longer simply classified into broad welfare categories. Instead, they were ranked using PMT—allowing for a more precise way to determine program eligibility. Rather than being placed into one of three or four fixed categories, households were ordered based on their estimated welfare levels. This ranking system made it possible to prioritize assistance more effectively. After ranking, households were grouped into deciles, dividing them into 10 segments based on their economic status. The first decile represented the poorest 10%, while the second covered those in the 10%–20% range, and so on, up to the wealthiest tenth decile. By 2011, Indonesia's UDB included households in the first four deciles—the bottom 40% of the population—ensuring that government assistance reached those with the greatest need.

Beyond unconditional cash transfers, the PPLS 2008 database became the foundation for multiple social welfare programs. The Family Hope Program (*Program Keluarga Harapan*: PKH) conditional cash transfer program, which started as a pilot in 2007 with 500,000 families, relied on PPLS 2008 data as it expanded to one million families in 2010 and 10 million a decade later. The government also used the database to target beneficiaries for the Raskin rice transfer program, the JAMKESMAS free healthcare scheme, and education assistance programs. Even local governments adapted the data for their own initiatives. For example, East Java's government used it to identify the poorest households eligible for *Jalinkesra*, a regional program providing additional support to improve household welfare.

In 2011, the Indonesian government prepared to raise fuel prices again but ultimately abandoned the plan. By this point, however, any major fuel hike was expected to come with a compensation package, so household data collection had already begun in anticipation. That year, Statistics Indonesia conducted the PPLS 2011 survey, leveraging the momentum from the 2010 census, which had recently updated the country's population data.[12]

[12] Hastuti et al., 2016.

The census provided a baseline that helped identify households for inclusion in PPLS 2011. In addition to households already listed in PPLS 2008, the survey expanded its reach by incorporating input from local community members and on-the-ground observations, ensuring that potentially poor households were not overlooked.

The PPLS 2011 introduced several methodological improvements in data collection and processing. Like PPLS 2008, it used PMT to rank households by welfare level, but with a more refined approach. Instead of the 14 variables used in 2008, the PPLS 2011 collected data on 26 variables, divided into household- and individual-level factors for greater detail. To improve accuracy, the ranking model incorporated data from the 2010 national socio-economic survey (*Susenas*), a nationally representative study that captured regional variations in household characteristics. This allowed for more precise, location-specific PMT models. For example, boat ownership might indicate wealth in a coastal village but would be irrelevant in an urban setting. By tailoring models to specific regions, the database more accurately reflected local poverty conditions. The coverage was also significantly expanded to 40% of Indonesia's population–far beyond the 12% poverty rate at the time–to account for economic vulnerability beyond those classified as poor.

Compared to earlier databases like PSE 2005 and PPLS 2008, PPLS 2011 offered several key advantages. First, its extensive coverage included 25.2 million families (about 96 million individuals), making it the most comprehensive household dataset to date. Second, because PPLS was not tied to a specific government program, it avoided biases linked to narrow program criteria. In contrast, earlier datasets, like the BKKBN database used for social safety net programs in 1998, were originally designed for family planning—leading to gaps in identifying households in poverty. Finally, by collecting more detailed welfare indicators, PPLS 2011 allowed for more accurate rankings and broader eligibility criteria, making it a stronger foundation for social protection programs.

The PPLS 2011 data collection followed clearly defined standards to ensure data accuracy and methodological rigor. This included careful selection of variables to improve the accuracy of household welfare estimation while also ensuring practical feasibility for field surveyors. Variables were chosen based on their predictive strength for household welfare, ease of observation, and resistance to manipulation by respondents. For example, surveyors could reliably assess the material of a house's walls, whereas self-reported ownership of valuable jewelry could be easily concealed or misrepresented. These refinements strengthened the reliability of the data in capturing actual household conditions.

A crucial factor in the success of PPLS 2011 was the role of TNP2K, which played a key part in preparing the targeting system and ensuring the quality of data collection and modeling. Under Boediono's leadership as vice president, TNP2K worked closely with Statistics Indonesia to refine the PMT models used to rank households by welfare level. His personal engagement in the process, such as directly inquiring about the progress of PPLS 2011 during discussions at official gatherings, underscored the government's commitment to improving social protection targeting. This strong coordination between policymakers and technical teams helped shape PPLS 2011 into a more robust and reliable system for identifying and assisting Indonesia's most vulnerable populations.

Following its launch in March 2012, the data resulting from the PPLS 2011 survey began to be referred to as the UDB. The UDB provided data on the distribution or aggregation of individuals, families, and households according to socio-economic variables collected in PPLS 2011 and subsequent Statistics Indonesia surveys. Most importantly, since the UDB not only contains welfare information but also the names and addresses of families registered in the database, it was used as a key targeting instrument for various government programs. This included the central government's flagship poverty relief programs: the PKH conditional cash transfer and the Raskin rice transfer scheme. At the regional level, the UDB was used for a range of programs managed by local governments, such as the regional health insurance program (*Jamkesda*) and the locally funded Raskin program (*Raskinda*).[13]

TNP2K played a critical part in expanding the UDB's reach and utilization across the government. Throughout its development, TNP2K provided quality assurance and technical support to Statistics Indonesia. Moreover, being strategically placed under the Office of the Vice President, TNP2K was in a place to coordinate poverty-alleviation programs across the government, with the UDB as its key policy targeting instrument. The UDB remained under TNP2K's management until its update in 2015 and subsequent handover to the Ministry of Social Affairs' Social Welfare Data and

[13] TNP2K, 2015.

Information Centre.[14] Although its strategic role was key in the UDB's expansive use across the government, the handover was deemed necessary due to TNP2K's ad hoc nature and concerns about the UDB's sustainability in the long run.

Despite the advantages of the UDB, challenges remained. Critics pointed out that its algorithm did not fully account for local socio-economic conditions, leading to some poor households being left out.[15] Without a built-in mechanism for continuous updates, a large-scale data revision was needed. In response, Statistics Indonesia launched the PBDT 2015 survey to refresh and improve the database.[16] To ensure accuracy and inclusivity, the update was conducted in two phases. The first phase involved community consultations where village chiefs, neighborhood heads, and local leaders reviewed the list of families in the database. They identified households that had moved away, those no longer in need of assistance, and new families struggling with poverty. This process helped make the database more reflective of real conditions and increased community trust in the system. The final list was then approved by district and city leaders before moving to the second phase: household visits by surveyors from Statistics Indonesia. This approach not only improved the accuracy of the data but also ensured that the poorest households, often overlooked in standard surveys, were recognized. By integrating local knowledge into formal data collection, the government made the database more reliable and responsive to real needs.

During the survey phase, Statistics Indonesia's surveyors visited households to collect socio-economic data and rank their welfare level. To ensure no families were overlooked, they also conducted local consultations and on-the-ground "area sweeping." While a similar effort was made in the PPLS 2011 survey, the introduction of public consultation forums in the Integrated Database Update 2015 (*Pemutakhiran Basis Data Terpadu*: PBDT 2015) set it apart. Previously, community involvement in data collection had been limited. In PPLS 2011, an attempt to reduce exclusion errors fell short because surveyors often skipped the area-sweeping process, considering it too time consuming. The PBDT 2015 approach improved on this by combining structured community forums with proactive field verification. Once the data was collected, it was processed using PMT testing to rank households by welfare level. This effort led to an updated UDB covering 92.9 million individuals

[14] Ministry of Social Affairs, 2020.
[15] Hastuti et al., 2016.
[16] TNP2K, 2019.

(28 million families). While still targeting the poorest 40% of the population, the updated list included 2.8 million more families than in 2011–reflecting a more comprehensive and inclusive dataset.

The PBDT 2015 was the last time that Indonesia's UDB saw a large-scale update. In the absence of a dynamic data updating process that allowed for recurrent data input and verification, the database's accuracy waned over time. By 2021, more than 93% of the entries in the UDB were identical to those in 2015, which suggested a lack of data updating despite the population's move in and out of poverty. COVID-19, in particular, had brought a great shock that unexpectedly drove people into poverty throughout 2020 and 2021. As a result, only about 35% of the poorest 10% of families in Indonesia received food assistance when the poorest 40% of families should have received the transfer (see Table 3.1). In addition, with a growing population, the UDB that was intended to cover the poorest 40% of the population was 2% short of reaching this target by 2021. This made it difficult to scale up safety net programs during the COVID-19 pandemic and reach more people, as the government had exhausted the entries in the UDB.

Despite the need for an updated database, the Ministry of Social Affairs was only able to cover about 33% of the data updating cost. A proposal to seek funding from the Ministry of Finance and BAPPENAS was floated early in 2020, but when the proposal was finally approved, the pandemic hit and the budget had to be redirected toward a range of social safety net programs. Even if the budget had not been redirected, movement restrictions during

Table 3.1 Share of *Program Sembako* Recipients by Expenditure Decile Group

Expenditure Decile Group	YEAR		
	2020	2021	2022
1	33.77	36.37	35.50
2	28.23	30.96	31.93
3	24.69	28.40	28.39
4	21.61	24.83	26.78
5	17.77	21.28	24.20
6	14.89	18.78	20.44
7	11.63	14.93	17.83
8	7.96	12.07	14.22
9	4.07	7.29	10.74
10	1.14	2.63	4.46

Source: SUSENAS (multiple years).

the pandemic would have posed logistical challenges to data collection. After the worst of the pandemic had passed, the idea to revisit the delayed data updating was once again floated in 2021. The momentum for data updating also came at the time President Joko Widodo set his eyes upon an ambitious goal to eradicate extreme poverty[17] by the end of his term in 2024. Despite this, the newly appointed Minister of Social Affairs did not go through with the planned data updating, partly due to a distrust of her predecessor, who had been embroiled in a high-profile graft case during the pandemic. With little trust in how the UDB was governed, and as an attempt to disassociate herself from her predecessor, the new minister limited other government bodies' access to the data and removed the households' PMT-processed welfare ranking.

With a vacuum in the ranked welfare data critical to targeting the extreme poor, BAPPENAS and the Ministry of Finance came forward to propose the creation of a Social Registry to cover an initial 60%, and 100% of the country's population. As an information system that supported the outreach, intake, registration, and determination of potential social program eligibility,[18] the Social Registry would effectively take over the UDB's role. Understanding the enormity of the task and time pressures for the extreme poverty-alleviation deadline that was fast approaching, TNP2K proposed a less ambitious but more timely database. Instead of focusing on broad data coverage, the Database for Extreme Poverty Alleviation focused on better capturing the country's poorest. This effort ran parallel to the agenda of BAPPENAS and the Ministry of Finance in creating the Social Registry. The two efforts highlighted two things about the state's optical project: while data coverage is one thing, data validity—or how accurate and reliable it is—is another.

Ensuring Data Validity

When access to government assistance can determine a family's well-being, accurate data becomes crucial. In poverty alleviation, failing to reach vulnerable populations can have serious long-term consequences. Take the PKH conditional cash transfer as an example. The program aims to improve

[17] Extreme poverty is defined by the World Bank as a condition where a person's daily consumption falls below the extreme poverty line (US$1.90 PPP).

[18] Leite et al., 2017.

children's health and development, particularly for expectant mothers, babies, and toddlers. Early nutrition is vital for brain and physical development, and missing out on PKH support could lead to stunted growth. This underscores the importance of precise targeting—although achieving it is far from simple.

Since income data is often unreliable, Indonesia relies on PMT to estimate household welfare. This method assesses asset ownership and housing conditions to estimate income, helping identify families most in need of government assistance. However, PMT primarily captures long-term economic status rather than short-term financial shocks. For instance, a family that owns a large house but loses its main source of income—whether due to illness, job loss, or economic downturns like the COVID-19 pandemic—may still be classified as non-poor, despite struggling to afford daily necessities.

In contrast, community-based targeting leverages local knowledge, allowing village heads or community representatives to help identify households in need.[19] While PMT assumes assets are harder to hide from surveyors than income, community-based methods operate on the belief that wealth is even harder to hide from one's neighbors. Both approaches aim to tackle the same problem—unobservable incomes—but each comes with its own strengths and limitations.

A bottom-up approach like community consultation, in particular, was incorporated into formal data-collection processes, as the method is particularly good in improving community satisfaction with the final database and the program beneficiary list derived from the database.[20] Incorporating community consultation into data collection not only improves public trust in the final beneficiary list but also helps identify the ultra-poor who may have been overlooked by surveyors. While some have questioned whether community-based targeting works consistently, evidence from both pilot programs and nationwide implementation suggests otherwise.[21] The results show strongly progressive targeting, as households with lower baseline consumption are more likely to be included. While the targeting in this case wasn't quite as precise as a fully up-to-date PMT, communities accounted for important local factors beyond just consumption—such as widowhood, recent illness, and high food expenditure shares. This reinforces the idea that community-based targeting can be effective at scale, not just in small trials.

[19] Galasso and Ravallion, 2005.
[20] Alatas et al., 2012.
[21] Sumarto et al. (2025).

The choice between the top-down and bottom-up approaches is often cast as a trade-off between the better information that communities might have versus the risk of elite capture, which is where local actors with power gatekeep access to programs to those they favor.[22] Nevertheless, the two need not be cast as an either/or situation as Indonesia did. By involving community discussion forums as a part of the data-collection process, the government can avoid losing legitimacy and fomenting political instability if the community perceives that the PMT result is wrong. At the same time, the government can also justify the UDB's final list by appealing to statistical rigor.

The combination of top-down surveys and bottom-up community-based targeting, however, does not mean that the database will be perfect. The government in this case, therefore, also created a mechanism where individuals who believed that they were falsely excluded or included from the program beneficiary list could ask local social agency workers to be added in or removed from program beneficiary lists. Local social agencies such as the Ministry of Social Affairs extension agents at the regional level would then pass this information into the ministry for assessment. This mechanism was designed to account for the change in household welfare level, composition, or address. In practice, however, this process was often criticized for lack of transparency, as individuals who appealed their removal from a program beneficiary list or requested inclusion in the list had no formal means to follow up on their cases. With the Ministry of Social Affairs holding an absolute authority to add or remove individuals from the UDB or program beneficiary list, local social workers often understood as little as local villagers did about their cases once they submitted their appeal to the ministry. This process could often take months to solve—if they ever got solved.

With top-down surveys costing a lot and taking months to complete, bottom-up data collection is key in data updating. With opacity in the bottom-up data updating process, however, other mechanisms are needed to continuously update data. This is especially true since poverty is a highly dynamic phenomenon; welfare level could change in a short space of time. For instance, 70% of people in extreme poverty in September 2020 were not considered as such as early as March 2020. On the other hand, 60% of those considered extreme poor in March 2020 were no longer considered so in

[22] Alatas et al. (2012).

September 2020. It is, therefore, no wonder that since the UDB had been last updated in 2015, the data's accuracy had waned over time.

Beyond the lack of an effective bottom-up data updating mechanism, the UDB's reliance upon monetary poverty has meant that various forms of vulnerabilities have not been sufficiently taken into account in designing a data entry and updating method. For instance, age- and life-cycle related vulnerabilities, such as pregnancy or old age, come with specific nutritional and healthcare needs that may not be sufficiently addressed by regular social assistance programs. This lack of a bottom-up data updating mechanism hampers the creation of a dynamic social protection system that could quickly respond to shocks or potential shocks in one's life. For example, since the PKH is aimed at poor families with expectant mothers and children, it is very closely tied to a person's life cycle as one moves from one stage of life to another. This makes program eligibility dependent on highly dynamic criteria such as age or pregnancy status. Administrative delays can hamper the program's efficacy in providing health and nutritional intervention in a child's early life. Even if administrative processes are efficient and benefits could be disbursed the next day, many families do not know that they are eligible, let alone do they sign themselves up. Other programs that are contingent upon one's life cycle are labor market interventions, such as the *Kartu Prakerja* re-skilling program or elderly persons' support like ASLUT,[23] and these also require dynamic targeting. Beyond programs related to one's life cycle but also require dynamic targeting are those related to disasters, which are projected to become more frequent in the future due to climate change. At this point, the multi-faceted nature of life that determine one's well-being and vulnerabilities makes it clear that maintaining data validity through updating is not a task that can be shouldered solely by a single government body.

An on-demand application system offers a flexible and dynamic way to update social program databases, thereby reducing targeting errors. This system allows individuals to report life changes such as pregnancies, deaths, or job losses, ensuring that assistance reaches those who need it most. By integrating national identification numbers, the system can cross-reference data with property tax records, mortgages, car loans, and utility usage to help screen out non-poor households automatically. It also enables

[23] ASLUT (*Asistensi Sosial Lanjut Usia Terlantar*) is the Ministry of Social Affairs social assistance program for elderly persons who are not receiving sufficient care and support.

self-selection, where families who feel economically stable can remove themselves from beneficiary lists or switch to a more suitable program—for example, opting out of PKH to access micro, small, and medium enterprise credit.

Indonesia's social protection system is fragmented across multiple government agencies, adding complexity to how assistance is delivered. While poverty is often defined as the inability to meet basic needs, a broader view includes vulnerability to risks and overall well-being that takes into account factors like nutrition, health, education, and social inclusion. Addressing these vulnerabilities requires not just safety nets but adaptive programs that respond to life changes.

To reflect poverty's multi-faceted nature, Indonesia has introduced various social assistance programs under different ministries. For example, the *Kartu Indonesia Pintar* (education scholarship) is managed by the Ministry of Education, *Program Sembako* (food assistance) by the Ministry of Social Affairs, and subsidized health insurance by the Ministry of Health. These national programs, along with local government initiatives, are designed to complement one another and ensure that a household does not receive duplicate benefits but, for instance, gets both food assistance and an education scholarship. Nevertheless, data-sharing challenges among ministries often hinder coordination—driven by bureaucratic silos and trust issues. This raises a critical question: What kind of data governance framework can foster collaboration and ensure that social programs work together to improve well-being?

Governing the Data

Evidence from other countries shows that social registries that list individuals in the population could be used to effectively and efficiently identify participants or beneficiaries for various government programs.[24] Learning from global best practices, Indonesia sought to build its own Social Registry to support program targeting. In 2021, the Ministry of Finance and BAPPENAS initiated the Social Registry's creation that would cover as much as 100% of the country's citizens. The database is designed to serve as a data source for both central and local government program beneficiaries.

[24] Mostafa and Sátyro, 2014; Acosta and Velarde, 2015; Lindert et al., 2018.

Its broad coverage beyond the UDB's reach to ~40% of the population means that programs could be expanded with relative ease if needed.

Indonesia's experience with the UDB highlights the need to balance data protection with independence from political influence. Instead of centralizing all aspects of data storage, maintenance, and updating under one institution, different government bodies should specialize in specific database functions to improve oversight and accountability. The Ministry of Social Affairs is currently responsible for managing social protection data which includes collection, system management, and updates, while Statistics Indonesia assists with non-routine data updates. Monthly updates, however, fall under the regional social agency that operates under the Ministry of Social Affairs. This concentration of multiple roles within a single body poses risks to data quality, as it lacks independent checks and balances. The Ministry of Finance cross-checks beneficiary data from the UDB with citizenship records through its state budget monitoring system, ensuring that program funding aligns with government priorities; however, it plays little role in verifying the accuracy of welfare data, even though precise data is crucial for determining program eligibility. To strengthen Indonesia's social protection system, a more decentralized and collaborative approach to data governance is essential.

Similar to the way central banks should be independent so that they can ensure effective monetary policies, the appropriate institution to host the Social Registry needs to be independent of, and different than, the organizations responsible for other facets of its data management processes. The separation of tasks would allow for a more accurate assessment of data quality and mitigation of political influence in data management. An organization that could fulfill this task in Indonesia is BAPPENAS. Unlike line ministries, BAPPENAS has a healthy degree of independence due to its primary mandate of planning, budgeting, and coordinating development efforts—instead of project implementation, where there may be vested interests for financial gains. Moreover, BAPPENAS is linked to government offices at both the central and regional levels and has the influence to improve social policies and monitor the implementation of social programs.

In terms of data collection, Statistics Indonesia would be an appropriate agency to be in charge. Law No. 16/1997 on Statistics stipulates that Statistics Indonesia is an institution that has the mandate to produce social and economic statistics, provide guidance to other agencies on the implementation of sectoral statistical activities, and coordinate with government agencies to standardize concepts and statistical measures. Since its inception in the 1920s, it has developed a reputation for effective data collection and analysis. Statistics Indonesia has conducted numerous censuses and surveys and has become one of Southeast Asia's most respected statistical agencies. Most importantly, its involvement in the UDB's evolution over time has endowed Statistics Indonesia with technical expertise over time. In addition, while the government could schedule regular top-down data updating, ministries and agencies that run various social programs also need to introduce bottom-up activities that allow for the data to be updated and verified throughout the year.

For the Social Registry to fulfill its role as a central data source for social programs, it must effectively serve all relevant government agencies—not just the Ministry of Social Affairs, but also ministries and regional governments that rely on accurate data for their programs. Ideally, the Social Registry should be interoperable with other key government databases, enabling efficient data-sharing while ensuring flexibility in access and updates. A modular approach to data management could address this need. Instead of unrestricted access, government bodies could retrieve relevant data and update specific sections within their domain. This two-way system would ensure that while the Social Registry aids in beneficiary targeting, it also receives regular updates from different ministries. For instance, integrating the Ministry of Social Affairs *Program Sembako* food assistance data with the Ministry of Health's subsidized national health insurance database would improve accuracy and coordination. By distributing responsibility for different data modules across agencies, this system could enable real-time verification, reduce duplication, and keep information up to date, ultimately strengthening the effectiveness of social programs.

A decentralized approach to data updating aligns with best practices from other countries. As social registries mature, they should move away from large-scale survey sweeps like those conducted by Statistics Indonesia, and instead rely on dynamic, local-level updates. While Indonesia's law assigns data updating responsibilities to regional social agencies under the Ministry of Social Affairs, experience has shown that this alone is insufficient. The main challenges include a lack of clear framework, financial support, and labor resources—particularly in remote areas with poor infrastructure. Relying solely on local governments to update data overburdens them and results in outdated records. A more effective approach would be for central ministries and agencies to share responsibility and distribute both costs and data ownership across government bodies. Although this model would enhance real-time data updates and foster interagency collaboration, implementation remains a challenge. Overcoming these hurdles requires a coordinated effort to build a sustainable and well-supported data updating system.

By 2022, as the 2024 election approached, competition and distrust among government agencies intensified. Politicians across ministries raced to gain public recognition through their own flagship programs, making collaboration more difficult than ever. Nevertheless, progress was not lost. Successful reform is as much about timing and strategy as it is about policy—it requires waiting for the right moment and finding key figures within the government who can champion the cause.

By 2025, the newly elected Prabowo Subianto government took a major step toward streamlining social program targeting by consolidating the country's three main social registries previously managed separately by the Ministry of Social Affairs, the Coordinating Ministry for Human Development and Cultural Affairs, and BAPPENAS. This was a significant milestone, but challenges remain. The new system still lacks a mechanism for dynamic updates, meaning that once data is collected it quickly becomes outdated, which was a key weakness of its predecessor databases. At the same time, Indonesia has spent more than two decades refining its approach to social protection targeting, accumulating valuable lessons along the way. At this stage, the hardest part is not the technical aspect but the politics: continue to build and leverage upon trust between technocrats and the government, foster cooperation, and ensure that reforms continue beyond political cycles. While much remains to be done, the foundation is stronger than ever, and the knowledge gained over the years will be crucial in shaping the next phase of reform.

Decades of investment in data collection, UDB development, and evidence-based policymaking has meant that institutions like Statistics Indonesia and TNP2K have amassed valuable expertise. While political leadership may change, institutional knowledge remains. The real challenge and opportunity lies in knowing when and how to deploy this expertise—building coalitions and ensuring that sound policies translate into lasting government action. Ultimately, the sustainability of reforms depends not only on technical solutions but also on the ability to navigate political realities. In a shifting landscape, progress is never linear; but the persistence of expertise, networks, and strategic policy-making ensures that the foundation for meaningful change endures.

4

Reforming Rice Transfer Policy, Feeding the Country

It is said that food security and political stability are often linked. While food security can be upset by a lack of political or social stability, the lack of food security resulting from a sudden shock like an international embargo or poor climate can also lead to political instability. Either way, these scenarios are challenging for any ruling government. In 1997, a financial crisis struck East and Southeast Asia. During the crisis, rapid depreciation of the Indonesian rupiah spurred inflation and made food imports prohibitively expensive. At the same time, growing unemployment undermined the purchasing power of large segments of the population. As a result, more people struggled with food insecurity. Amidst this crisis, the Indonesian government launched a food transfer program—in part to maintain political stability.

From serving as a critical component of the Indonesian government's crisis mitigation strategy during the 1997–1998 Asian financial crisis and the COVID-19 pandemic in 2020, to being utilized as the government's poverty-alleviation strategy, food assistance—particularly rice—has always been a key element of the Indonesian government's welfare spending. With rice expenditure amounting to as much as 30% of a poor household's monthly budget, rice transfer schemes could potentially have a large impact on the household's well-being.[1] The program itself has seen various changes since it was first conceived in 1998, mainly in its targeting and delivery mechanisms. However, it remains an integral part of the Indonesian social protection system. This chapter examines the evolution of Indonesian food transfers and analyzes the political and economic factors surrounding the program's many reform cycles.

Indonesia's food transfer program started out as a subsidized rice scheme in the wake of the 1997–1998 Asian financial crisis. With millions of people

[1] Satriawan and Shrestha, 2018.

Evidence and the Politics of Reform. Sudarno Sumarto, Oxford University Press.
 DOI: 10.1093/9780197831717.003.0005

thrust into poverty at that time, the shock resulted in almost a quarter of the country's population living below the poverty line. Thus, the government launched a number of social safety net programs (*Jaring Pengaman Sosial*; JPS) to soften the impact of the crisis on household welfare. A rice subsidy program called OPK (*Operasi Pasar Khusus*) was the largest of these safety net programs. This highlights the transfer's significance to household welfare.

After the crisis, the Indonesian government maintained OPK but renamed it to Raskin, which is short for *Beras Miskin* (Raskin) or "Rice for the Poor." This shift also signaled a change in the program's objective from a cushion for welfare shock to a program designed to alleviate poverty, as it specifically targets the poor. In 2015, the Indonesian government once again rebranded the program as Rastra (*Beras Sejahtera*) or "Rice for Prosperity." While thus far the program has remained as in-kind transfers that give out subsidized rice to its beneficiaries, in 2017 the government started to replace the transfer with *Bantuan Pangan Non-Tunai* (BPNT), a voucher-based non-cash food assistance program; it broadened its transfers to also encompass items beyond rice in 2020.

The Indonesian food transfer programs enjoyed relatively lax governance when compared to other social programs in the country, ranging from the lack of governance over the program's design and administration to freedom to scale the number of beneficiaries up or down almost arbitrarily. The only constraint that the government placed on making changes to the program was mainly budgetary in nature. Democratic competition after the fall of Suharto's New Order government in 1998 became one of the drivers in the program's many reforms and expansions. In just over two decades after it was first introduced, the program had transformed into the country's largest permanent targeted transfers.

In setting up a food transfers infrastructure, over time the Indonesian government has also set up an infrastructure for a comprehensive social protection system. This ranges from a household welfare database for targeting purposes to an efficient digital delivery mechanism. Furthermore, this infrastructure has given the government some flexibility to mobilize the food transfers program to mitigate various crises. The Indonesian food transfer program's evolution over time demonstrates how a politician's political interest can sometimes facilitate welfare expansion.

The Emergence of the Indonesian Food Transfer Program

Prior to the Asian financial crisis, large-scale targeted transfers for the public were virtually non-existent in Indonesia. At that time, the government relied upon fuel subsidies to get inflation under control and to provide public welfare. Thus, the OPK represented the country's early effort to run a large-scale targeted transfer program. The OPK allowed eligible households to purchase 20 kilograms of rice at the price of Rp 1000/kg, which was about a third of the market price for medium-quality rice in August 1998. For a typical poor household, receiving the full 20 kilograms of rice at the subsidized price would be equivalent to approximately 10% of their monthly household expenditure. The lack of beneficiary registry lists to target eligible households meant that eligibility for this program was determined using household survey data gathered by *Badan Kependudukan dan Keluarga Berencana Nasional* (BKKBN), the national family planning agency.

The BKKBN's household survey data classified households into four "prosperity" groups from the least to the most prosperous. A household would be classified in the lowest welfare category ("pre-prosperous") if (i) they could not practice their religious principles; (ii) all household members did not eat at least twice a day; (iii) not all household members had different sets of clothing for home, work, school, and visits; (iv) the household could not seek modern medical assistance for sick children and family planning services for contraceptive users; and if (v) the largest floor area of their house was made of earth. The BKKBN usually used these indicators to target households that could potentially receive contraceptive subsidies and campaigns. However, during the financial crisis the government decided that households in the two lowest BKKBN welfare categories were eligible to receive the subsidized OPK rice. Although these indicators may not have been the best proxies for the households' economic welfare, the government had little time and few options to do better targeting and refine their targeting algorithm.

Despite its limitations, the BKKBN's list of households had been compiled and updated annually by the BKKBN's cadres at the village level, which is the smallest administrative unit in the country. Assuming that this data collection was reliably done, the government would at least have updated household data. However, despite the government's reliance on the BKKBN's household data, to call it a survey would be an overstatement of the data collection's rigor. Rather than a household survey, this dataset consisted of household names compiled by BKKBN's village cadres, and the higher levels of government only had access to summary reports of the number of households in each category. Thus, instead of precise household-level targeting, the central government determined the amount of rice to be disbursed to each village by setting a quota according to the number of eligible households in each region and letting village officials be in charge of the OPK rice distribution.

Each month, OPK rice was delivered to the villages, either directly by the warehouse managed by the local district logistics agency (*Badan Urusan Logistik*, BULOG) or by the village staff, who retrieved the rice from the *kecamatan*[2] office. Households then purchased this rice in the village at the determined price, with some allowance for transportation costs. Though the list of rice recipients was supposed to follow the BKKBN's household prosperity classification, village officials had almost complete authority to determine how the rice would be distributed within their villages. As a result, the implementation of the OPK program varied from village to village, even in the same *kecamatan*.[3] In some areas, the rice was well-targeted toward poor families. Meanwhile in other areas, the rice was divided equally among recipients. In still other areas, village officials would announce that cheap rice was available for sale and that whoever could afford to buy it was allowed to do so.

In practice, OPK distribution guidelines were often not followed. The rice allocated by the central government to a village was indeed almost always based on the number of eligible households that were determined through the BKKBN's survey.[4] However, in practice, the rice was allocated beyond the eligible households at the village level. When the Indonesian households were ranked from the richest to the poorest based on their monthly expenditure and divided into five "quintiles," households in the middle quintile were 80% as likely as a household in the bottom quintile to have received the subsidized rice. Meanwhile, the richest, or those in the top expenditure quintile, were 46% as likely as those in the lowest quintile to have received the subsidized rice. This discrepancy meant that OPK's targeting was imperfect and that its coverage among the poorest was less than expected. Indeed, only

[2] Administratively, Indonesia is divided into provinces, municipality-level cities or districts (*kabupaten*), sub-districts (*kecamatan*), and wards (*kelurahan*) or villages (*desa*).

[3] Olken et al., 2001.

[4] Suryahadi, Suharso, and Sumarto, 2001.

53% of households in the lowest quintile, representing the poorest, actually received the subsidized rice.

This poor targeting, however, was not fully unintentional. The centrally planned administrative guidelines were deemed socially unacceptable at the community level.[5] Those deemed ineligible for OPK by the government's guidelines were oftentimes deemed eligible by community standards. Thus, in many cases eligible households received smaller amounts of rice than stipulated in the program design, as their share was divided up with households that were not officially eligible to receive the subsidized rice. However, for a number of reasons it is not clear whether these deviations at the local level were "good" or "bad."[6] First, the official list of OPK beneficiaries compiled by the BKKBN was not an accurate list of those who were in need to begin with. Due to the suddenness of the economic shock, many households that were not poor during BKKBN's data collection might have experienced welfare shock and were in need of assistance by the time the OPK was disbursed. In this case, community targeting might have been justified to better identify those in need. Second, even if the list was accurate, the distinctions drawn between those deemed eligible and not were too fine.[7] The differences between households who were entitled to receive the subsidies and those who were not were difficult to justify. When one group received 10kg–20kg of rice and the rest received nothing, this could potentially foment jealousy between households in the village and damage the social fabric.

Further, these arguments for deviating from the centrally determined OPK program guidelines raised important questions about community involvement in seeking to achieve "optimally feasible" targeting. Community members may be better judges of which households should be deemed eligible to receive OPK, compared to the central government, which had to rely on the BKKBN household classification. OPK's leakage beyond the BKKBN listed households due to community-based mistargeting may have resulted from community members having different perceptions about poverty that might not be fully captured by expenditure-level measures to proxy for household welfare.[8] Local village leaders, for instance, may know more about what is socially and politically feasible, especially when household data was not as detailed as the BKKBN's list. Rice that went

[5] Sumarto and Suryahadi, 2002.
[6] Pritchett, Sumarto, and Suryahadi, 2001.
[7] Pritchett, Sumarto, and Suryahadi, 2001.
[8] Alatas et al., 2012.

to "non-eligible" households might have not been mistargeted despite discrepancies with the OPK's program guidelines. On the flipside, local social pressures around "fairness" that led to more uniform distribution also caused fewer benefits for households that actually were in poverty. Moreover, providing too much discretion—particularly discretion in the absence of adequate local oversight—could lead to abuses. Powerful individuals in the community, such as village leaders, could prioritize rice distribution to their family or friends instead of those who were in greater need. Indeed, there is some evidence suggesting local politics played some role in the way certain village heads distributed the subsidized OPK rice.[9]

Beyond mistargeting, there were also problems of rice going "missing." It is estimated that 17.8% of the rice from BULOG distribution centers did not reach beneficiaries.[10] Villages that were poorer, more ethnically fragmented, and had lower population densities were more likely to be missing rice. Along with mistargeting, this issue further eroded the OPK benefits that should have been received by the needy.

Poor targeting and issues with distribution diluted benefits received by the poor. The lack of adherence to the beneficiary list, targeting criteria deemed insufficient by local village officials, and these officials' largely unchecked discretion over benefit disbursement were factors that contributed to this problem. Additionally, there was also some arbitrary rice pricing on the ground. However, these problems were not grounds to revoke the program. In 2002, Indonesia's poverty rate still hovered at 18.2%, which was still above the pre-crisis levels. Revoking the program would surely have hurt the newly elected President Megawati Soekarnoputri. Thus, in 2002 the Megawati administration retained the rice transfers program and rebranded it to "rice for the poor" (*Beras Miskin*, Raskin).

From Temporary to Permanent Transfers

If initially Indonesia's rice transfers under OPK were intended to serve as a shock-absorbing mechanism for poor and vulnerable households during the Asian financial crisis, as the country recovered from the crisis the program became a more permanent part of the Indonesian welfare system.

[9] Olken, 2006.
[10] Olken, 2006.

In 2002, OPK's rebranding as Raskin signaled a change in its objective as a program designed to alleviate poverty. Not only was this policy popular, given that nearly 20% of the country's population were in poverty, but it also was strategic, as nearly a third of a poor household's income was being spent on rice.

By changing the program's name, the government sought to make it more precisely geared toward a specific socio-economic group through a self-targeting mechanism. The government expected that families who were not poor would be discouraged from joining the queue for the Raskin rice ration. However, whether this mechanism was effective in improving targeting remained a question. In 2002, the government aimed to disburse rice to 9,790,000 households. However, 20,943,085 households claimed to have received the disbursements. This meant that 114% more households received Raskin than the number planned. This mistargeting issue never ceased to plague Raskin (see Table 4.1). In 2005, the ratio between Raskin's actual and intended beneficiary number reached as high as 176%. With a fixed amount of rice reaching more households than intended, each household received less rice than the program planned for. In 2010, for instance, the average amount of rice that households received was 4.5 kilograms—well below the 15 to 20 kilograms of rice per month that eligible households were entitled to, per Raskin's program guidelines.

Beyond targeting efficacy issues, there were also issues with rice distribution. The Raskin program provided subsidized rice per month, to poor and near-poor households, at prices 75% to 80% below the regular market price. However, substantial variability in the actual price existed across regions. For instance, although Raskin rice's price was set at IDR 1000 per kilogram in 2007, in 2006 the price already had reached as high as IDR 2900 per kilogram.[11]

Despite its problems, the Raskin program remained the largest government social transfer program fully funded through the national budget. After it was first launched in 2002, Raskin consistently received a third or more of the Indonesian government's entire poor-relief social transfers budget. When Raskin was first launched in 2002, the program's budget was around IDR 4.24 trillion. This number more than quadrupled to IDR 18.8 trillion by 2014 before it was reformed in the following year (see Table 4.2). Spending for Raskin peaked in 2013. This increase was related to the government's

[11] Hastuti et al., 2006.

Table 4.1 Targeted and Actual Number of Raskin Beneficiaries

Year	Targeted Beneficiaries	Actual Number of Beneficiaries*	Difference	Ratio of Difference to the Actual Number of Beneficiaries	Targeting Reference
2002	9,790,000	20,943,085	11,153,085	114	BKKBN
2003	8,580,313	22,519,131	13,938,818	162	
2004	8,590,804	19,537,271	10,946,467	127	
2005	8,300,000	22,939,778	14,639,778	176	
2006	10,830,000	24,545,069	13,715,069	127	
2007	15,781,884	29,412,414	13,630,530	86	PSE 2005
2008	19,100,000	30,542,384	11,442,384	60	
2009	18,497,302	30,171,692	11,674,390	63	
2010	17,488,007	31,021,803	13,533,796	77	PPLS 2008
2011	17,488,007	31,747,723	14,259,716	82	
2012	17,488,007	33,639,699	16,151,692	92	
2013	15,530,897	33,346,713	17,815,816	115	BDT
2014	15,530,897				PPLS 2011

*Estimate based on SUSENAS
Source: BULOG and SUSENAS.

effort to mitigate pushback against its attempt to revoke fuel subsidies in that same year (see Chapter 2). As a part of this mitigation effort, the government distributed Raskin rice 15 times for a year instead of the regular once-a-month schedule (see Table 4.3). With issues hampering a program at that scale, the government made substantial changes to Raskin in 2007.

Learning from shortfalls in OPK rice distribution—from inadequate determination mechanisms for eligibility to a lack of room for community input in determining program recipients—the government modified Raskin's targeting mechanism. The Indonesian government tasked Statistics Indonesia to create a database for beneficiary targeting purposes. First, Statistics Indonesia listed potential benefit recipient households through consultation with village chiefs and neighborhood heads. Then, local communities were involved in data collection through village consultative meetings designed to identify households not included in the initial list. Statistics Indonesia's enumerators would then visit listed households to collect data on 14 variables used to proxy for the household's welfare level, such as asset ownership and housing conditions.[12] Afterward, families would be ranked

[12] Hastuti et al., 2006.

Table 4.2 The Value of Various Government Regular Social Transfers in IDR Trillion (2007–2020)

Program Type	Year													
	2007	2008	2009	2010	2011	2012	2013	2014	2015	2016	2017	2018	2019	2020
Food subsidy (Raskin/Rastra/BPNT/Program Sembako)	6.6	12.1	13	15.2	16.5	19.1	20.3	18.8	18.9	19.2	19.3	28.1	43.1	43.9
Askeskin/Public health insurance (inc Jampersal)	4.4	4.7	4.5	5.1	6.3	7.2	8.1	–	–	–	–	–	–	–
Beneficiary contributions (PBI) Health Insurance	–	–	–	–	–	–	–	19.9	24.8	25.4	25.5	35.8	48.8	48.8
Cash transfers for poor students (BSM/PIP)	–	2.3	3	3.7	4.7	6.2	11.59	6.6	11.16	10.77	10.7	10.97	11.17	47.7
Conditional Cash Transfers Program for Poor Families (PKH)	0.9	1	1.1	1.3	1.6	1.9	5.6	7.6	11.4	17.5	32.7	29.1	37	28.7
Total	11.9	20.1	21.6	25.3	29.1	34.4	45.59	52.9	66.26	72.87	88.2	103.97	140.07	169.1
Total Food Subsidies (%)	55.5	60.2	60.2	60.1	56.7	55.5	44.5	35.5	28.5	26.3	21.9	27.0	30.8	26.0

Notes:

- Figures: LKPP (2012); APBN-P (2013) and Annual National Budget (APBN) (2014).
- Rastra replaced Raskin in 2015, then between 2017 and 2019 Rastra was gradually transformed into BPNT, and in 2020 Program Sembako replaced BPNT.
- PBI health insurance has replaced the budget for Askeskin/Jamkesmas since 2014.
- Does not include minor social protection programs, such as Social Security for Elderly (JSLU), Social Assistance for Disabled People (JSPACA) or other programs within the Ministry of Social Affairs, as well as non-regular transfers like Kartu Prakerja.
- Askeskin = health insurance for the poor; Jampersal = program to accelerate the reduction of maternal and newborn deaths; Jamkesmas = public health insurance; PBI = beneficiaries of government assistance toward payment of health insurance premiums.

Source: Government Goods and Service Procurement Policy Agency (LKPP) (2012, 2015, 2016, 2017, 2018, 2019, 2020); Financial Note—National Budget (2010, 2012, 2013, 2014)

based on their proxied welfare level. Finally, this ranking would then be used to determine a family's eligibility to receive Raskin. This data collection and the resulting ranked database was dubbed the 2005 socio-economic data collection (*Pendataan Sosial Ekonomi*, PSE 2005). The PSE 2005 dataset was then used to update the list of beneficiaries compiled by the BKKBN to target Raskin beneficiaries.

Beyond a change in its targeting instrument, in terms of program administration the Coordinating Ministry for People's Welfare (Kemenko Kesra) was appointed to oversee the implementation and budgeting of the Raskin program. Prior to 2007, the national logistics agency (*Badan Urusan Logistik*, BULOG) was responsible for program planning as well as the availability and delivery of rice stock at the district and city levels, while local village governments were responsible for distributing the rice to households. In 2007, while much of the government moved the program's administration to the Coordinating Ministry of Social Affairs, BULOG continued to be responsible for delivering the rice to around 50,000 distribution points at the subdistrict or village level across Indonesia.[13]

Despite changes to the program's targeting and administration, problems remained in the implementation of the program at the local level. This led to widespread rice misallocation.[14] Since PSE 2005's ranking system was based on household assets and other observable characteristics, such as the occupation and education level of the household head, the PSE 2005 dataset was not perfect and excluded many poor households. The choice of the 14 variables used to proxy for household welfare may not have reflected short-term changes in the households' economic situation. This provided local bodies the leeway to deviate from the list in distributing the rice. Furthermore, the 2006–2007 Raskin program guidelines did not mandate that local bodies use the list of poor households to determine beneficiaries, nor did it state that the beneficiaries had to be poor.[15] This led to discrepancies between the practice of rice distribution and the Raskin program's objective to alleviate poverty.

Although the program aimed to provide food security to the poor and near-poor, there was significant leakage of the rice to the non-poor due to weaknesses in program targeting and implementation.[16] In many places, rice

[13] Satriawan and Shreshtha, 2018.
[14] Satriawan et al., 2015; Satriawan and Shreshtha, 2018.
[15] Hastuti et al., 2008.
[16] Hastuti et al., 2008.

distribution was irregular, especially in regions that were more difficult to reach. Moreover, some villages did not receive enough rice for distribution to all the poor households. Additionally, there was variability in distribution schemes. Some villages would distribute rice equally among households while others used a rotational system where different households would become eligible to purchase rice in different distribution cycles.

In 2010, the Indonesian government updated the beneficiary list with hopes to improve program targeting. Between 2010 and 2012, the government used data from the 2008 Data Collection for Social Protection Programs (*Pendataan Program Perlindungan Sosial*, PPLS 2008) conducted by Statistics Indonesia to update Raskin's beneficiaries list, which totaled around 17.5 million households.[17] In July 2012, the government again updated the list of beneficiaries for the Raskin program, using new data from the Unified Database for Social Protection Programs (*Basis Data Terpadu*, the Unified Database).

In 2011 the National Team for the Acceleration of Poverty Reduction (*Tim Nasional Percepatan Penanggulangan Kemiskinan*, TNP2K) created the Unified Database from the 2011 Data Collection for Social Protection Programs (PPLS 2011) survey conducted by Statistics Indonesia. TNP2K used proxy means testing to rank households according to their levels of poverty or vulnerability. Due to government budgetary constraints, not all households listed in the 2011 data were able to benefit from Raskin. Consequently, TNP2K had to process the 2011 data to establish the final list of Raskin beneficiaries, which only included 61.58% of households from the original list in PPLS 2011. Beneficiaries were drawn from a total of 15.5 million households and constituted about 28% of the poorest households in the country. As in the PSE 2005 survey, village meetings were also incorporated into the data collection process to accommodate local social, economic, and demographic changes that might not have been captured by Statistics Indonesia's list of potential beneficiaries. Through these meetings, village administrations were able to replace some households in the initial list with those considered in greater need of Raskin support. This process was necessary, as the number of beneficiaries in each region could not exceed the total allocation stipulated in the pre-approved program budget. Since it was first launched in 2002, Raskin only deviated from its pre-approved budget twice—in 2008 and 2013. On both occasions, the Indonesian

[17] Hastuti et al., 2012; TNP2K, 2015.

Table 4.3 The Frequency of Disbursement, Beneficiary Data Source, and Number of Recipient Families for Government Regular Rice Transfers (2007–2020)

Year	Program Name	Number of Disbursement per Year	Data Source	Number or Recipient Families (millions)
1998	OPK	9	BKKBN	9.3
1999	OPK	12	BKKBN	10.5
2000	OPK	9	BKKBN	7.5
2001	OPK	12	BKKBN	8.7
2002	Raskin	12	BKKBN	9.8
2003	Raskin	12	BKKBN	8.6
2004	Raskin	12	BKKBN	8.6
2005	Raskin	12	BKKBN	8.3
2006	Raskin	10	BKKBN	10.8
2007	Raskin	11	PSE 2005	15.8
2008	Raskin	12	PSE 2005	19.1
2009	Raskin	12	PSE 2005	18.5
2010	Raskin	13	PPLS 2008	17.5
2011	Raskin	13	PPLS 2008	17.5
2012	Raskin	13	PPLS 2008 & 2011*	17.5
2013	Raskin	15	PPLS 2011	15.5
2014	Raskin	12	PPLS 2011	15.5
2015	Rastra	15	PPLS 2011	15.5
2016	Rastra	12	PBDT 2015	15.5
2017	Rastra/BPNT**	12	PBDT 2015	15.5
2018	Rastra/BPNT**	12	PBDT 2015	15.4
2019	Rastra/BPNT**	12	PBDT 2015	15.3
2020	Program Sembako	12	PBDT 2015	20

Note: OPK = Operasi Pasar Khusus; Raskin = Beras Miskin; Rastra = Beras Sejahtera; BPNT = Bantuan Pangan Non-Tunai; BKKBN = National Family Planning Coordinating Board; PSE = Socio-economic Data Collection; PPLS = Data collection for social protection programs; PBDT = Unified Database updating.
*Between January–May PPLS 2008 data was used for beneficiary targeting, while between and June–December the Unified Database based on the PPLS 2011 data collection was used.
**Starting in 2017, the Indonesian government began transforming Rastra to BPNT.
Source: Tabor and Sawit (2001), Suryahadi et al. (2010), Ministry of Finance Financial Report (various years), Raskin/Rastra/BPNT/Program Sembako general guidelines (various years).

government increased the frequency of Raskin rice distribution to compensate for fuel price increases (see Table 4.3 and Chapter 2 for fuel subsidies revocation).

Since it was first launched in 2002 to replace the OPK, Raskin has been marred with issues in its distribution, partly due to mistargeting. Despite efforts to continuously update the beneficiary list in 2007, 2010, and 2011, the problem has persisted. There was even evidence that Raskin was, in fact, regressive among the poor. Although poor households as a whole are more likely to participate in the program compared to the non-poor,[18] the poorest in this group benefit less from the program than those in the group with higher incomes.[19] The poorest households are less likely to participate in the program, they purchase lower quantities of rice, and they purchase rice fewer times per year. Part of the problem was the lack of program transparency and information accessible to program recipients. In practice, beneficiaries seldom received their full entitlement, and they paid 42% more than the official co-pay price.[20] As a result, eligible households received only about one-third of the intended subsidy on net.

Over time, the Indonesian government enacted changes to the program, especially to improve its targeting mechanism. Providing information directly to households on eligibility and the quantity of rice they were entitled to increased the amount of subsidy they received.[21] An experiment attempted to provide information directly to eligible households. In 378 randomly selected villages, the central government mailed "Raskin identification cards" to eligible households to inform them of their eligibility and the quantity of rice they were entitled to. The government also experimentally varied how the card program was run along three key dimensions: whether an additional rule (the co-pay price) was also listed on the card, whether information about the beneficiaries was made public, and whether cards were sent to all eligible households or to only a subset. On net, across all the variations of the program, the study found that the cards led to a large increase in the amount of subsidy received by eligible households. Eligible households in treatment villages received an increase in subsidy due to both an increase in quantity and a decrease in the co-pay price. Moreover, the information listed on the card mattered: Printing the co-pay price nearly doubled the additional subsidy that eligible households received relative to the effect of providing a card without the co-pay information.

By 2014, Raskin already covered 15.5 million beneficiary families out of around 65.4 million families in the country[22] and amounted to nearly 20% of

[18] Pritchett, Sumarto, and Suryahadi, 2001.
[19] Satriawan and Shreshtha, 2018.
[20] Banerjee, et al. 2018.
[21] Banerjee, et al. 2018.
[22] We divided Indonesia's population in 2014 of 225.1 million by 3.9, or the average family size in Indonesia on the same year

Indonesia's social welfare expenditure. This program's size makes targeting accuracy even more important. Beyond changes to targeting mechanisms, in the following years discourse has shifted from the use of rice transfers for poor-relief toward the use of social protections. While the former refers to programs that alleviate poverty and are exclusive to persons living under the poverty line, the latter refers to programs designed to guarantee a minimum standard of living. Social protection programs are usually not exclusive to those in poverty and often extend to the entire population. This change in discourse is also closely related to changes in the program's beneficiary list, which eventually led to the precursor of the country's social registry system.[23]

From Raskin to Rastra, from Poor-Relief to Social Protection

In 2015, the Indonesian government rebranded Raskin as Rastra (*Beras Sejahtera*) or "Rice for Prosperity." This change reflected a shift in the government's rice transfer from poor aid to being a part of a social protection system aimed to ensure general household welfare. This shift was coupled with an expansion of the database used to target the program's beneficiaries. The new database was set to cover more than just households in poverty, specifically 40% of the households in the country with the lowest welfare level. Not everyone listed in the database would necessarily receive rice transfers. However, the program could be expanded if needed since household data beyond the program's beneficiary list would already be available.

Moreover, Rastra's delivery mechanism was a significant departure from OPK and Raskin's design. Instead of gaining access to purchase heavily subsidized rice, Rastra beneficiary families could receive 10 kilograms of medium-quality rice per month without having to pay a co-pay price at all. This change was expected to alleviate issues with arbitrary rice pricing that plagued Raskin. Rastra's benefits at that time were valued at about IDR 100,000 or USD 8 per month, depending on the market price of rice, which

[23] "Social Registries are information systems that support registration and determination of potential eligibility for social programs." See Leite et al., 2017. "Social Registries for Social Assistance and Beyond: A Guidance Note & Assessment Tool." Social Protection & Labor Discussion Paper No.1704. World Bank.

was around IDR 9,700 per kilogram back then.[24] This benefit equated to around 6.5% of the poverty line for a family of four.

As in OPK and Raskin, the central government procured rice through BULOG, the central logistics agency. BULOG sought to procure rice at approximately the market price. Procured rice would then be stored at district-level warehouses before being delivered to villages, usually in 50kg sacks. Local officials, consisting of the Ministry of Social Affairs social workers and village government personnel, were tasked with dividing the rice. They were also in charge of delivering the rice to beneficiaries on the list, either at the village office, at neighborhood distribution points, or door-to-door.

As stipulated in the program's guidelines, targeting to determine eligibility for Rastra was conducted through proxy means testing conducted by the central government. The Ministry of Social Affairs would then provide the final benefit recipient list. In 2015, Statistics Indonesia conducted the Unified Database Updating (PBDT 2015) census of more than 28 million households, or about 43% of all households in Indonesia at that time. As in PPLS 2011, this census also collected a variety of indicators that were predictive of the household's consumption level, such as asset ownership, education, housing conditions, and others.[25] Afterward, TNP2K estimated each household's welfare level and ranked them using proxy means tests computed using these indicator variables. Households with lower PMT scores were generally eligible for the program, with the rules varying by district and urban/rural status. Furthermore, villages were allowed some minimal changes to the recipient list through village meetings to replace households that had moved, were deceased, or were double-counted. Excluded households could also apply to their local social services office to enter the beneficiary list if they believed they had been excluded from the proxy means testing. Furthermore, according to Rastra's program guidelines, villages were not officially allowed to subdivide the rice, and benefit recipients had to receive the full 10 kilograms they were entitled to.

Despite a continuously updated benefit recipient list and rules stipulated in Rastra's program guidelines, mistargeting remained a problem, and many eligible beneficiary families still received less than the amount that they

[24] Banerjee et al. (2020)
[25] See Alatas et al., 2012 and Banerjee et al., 2020 for more details.

were entitled to, or even none at all. A government monitoring survey of the Rastra program conducted between January and February 2018 found that only 77.3% of the beneficiary families received the transfers.[26] Approximately one-third of them stated that they did not receive the transfer because they were not registered as program beneficiaries, while the other one-third stated that no Rastra rice had been delivered to their areas. This suggests that beyond issues with beneficiary data, delivery mechanisms were also an issue with the food transfer program.

This was by far the largest and most significant change to the Indonesian government's food transfers program so far. Beyond adding to the value of the transfers, changes under the new BPNT program marked a greater shift in the government's social welfare infrastructure and its ability to deliver more complex program designs. This was not a piecemeal change.

Breaking the Ground

In the policymaking world, there are piecemeal changes that lead programs to move incrementally. This had categorized Indonesia's rice transfers program thus far, as it mostly saw incremental change in its benefit value or program scope. On the flip side, there are groundbreaking changes that shift a lot of things at once that are often at a more fundamental level. The latter is more uncommon than the former. A devastating shock was needed to launch the first Indonesian government food transfers program in 1998. The launch of BPNT, however, was a matter of all things falling into the right place at the right time.

In 2016, talks on reforming the problem-plagued but popular rice transfers program were floated in the government. At that time, Joko Widodo, who won the presidency under a government opposition party, had all the incentive to rebrand Rastra since it was deemed part of the previous president's legacy. Moreover, Widodo's vice president, who headed the national poverty-alleviation task force, was a seasoned politician familiar with the country's rice transfers, having been vice president as well under the previous president. This was fertile ground for policy reformers to make changes to the program. Policy reformers under the vice president took this opportunity to reform Rastra to an extent never seen before.

[26] TNP2K, 2018.

Instead of providing heavily subsidized rice, the BPNT was designed to provide beneficiary families with a debit card. The government would then top up the card with a voucher that amounted to IDR 110,000 per beneficiary family per month. This voucher could be used to purchase rice and eggs from selected vendors in the village. These vendors were local shops that partnered with state-owned banks who provided them with a debit card reader. These machines would allow beneficiary families to redeem their vouchers for rice and eggs. The voucher could not be cashed out, but its value could be saved for future months. These vendors were allowed to source rice and eggs from the private market as they saw fit. Although in practice there was pressure in some areas to source rice from BULOG as a government-owned logistics agency, rice was sourced through a relatively broad range of suppliers under BPNT when compared to the program's previous iterations.

The government made these changes to Rastra for a number of reasons. First, while a robust targeting procedure existed, in practice it was often not adhered to. There were many cases in which non-poor households received rice, while many beneficiaries received only a fraction of what they were entitled to.[27] Rice redistribution to non-poor households in OPK, Raskin, or Rastra had been a perennial challenge that the government was unable to fully resolve, despite major beneficiary data updating in 2005, 2008, 2011, and 2015. The government believed that the voucher program could reduce the improper inclusion of non-beneficiary households by directly sending the voucher to eligible households and only allowing them to access the benefits. By doing so, the BPNT removed the involvement of local governments in benefit disbursement and avoided the chance that rice went "missing" or was redistributed to ineligible households. While an updated beneficiary list improved program targeting accuracy, a revamped program design meant that it was more efficient in doing so.

Second, "in-kind" programs that transfer rice directly to households like Rastra were known for having high levels of leakage, where a substantial share of the rice went missing.[28] The government thought that the switch to vouchers could reduce this leakage. Third, the Rastra rice was of poor quality.[29] Although this could have self-targeting properties, there was a belief that the move to vouchers could improve program satisfaction by increasing rice quality. Finally, Indonesia has high levels of stunting, even

[27] Banerjee, et al. 2018.
[28] Olken, 2006.
[29] Banerjee et al., 2023.

conditional on income levels,[30] and it was thought that the vouchers could increase food diversity by allowing households to also purchase eggs.

Indeed, households which were eligible to receive the BPNT consumed more egg protein.[31] For poor households who received BPNT in particular, there was a 4.3% increase in total egg protein consumption. The poorest experienced an 8.4% increase, while the very poorest saw an 11.7% increase. This implies that the government's decision to add eggs as a component in the transfers program worked to actually encourage protein consumption among the poor.

Instead of at once enacting the reform at a nationwide scale, the government converted Rastra to BPNT over approximately four years. This conversion was based upon the government's annual budget availability. In the first rollout phase in 2017, the voucher program was initially piloted in 44 cities.[32] For the second phase of the rollout, in 2018, the government ranked all the remaining districts by using a conversion readiness indicator. Based on this indicator, 105 districts were deemed ready to be converted. However, the government only had the budget to convert the program for about 8.3 million beneficiary households; thus, they randomized 42 of the 105 districts to be converted in 2018, and the rest to be converted in 2019. These 105 districts encompass about a fifth of Indonesia's population, which was about 53 million individuals and about 3.4 million targeted beneficiary households.

Switching from the in-kind Rastra program to the BPNT vouchers greatly increased the government's ability to target eligible households. Poorer households experienced substantial gains in the total amount of subsidy received. On average, poor households in areas where Rastra was already converted to BPNT received a subsidy that was IDR 13,235 greater than that of poor households in areas that still had Rastra. This was a 45% increase in the value of subsidy received. The gains were most pronounced for the poorest 18% of the population. While households in the middle of the distribution received about the same amount of subsidy on average, those at the top saw the amount fall considerably.

Furthermore, although there was a reduction in the number of people who received benefits under the BPNT, this reduction was larger for those who were not eligible for the transfers. The probability of receiving any assistance fell by 16% for the poor and by 49% for the more well-off, who should not

[30] Cahyadi et al., 2020.
[31] Banerjee et al. (2023)
[32] Banerjee et al., 2023.

be eligible to receive the transfers. However, conditional on subsidy receipt, beneficiaries received 85% more rice under BPNT than under Rastra. What these findings imply is that benefit was more concentrated in poor families under BPNT vouchers than under the in-kind Rastra program. Under BPNT, not only was more of the subsidy was going to the targeted households but also, conditional on receipt, households were much more likely to receive the program's full amount.

With a program design more effective in targeting the poor, there were substantial reductions in poverty associated with the move from the in-kind Rastra program to the BPNT voucher program. This was particularly apparent for the poorest households, who saw their poverty rates fall by about 6.5 percentage points for those in the poorest group, and around 4 percentage points for those in the next-poorest group. This occurred both because more of these households were close to the poverty line to begin with and because the impact of the transfer was largest for these groups.

Beyond alleviating poverty, the BPNT program seems to have improved the quality of the rice received by families. Rice distributed under the Rastra program tended to be of lower quality.[33] Poor rice quality could have self-targeting properties, especially compared to cash, which everyone might want.[34] However, under the BPNT programs, targeted households not only received larger quantities of rice, they also received rice of higher quality. Quality improvements in the voucher program were likely related to the fact that rice sourcing was more flexible. Under Rastra, the subsidized rice was sourced and distributed by BULOG as a government-owned logistics agency. In that case, rice vendors had little say in determining the rice's quality, as the suppliers had already been pre-determined. By contrast, in the voucher BPNT program, local food vendors had a greater ability to source rice where they saw fit. This meant that they could shop around for rice vendors with the best value for money, balancing quality and price.

Finally, BPNT not only was more effective in delivering assistance to targeted beneficiaries, it was substantially less costly to administer. On net, administrative program costs for the in-kind delivery were about 4.1% of the total benefits. Meanwhile, the administrative costs of the BPNT voucher program were 0.74% of the benefits disbursed, or about 18% of administrative costs for the in-kind Rastra program. This was due to the simplified

[33] Banerjee et al., 2019.
[34] Nichols and Zeckhauser, 1982; Besley and Kanbur, 1988.

benefit delivery mechanism, which cut the direct involvement of village officials and BULOG in a massive logistics operation, moving millions of tons of food to different parts of the country.

By 2019, all districts across Indonesia had adopted BPNT. There were 15.6 million recipient households. This was practically the largest food transfers reform in the country in nearly two decades, having dramatically changed the program's design and benefit component, and it was also the most significant. In 2020, the government rebranded BPNT as Program Sembako (staple foods program). The government retained its digital benefit disbursement mechanism, and it increased the program's benefit from IDR 100,000 to IDR 150,000. While this was a relatively minor change when compared to the previous reform, this change could be implemented immediately instead of in stages.

Moreover, learning from BPNT's design, which effectively changed the protein consumption pattern among beneficiaries, the government further broadened the variety of commodities that the beneficiaries could redeem through their food transfer program. Under Program Sembako, beneficiary families could redeem their vouchers for sources of carbohydrate, animal-based protein, and plant-based protein, as well as vitamins and minerals. This expansion aimed to broaden the beneficiaries' options in fulfilling their dietary needs. Although the government had intended the changes in BPNT to give beneficiaries more options to select their choice of food items, in practice beneficiary families often had little say in determining the kind and quantity of food that they could redeem.[35] Food vendors often provided pre-packaged goods, with set amounts and types of food, and there was some pressure on vendors to source from them, or pressure from local government bureaucrats to source from selected distributors. As a result, beneficiary families often had little say in choosing vendors who could provide them with the best goods with the best value for money.

BPNT's digital infrastructure and pre-existing beneficiary database as a targeting instrument allowed the Indonesian government to implement the program with some flexibility and to swiftly modify the program's design and launch Program Sembako at the start of 2020. Later on, in March 2020 when the Indonesian government acknowledged COVID-19 as a pandemic, the announcement was soon followed by the launch of a special disaster mitigation budget. Under this budget, Program Sembako's benefit value was

[35] TNP2K, 2020.

increased from IDR 150,000 to 200,000 per family per month. Moreover, Program Sembako's beneficiaries saw an expansion from 15.2 million to 20 million families, which exhausted the number of families in the government's Unified Database listing potentially eligible recipient households. While this expansion illustrated the flexibility of Indonesia's social protection system, it also exposed its limitations. No matter how much the government wanted to expand Program Sembako, when it had exhausted the names in the list, it had to take time to identify and enlist new program beneficiaries.

Beyond the database's limited scope, it was last extensively updated in 2015 prior to BPNT's launch and had not been regularly updated since. As a result, the database no longer accurately reflected the listed households' current welfare conditions (see Chapter 3). This was a problem during the pandemic when millions were potentially pushed under the poverty line due to the sudden economic shock, which tested the food transfer program's ability to provide social protection for the population. While the database's inaccuracy was not a new problem, and the food transfer program's mistargeting had plagued it from the start, the pandemic revealed the program's limits. Not just that the program's flexibility and targeting accuracy hinged upon the availability of a reliable database, it also needed a database with enough buffer to scale the program up or down as needed to be effective.

More than two decades since its inception in 1998, Indonesia's food transfers have seen numerous changes. Varying in scope of change, many of these reforms were not merely cosmetic in nature. They included changes in targeting methods, delivery mechanisms, and benefit value. What allowed a government social program to endure for so long and to change relatively frequently and, at times, to such an extent? Beyond the technical considerations, Indonesia's food transfers reform is also a political story.

The Political Economy of Reform

Since the fall of the New Order Suharto regime in 1998, Indonesia has experienced a dramatic increase in the scale and reach of its food transfers program. Although it began as part of the government's social safety net programs designed to dampen the impact of the 1997-1998 Asian financial crisis on the poor, the program has expanded, seen numerous reforms, and turned into a permanent feature of the Indonesian social protection system. Since the fall of the authoritarian regime, democracy has altered the political game.

The advent of democratic elections changed the incentive structures within which new and old political actors alike operated.

Under democracy, expanding social welfare policies to reach out to voters—and particularly the poor—has been a strategy for politicians to compete in elections. This was visible during the first phase of the food transfer policy expansion during the BJ Habibie administration (1998–1999) and has been followed by others. For instance, the Megawati Soekarnoputri (2001–2003) administration launched a major free healthcare initiative; the Susilo Bambang Yudhoyono (2004–2014) administration reformed and expanded Raskin and later on Rastra; the Joko Widodo (2014–2024) administration continued Rastra before revamping it. Although the Indonesian food assistance reform is a part of a larger pattern of politicians competing for public support, factors outside of politics also contributed to this expansion.

The catalyst for initial policy expansion was the Asian financial crisis. Some literature depicted Indonesia's social protection policies as an outgrowth of temporary safety net programs. The subsequent policies have become a more permanent feature of the country's social protection system.[36] However, these factors cannot be separated from their political context. Thus, though the JPS social safety net program was a response to the economic crisis—and was initially largely funded by and planned in conjunction with, the World Bank—it was highly political from the start. The JPS was seen by both supporters and opponents of President Habibie and Golkar Party's attempt at political survival in the midst of the political storm triggered by the crisis, at a time when the first post-Suharto elections were looming.

Once the policies were introduced, it became difficult for politicians who were subject to regular elections to repeal or retrench them, especially as they feared losing political support from their voter base. Accordingly, both Megawati (2001–2004) and Yudhoyono (2004–2014) viewed the social safety net policies they inherited as crucial to maintaining their government's popularity. This was evident in Megawati's decision to establish a National Social Security System Working Committee in March 2001 to prepare a sweeping reform where a national system covering health, pensions, and other benefits would be run by a single trust fund responsible to the

[36] Barrientos and Hulme, 2009; Sumarto et al., 2010.

president.[37] The end of Megawati's term saw the legislation of Law No. 40 of 2004 on the National Social Security System. Beyond establishing the basic principles for the new system, it guaranteed healthcare, workplace accident, old-age, and death benefits for all Indonesian citizens, to be provided by compulsory insurance. The government was obliged to pay premiums for those who could not afford it. This was in line with Megawati and her party's populist traditions and desire to appeal to the working class. Meanwhile, in terms of food transfers, how the policy has become a part of the government's policy repertoire was evident in Yudhoyono's reliance on the program to assuage the public when his administration scaled back fuel subsidies. However, a desire to appeal to the voters alone cannot explain how changes at this scale were able to happen relatively frequently.

Since the governance of food transfers is not clearly prescribed by the law, those holding office tend to have the flexibility to determine the way the program is administered. Such flexibility is not equally distributed across all social programs, regardless of whether they similarly stem from the 1997–1998 crisis and its social safety net programs. This is partly due to the nature of power separation in a democracy. Democracies like Indonesia are usually characterized by separation of powers in the government to keep different parts of the government in check. The power balance between the executive, legislative, and judicial branches of the government would usually reflect political coalitions. In the context of social welfare, this means that the kinds of policies passed are also shaped by the country's political landscape.

When the interests of the president in the executive branch and the interests of the "median legislator" in the Indonesian People's Representative Council (*Dewan Perwakilan Rakyat*, DPR) are not aligned, conflict arises.[38] The median legislator reflects the preferences of the majority in the DPR, which makes them the most decisive legislators. Disagreements may occur when the president and the median legislator come from opposing political parties. Conflict may also arise when the president and median legislator are from different factions in the same party. A legislator from an opposition party or faction knows that if they fund a transfer program with a lax design, the president can claim the credit for welfare gains linked to that policy reform. Moreover, the president can take greater advantage of the opportunities offered by a lax transfers program to build and strengthen their

[37] Wisnu, 2007.
[38] De La O, 2015.

support base. Thus, if the president proposes a transfer program with a weak design that allows for a lot of executive discretion, an opposing legislator has incentives to refuse to support it.

On the other hand, if a legislator from the opposition funds a transfer program with a design that suppresses political discretion, the president can still claim credit for innovating to fight poverty. However, the more rigid operational rules would also limit opportunities to use the program's resources in a clientelist manner. To anticipate the reaction of the median opposition legislator, the president would be better off proposing a program with a rigid design. With this course of action, the president would limit their own discretion over the policy.

Anticipating the reaction of the opposing politicians, the president may be better off proposing a program with a stringent design. With this course of action, the president would limit their own discretion over the policy, but would also limit other politicians' ability to use the program to build and strengthen their support bases. This was the case with the expansion of the national social security system under Megawati. Megawati's administration was then counterbalanced by a fragmented parliament she inherited from her predecessor, Abdurrahman Wahid (1999–2001). During Wahid's presidency every single large and medium-sized party held cabinet positions in his administration, which he shared with Megawati who was herself General Chair for a major party. It was only when Wahid replaced his ministers with people close to him that several parties stood in opposition and sought to impeach him. Against this politically fragmented parliament, Law No. 40 of 2004, on the national social security system, was passed.

Under this law, the governance of the social security system is rigidly spelled out. This ensures the program is not politicized. This stands in contrast with the food transfer program's reform and expansion under Yudhoyono and Joko Widodo's (2014–2024) administration.

Instead of being governed by a set of rigid laws and regulations, the food transfer program was loosely governed by Law No. 18 of 2012 on Food. The law itself referred to food as the most important basic human need and that its fulfillment is a human rights guarantee in the country's constitution—without spelling out the way the program is to be governed or its scope of coverage. The law only stipulates that central and local governments are responsible for ensuring food affordability through food distribution, trade, price, supply stabilization, and aid policies. Based on this law, food transfers are usually governed by presidential or ministerial regulations, which in practical terms allows the ruling administration to govern the program. The Joko Widodo administration is a case where the president and the median legislator's interests were aligned. With his party holding the House of Representatives, President Joko Widodo could adopt a transfer program that did not require him to tie his own hands with stringent operational rules. Policies passed under such a circumstance would leave open the opportunity to use program resources for building and strengthening his support base.

In such a political context that is favorable to the administration, the program has often been scaled up and down according to the government's available budget. For instance, in 2013 the government distributed rice 15 times per year instead of the usual 12 times per year to compensate for increased fuel prices. With the program's transformation into vouchers rather than in-kind transfers, benefits could be disbursed swiftly and did not require moving tons of rice across the country. In 2020, Program Sembako's value was increased twice from IDR 110,000 to IDR 150,000, with the latter addition serving as a cushion for welfare shocks due to the COVID-19 pandemic. At that time, Program Sembako's coverage increased from 15.2 million families prior to the pandemic to 20 million families. This was facilitated by a newly launched COVID-19 mitigation emergency budget.

Beyond politics, changing attitudes toward social protection on the part of international agencies and donors like the World Bank, the United Nations Development Program, and USAID also shaped the policy debate.[39] Starting as a temporary safety net program, Indonesia's food transfer had become the government's key program for poverty alleviation after the Asian financial crisis, and later it became a part of the country's social protection infrastructure that could be mobilized in times of need. TNP2K, a government think tank set up by President Yudhoyono in 2010, reflected such a shift in attitude. Mandated to coordinate the country's poverty-alleviation efforts, TNP2K played a key role in the food transfer program's transformation into a permanent structure. This entailed establishing a targeting system that encompassed a database for social assistance programs and improving the efficiency and effectiveness of various poverty-alleviation programs. To tread the political waters in bridging many interests across the government, TNP2K relied on evidence from research to make recommendations to policymakers. Its role has been instrumental in reforming and evaluating Indonesia's food transfer program and the broader social protection system

[39] Barrientos and Hulme, 2009.

infrastructure. In Rastra's transformation from BPNT, for instance, TNP2K played an instrumental role in designing the policy, as well as staggering its rollout in a way that allowed the program's impact to be robustly measured.

Due to a steady decline in poverty rates over the years, TNP2K began advocating for broader welfare system reform that also covered middle-class households at risk of falling into poverty. This has included mobilizing the country's food transfers program for contingent safety net programs—similar to OPK in the aftermath of the 1997–1998 Asian financial crisis but with more efficient targeting and more effective delivery—rather than using the transfers merely as a means to alleviate poverty. This was the case with Program Sembako that the government mobilized during the COVID-19 pandemic in 2020 and 2021.

Over time, Indonesia's food transfers program has evolved from a rice subsidies scheme to one using voucher-based transfers. The food transfer program's changes and expansions could be perceived as an attempt to strengthen the president's patronage bases; but at the same time, the program's lax administration has enabled it to work as a shock-absorbance mechanism if needed. This shows how political interest may not always be detrimental to welfare, or might even pave ways toward the development of a full-blown social protection system.

An Afterthought

Indonesia's food transfer program started out as a subsidized rice scheme in the wake of the Asian financial crisis. Over time, it has transformed into a permanent feature of the Indonesian social protection system. This transformation entails not only nominal changes but also a more extensive infrastructural change. Expansion of the program's coverage and delivery mechanism does not just represent surface-level changes, but rather a whole set of reforms that entail setting up a database for targeting and an electronic delivery system. Beyond food transfers, other programs across the government also benefit from these reforms by attaching its own design and implementation to the same infrastructure. For instance, the Family Hope Program (*Program Keluarga Harapan*, PKH) conditional cash transfer, and Smart Indonesia Program (*Program Indonesia Pintar*, PIP) used the database created to target rice transfer program's beneficiaries in order to determine beneficiary eligibility for their programs, and used the same digital benefit disbursement channels.

What is interesting was that changes to Indonesia's food transfer program occurred not just extensively but also relatively frequently. A part of what enabled this change was political competition under democracy. The incentives for policy reform—particularly program expansion—emerged as politicians were vying for popular support following Indonesia's transition into democracy. The development of the social protection system infrastructure not only meant coverage expansion or additions to benefit value could be achieved relatively easily for political ends, but it also has meant that the food transfer program could be mobilized as a part of the government's crisis mitigation strategy, as seen during the COVID-19 pandemic. The shift from Rastra to BPNT significantly improved Indonesia's benefit delivery capacity when the government implemented a new digital delivery system, which substantially altered the existing benefit delivery mechanism. Once the new digital system was set up, modifying benefit value or beneficiary lists could be done almost instantaneously. This was the case with the transformation from BPNT to Program Sembako early in 2020 and when the beneficiary list was expanded in March of the same year. However, the scope and success of these expansions hinges upon the quality of the welfare system infrastructure itself, such as an updated beneficiary database or robust benefit delivery systems. This tells us that political drives to expand popular social programs need to be extended to a commitment to improving the welfare system infrastructure as well.

Despite the largely political nature of Indonesian food transfer program reform, democratization does not explain the direction of the reform. Instead of being purely populist in nature, reforms were guided by lessons learned from research. This was partly due to the changing discourse in welfare expansion with the involvement of international financial institutions and donors in the Indonesian welfare policy discourse. Aside from external actors, the role of TNP2K as the government's internal government think tank, producing evidence and advocating for collaboration across government units, was also instrumental in shaping policy outcomes. If there is anything to take away from Indonesia's food transfer reform, it is that good reforms may not always conflict with political interests. In this process, evidence from research needs to inform policy decisions to ensure that changes are not just political or cosmetic in nature.

5

Spending More, Spending Better

Reforming Education in a Fragmented System

Since 2009, Indonesia has allocated one-fifth of its annual national budget to the education sector, marking a significant increase compared to previous years. However, despite this substantial investment in its education system, the country's educational attainment remains sub-par. According to the 2022 assessment by the Programme for International Student Assessment (PISA) on literacy and numeracy, Indonesia is ranked 68th out of 81 countries. The same report also found that only one out of three Indonesian children has basic reading comprehension skills. PISA results have often been regarded as a reliable indicator of student capabilities and have played an important role in shaping Indonesia's education policies.[1]

At this point, it is clear that the amount of money spent on education cannot readily translate into educational attainment. Part of what made reforming the country's education system less straightforward is its fragmented political system, whereby authority over matters of education falls under multiple government bodies both at the central and regional levels. An understanding of the locus at which reformers seek to make changes, and its limits, as well as engaging the right stakeholders, are key to any change in a positive direction.

Increasing the budget for education surely is not a bad thing, as over the years this has translated into broader access to education for Indonesia's population. For instance, between 1974 and 1978, the Indonesian government built over 61,000 primary schools, which led to an increase in education enrollment.[2] Moreover, the government also abolished primary school fees in 1977 and, by the mid-1990s, mandated nine years of compulsory basic education. By 2000, Indonesia had already reached close to universal primary school enrollment (Figure 5.1). At this point, the government

[1] Pratiwi, 2019.
[2] Duflo, 2001.

Evidence and the Politics of Reform. Sudarno Sumarto, Oxford University Press.
 DOI: 10.1093/9780197831717.003.0006

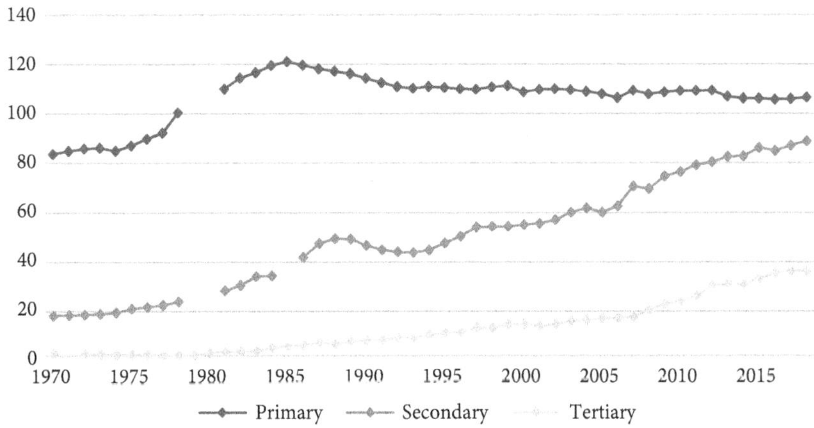

Figure 5.1 Gross Enrollment Rates, %, 1970–2015

Note: Gross enrollment rates can be greater than 100 if students enroll early or late, or repeat a grade.

Source: World Bank, World Development Indicators, https://databank.worldbank.org/source/world-development-indicators

began to shift its policy from broadening education access toward improving the quality of educational input and processes. These policies included reforms related to teacher recruitment,[3] teacher professional development,[4] teacher certification and remuneration,[5] and national examination methods.[6] In terms of spending, the government has consistently invested a fifth of its budget in the education sector since 2009.[7] Surprisingly, despite all of these policies, educational output has remained poor.

PISA is a study conducted by the OECD to evaluate education systems across the world by measuring the scholastic achievement of 15-year-old school students in mathematics, science, and reading. Indonesia's PISA results across all testing components in 2022 are among the lowest ever measured for the country.[8] Indonesia's reading and mathematics achievements in 2022 are comparable to results observed in 2003, and Indonesia's science achievements in 2022 are comparable to those recorded in 2006. Although

[3] Huang, Revina, and Fillaili 2020.
[4] Revina et al. 2020.
[5] de Ree et al. 2018.
[6] Berkhout et al. 2020.
[7] Kurniawati et al. 2019.
[8] OECD, 2023.

results from some previous assessments were higher than those observed in earlier years, Indonesia's results have tended to show a decline since 2015.

In contrast to Indonesia's achievements in increasing access to education, there is evidence that Indonesian children learn very little, even after several years of schooling, more than a decade later. Echoing PISA's findings, an assessment of how children and young adults developed their learning profile within 15 years between 2000 and 2014 found that higher levels of school enrollment and attainment have not translated into improvements in the students' basic numeracy abilities.[9] A large gap remains between students' mathematical abilities and expected knowledge based on the education curriculum.[10] Absolute learning levels as well as marginal learning levels are low. This means that students are not learning much despite having moved along grade levels. Even high school graduates struggle to correctly answer numeracy problems that they should have mastered in primary school.

The problem is that schooling does not always translate into learning. While in the 2010s elementary school and secondary school enrollment rates continued to rise, children's learning did not truly match their grade level.[11] In 2020, on average, Indonesian students had already completed 12.4 years of schooling by the time they had their 18th birthday.[12] However, their learning levels remained equivalent to only 7.8 years of schooling. The contrast between high enrollment, growing education budget, and the disappointing educational outcomes in Indonesia has certainly puzzled policymakers.

Beyond the country's general issue with educational input and output quality, the tendency to report educational attainment as averages—such as the enrollment rate or PISA score—masks heterogeneity across the country and between students of different socio-economic backgrounds.[13] For instance, students from families within the richest quintile in the country have much higher school participation rates than their less well-off peers (Figure 5.2). Additionally, according to the 2022 PISA test report, Indonesia's socio-economically advantaged students (the top 25% in terms of socio-economic status) outperformed its disadvantaged students (the bottom 25%) by 34 score points in 2022.[14] The same report also found that socio-economic status was a predictor of performance in mathematics.

[9] Beatty, 2018.
[10] Beatty et al., 2021.
[11] Beatty et al., 2021; Afkar, de Ree, and Khairina, 2018.
[12] World Bank, 2020.
[13] Dharmawan and Suryadarma, 2021.
[14] OECD, 2023.

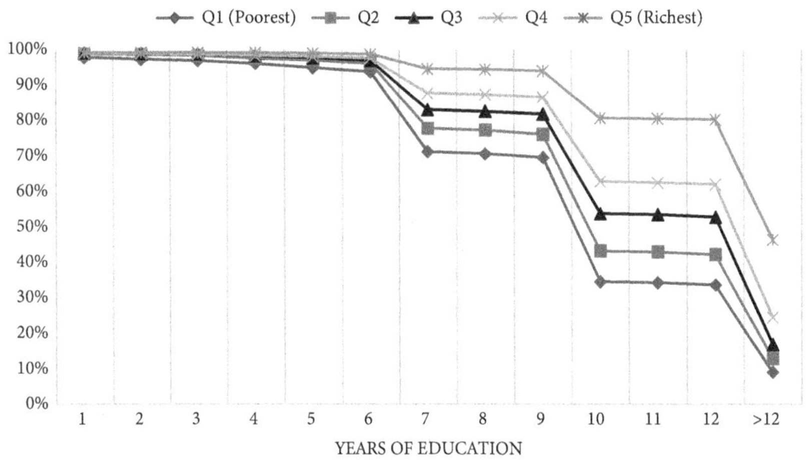

Figure 5.2 School Participation (%) Based on Quintile Year 2021
Source: SUSENAS 2021, author calculation.

Although Indonesia has witnessed gains in school participation, the quality of education measured by performance on standardized tests remains low and is stagnating. To make matters worse, the quality of education has declined over the past two decades.[15] In short, higher public investment in education and many of the reforms over the past two decades have not led to higher-quality education. Instead of looking at all these reforms as a failure, there needs to be a closer look at why these policies do not "work." Education policies to expand enrollment, for instance, worked to increase enrollment. Meanwhile, an expanded education budget was accompanied by improvements in school physical infrastructure. These policies worked to meet their very specific set of goals. However, new times call for different policies. From increasing enrollment, policymakers now need to translate enrollment into learning, to actually improve the country's learning outcomes. Yet, reforming the country's education system is not as straightforward as it used to be.

In Indonesia, education policy is set at the national level by the Ministry of Education, but its implementation is highly decentralized, limiting the ministry's direct control. Since the 2001 decentralization policy, responsibility for delivering education services has largely shifted to regional governments. Provincial governments oversee senior secondary education, while district governments manage basic education (primary and junior

[15] Beatty et al., 2021.

secondary schools). However, these local governments report to the Ministry of Home Affairs, not the Ministry of Education, creating an additional layer of complexity. Further complicating governance, civil servant teachers and school principals are primarily accountable to the Ministry of Administrative and Bureaucratic Reform, while budget allocations fall under the authority of the Ministry of National Planning and Development and the Ministry of Finance.

Despite Indonesia allocating 20% of its annual budget to education, the Ministry of Education directly receives only about 15% of this funding, with the rest distributed to local governments and other national ministries. With so many stakeholders involved across different levels of government, diagnosing problems in education policy is only the first step. Finding solutions requires identifying the right locus for reform, understanding which agencies hold decision-making power, and ensuring that the right stakeholders are engaged to make meaningful change possible.

Diagnosing What Has Gone Wrong

Before 1998, Indonesia's main education challenge was access. In 1970, nearly half of the population aged 15 and above had not completed primary school.[16] To address this, the government launched a massive school expansion effort that led to the construction of tens of thousands of primary schools across the country. Fueled by an oil boom, the government also aggressively recruited teachers throughout the 1970s and early 1980s. However, this period of heavy investment ended abruptly with the 1997–1998 Asian financial crisis, which strained public resources and reshaped the country's education priorities.

When the crisis hit and pushed millions into poverty, the government launched a series of social safety net programs, including education assistance. To keep children in school and prevent long-term learning loss, the government provided block grants to improve school infrastructure in disadvantaged areas and introduced scholarships to help students from low-income families stay enrolled.[17] These scholarships ranged from IDR 10,000 to IDR 30,000 per month, depending on the education level.

[16] Lee and Francisco, 2012.
[17] Pritchett, Sumarto, and Suryahadi, 2002.

Payments were made directly to students or their families twice a year through local post offices. Schools received a scholarship quota and were responsible for distributing aid based on guidelines set by the central government. Selection criteria prioritized students from the poorest households, with additional considerations such as family structure, gender quotas for girls, and risks of dropping out.[18] However, some factors—like assessing a student's dropout risk—were subjective, leading to mistargeting. In practice, only a small fraction of the poorest students received scholarships—5.8% in primary, 12.5% in lower secondary, and 5.4% in upper secondary schools. Meanwhile, students from middle-income households were still 60%–70% as likely as the poorest students to receive aid.[19] Despite these targeting challenges, the program had a measurable impact, particularly for vulnerable groups such as students in rural areas and those living in poverty, helping to sustain school enrollment during the financial crisis.[20]

After 1998, the Indonesian government continued to construct new schools, though at a much slower rate than during the 1970s and early 1980s and with a focus on junior secondary and senior secondary schools. By 2021, the country had over 165,000 public schools and two million teachers in these schools.[21] These efforts to expand the supply of education have intersected with rising income levels, demographic changes, and government efforts to provide free education, all of which have served to increase the demand for education. The result has been a marked increase in student enrollment rates at all levels of the education system. For example, between 1972 and 2015, the country's gross enrollment rate[22] increased from 85% to 105% for primary schools and from 18% to 85% for secondary schools. Importantly, this growth in enrollment is closely associated with increased female participation in education, which improved gender equity in the education sector (see Figure 5.3).

As the country's economy recovered in the 2000s, education spending was largely focused on improving educational inputs. During this period, the government maintained the school subsidies scheme that was a part of the

[18] "Welfare level" is determined by the BKKBN's "prosperity" ranking. More details about how this ranking is set up can be found in Chapter 3.

[19] Pritchett, Sumarto, and Suryahadi, 2002.

[20] Sparrow, 2007.

[21] Ministry of Education and Culture, 2021. *Statistik Pendidikan*. Available at: statistik.data.kemdikbud.go.id

[22] Gross enrollment rate refers to the ratio of total enrollment, regardless of age, to the population of the age group that officially corresponds to a certain level of education.

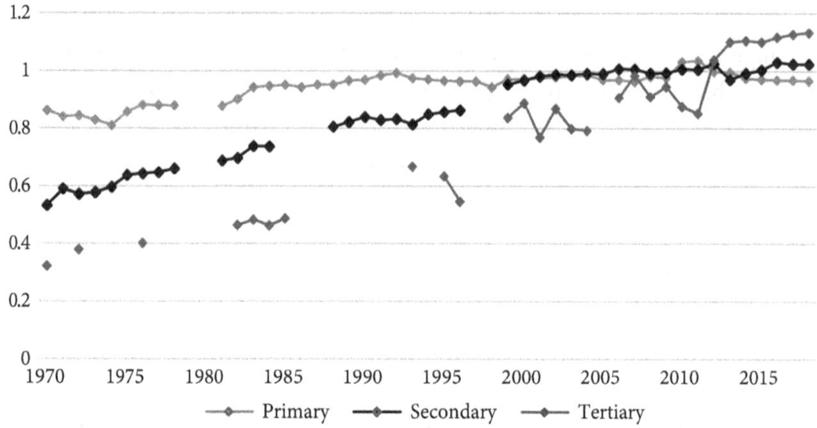

Figure 5.3 Gender Parity Index, 1970–2015

Note: The Gender Parity Index measures the ratio of girls to boys enrolled at the relevant level of schooling in public and private schools.

Source: World Bank, World Development Indicators, https://genderdata.worldbank.org/en/indicator/se-enr?view=trend&geos=IDN&education=Tertiary

social safety net. On top of that, law No. 20/2003 on the National Education System was passed in 2003, which mandated that 20% of the national budget be allocated for education. Education spending increased by 200% in real terms from 2002 to 2018,[23] which financed various reforms. This entailed efforts such as expanding access to education from early childhood to higher education levels and improving teacher qualifications through a teacher certification program.

In this period, Indonesia also saw a shift in its educational policy paradigm from giving schools the authority to identify transfer beneficiaries to providing direct transfers to students. The rationale was that this would improve targeting, ensuring that the needy were not excluded and the well-off were not included in the transfers beneficiary list. In 2008 the government launched the Bantuan Siswa Miskin (BSM) cash transfers for poor students to complement the school subsidies scheme. While the school subsidies were designed to cover education's direct costs, such as tuition fees, the BSM was designed to cover its indirect costs, such as transportation fees. However, the BSM program's targeting was weak, as just 4% of benefits for primary and junior secondary school-aged students reached students

[23] World Bank, 2018.

from the poorest 10% families. In the senior secondary school-age category, the ratio was half that.[24]

Prompted by these findings, TNP2K proposed a number of recommendations to the Ministry of Education and Culture and the Ministry of Religious Affairs (which were in charge of religious schools) to reform BSM's targeting. Using the Unified Database managed by TNP2K (see Chapter 3), the implementing ministries modified BSM's targeting from school-based selection to direct selection of students in poor households. Selected students were then issued with social protection cards to note their entitlement to benefits. By 2014, the number of BSM-eligible students reached nearly 15.4 million.

In the same year, the Joko Widodo administration launched the *Program Indonesia Pintar* to replace the BSM, around the same time as its decision to revoke fuel subsidies (see Chapter 2). While the mechanics of the Program Indonesia Pintar were not much different from those of the BSM, new recipients were added into the beneficiary list. By 2015, the program reached 19 million students. Eight years after it was first launched, the Program Indonesia Pintar remained the administration's flagship educational assistance for the needy. However, ensuring that social assistance reaches intended beneficiaries is not a panacea. No matter how well designed, an educational transfer program still does not address problems in educational service delivery.

In reality, education policy and service delivery fall upon multiple governing bodies. This bureaucratic complexity directly shapes the country's educational output. For one, Indonesia's decentralization policy means that authority over education policies falls in the purview of three levels of government, which are the central, provincial, and district/municipal governments. At the national level, the government is responsible for policies concerning higher education and for setting up educational standards, control, and quality assurance. Meanwhile, at the provincial level, the government is responsible for teacher management. Finally, at the district/municipal level, the government is responsible for policies concerning elementary school, middle school, and pre-school. Although these separations of authorities are meant to best accommodate local dynamics in educational policies, in practice a mismatch between different levels of government could pose problems. The result of this fragmented system is Indonesia's poor learning outcomes.

[24] Based on an evaluation conducted by TNP2K in 2011, using data from the 2009 National Socioeconomic Survey (*Survei Sosial Ekonomi Nasional—Susenas*).

Teacher competence and professionalism play a key role in the success of student learning, which then translates to educational achievements.[25] Yet complaints about low teacher pay—let alone efforts to address more specific concerns relating to teacher quality improvements—reflect the government's lack of commitment to the welfare and quality of educators. As long as the government does not prioritize improving teaching quality and mapping teacher competencies, Indonesia's quality of education is going nowhere. The Teacher Competency Test is the government's evaluation tool to measure teacher performance in Indonesia. This test assesses a teacher's pedagogic competence, their ability to manage classes and prepare learning strategies for students, and professional competence, as well as their mastery over the materials and their ability to evaluate learning. Based on the test's 2015 results, the average teacher competence score was not particularly promising.[26] On average, elementary school, middle school, and high school teachers scored 40.14, 44.16, and 45.38 respectively, which were all below the minimum standard that the Ministry of Education set at 55 at that time. In 2018, this minimum standard was increased to 75.[27] However, efforts to turn things around have yet to come to fruition.

Indonesia's fragmented education system has long been a barrier to improving teacher quality and student learning. Despite significant investments in education and rising enrollment rates, learning outcomes remain stubbornly low. This issue is not unique to Indonesia—globally, many education systems struggle with a "learning crisis" in which more children are in school, but too few are actually learning. To better understand these challenges, the RISE Programme Indonesia—part of a multi-country research initiative launched in 2015—set out to diagnose the root causes of Indonesia's education problems. What makes RISE's approach distinctive is its deep engagement with local research institutions and policymakers. By working closely with the Ministry of Education and Culture, local governments, and education agencies, the program ensures its research remains policy-relevant and grounded in Indonesia's realities.

A key insight from RISE's work is that piecemeal reforms are unlikely to work in Indonesia's highly decentralized system. Effective change requires a holistic understanding of the education landscape, including how policies

[25] Huang et al., 2020.

[26] Ministry of Education and Culture, 2022. Neraca Pendidikan Daerah. Available at: https://doi.org/10.64628/AAN.m5x5r3chu

[27] Revina, 2019.

are formulated and implemented across different regions. With this in mind, RISE's research has focused on leveraging local resources and institutional structures to enhance teacher accountability and student learning outcomes. By embedding research within Indonesia's political and institutional context, RISE has provided valuable insights into what works—and what doesn't—in improving education quality. Its findings offer important lessons for policymakers navigating the complexities of reform in a decentralized system.

RISE Programme researchers took a deep dive into teacher quality in Indonesia, starting with teacher competency exams, education, and recruitment. Despite requiring prospective teachers to complete a one-year professional education program after their undergraduate studies, RISE's results were concerning. A 2018 study found that only 12.4% of primary school teachers felt confident in their literacy skills, and just 21.3% felt competent in numeracy.[28] These figures highlight a troubling reality: many teachers lacked confidence in their own ability to teach, even after completing training and gaining classroom experience. If teachers themselves struggle with basic skills, it's little surprise that Indonesian students consistently rank among the lowest in international assessments like PISA. Adding to the problem, teacher recruitment is handled by the Ministry of Home Affairs rather than the Ministry of Education or regional education agencies. This means hiring decisions often overlook teaching ability and subject mastery, further weakening the education system. Without addressing these fundamental issues, improving student learning outcomes will remain an uphill battle.

Indonesia's teacher education system is failing to produce graduates with the necessary skills to be effective educators. This issue is especially critical at the elementary level, where teachers must master and teach a broad range of subjects which serve as the foundation for students' future learning. Beyond gaps in subject mastery and teaching skills, teacher absenteeism is widespread, further weakening education quality.[29]

While Indonesia has attempted to map teacher competence through the Teacher Competency Test, this approach has not led to sustainable improvements. One major flaw is that it does not assess skills by grade level, making it difficult to tailor training to specific teaching needs. If training programs fail to improve teacher quality, then the solution should start at the source—recruiting better teachers in the first place. Ideally, an effective recruitment

[28] Yusrina et al., 2022.
[29] McKenzie, 2014.

system would attract and select the most competent candidates. However, RISE Programme Indonesia found that two major obstacles stood in the way: flaws in institutional design and political-economy pressures. These structural issues make it even harder to build a strong, professional teaching force.

Indonesia's teacher recruitment process is mired in bureaucratic complexity, with laws and regulations that create more confusion than clarity. Institutional responsibilities are fragmented, discouraging collaboration between political authorities who lack both the mandate and guidance to improve the system. Even when reform is attempted, rigid regulations narrowly define what constitutes a "good teacher," leaving little flexibility to select candidates based on real classroom needs.

The centralized control over the teaching profession is a legacy of Indonesia's authoritarian past when teachers were classified as state civil servants, which was a status that ensured stable pay and benefits but also secured their loyalty to the regime.[30] Decades later, this system remains largely intact, with three ministries dividing control over teacher management. The Ministry of Administrative and Bureaucratic Reform oversees recruitment, ensuring a formal merit-based process, while the Ministry of Finance manages teacher salaries and funding. Meanwhile, the Ministry of Education and Culture, which might be expected to play the most active role, has limited authority, largely confined to professional development. This bureaucratic fragmentation has left Indonesia without a coordinated approach to attracting and retaining high-quality teachers. Without systemic reform, recruitment will continue to follow outdated processes, reinforcing the very challenges that keep Indonesia's education system from realizing its full potential.

Indonesia's fragmented teacher management system presents a major barrier to reform, as no single ministry has full authority over teacher supervision. In theory, this separation could allow for independent oversight, but in practice, poor communication and coordination among ministries has hindered meaningful change. As a result, teacher recruitment often fails to align with the competency standards set by the Ministry of Education's Teacher Competency Test.

This bureaucratic entanglement means that efforts to improve teaching quality are often driven more by political negotiations than by educational priorities. Any reform must navigate the competing interests of the Ministry

[30] Nielsen, 1998.

of Administrative and Bureaucratic Reform, which oversees recruitment; the Ministry of Finance, which controls funding; and the Ministry of Education and Culture, which is responsible for professional development. The challenges surrounding contract teacher recruitment illustrate this tension, as each ministry operates within its own silo, making it difficult to implement cohesive and effective policies.

Indonesian teachers in public schools consist of permanent civil servants and contract teachers, who are teachers that have not been appointed as civil servants. While the former are entitled to various work benefits and pensions, the latter are not. Moreover, these contract teachers tend to be paid less and lack job security, with little guarantee in regard to their promotion as a civil servant.[31] Despite disparities in income levels between the two kinds of teachers, contract teachers do not perform any worse when compared to civil servants.[32] However, this does not say much, since teacher quality is insufficient to begin with. Where the problem arises is that it is unclear to whom these contract teachers should be answering. In particular, the sense of job security is accompanied by a lack of consequential performance evaluation, which has led to little—if any—incentive for teachers to improve their teaching once they are promoted to civil servant status. On the other hand, faced with poor compensation, job security, and clarity over career progression, contract teachers may become demotivated over time.[33]

When publicly questioned about the teacher recruitment system and mandated to only select tenured civil servants, the Ministry of Administrative and Bureaucratic Reform would refer to their mass teacher recruitment drive into civil service. However, at the same time they would also evade the dilemma of having to promote contract teachers who did not qualify for civil service. The ministry would leave the decision of contract teacher promotion to local governments. Further complicating matters, the Ministry of Finance was opposed to such recruitment drives due to budgetary concerns. This push and pull between ministries demonstrates how the dynamic between various political powers allowed each to deny responsibility over teachers' employment within the recruitment process.

In terms of political economy, teacher recruitment is closely tied to Indonesia's decentralization process. The newly rolled out decentralization policy allowed a vacuum of authority. As Indonesia transitioned from

[31] Alifia et al., 2022.
[32] Huang et al., 2020; Yusrina et al., 2022.
[33] Alifia et al., 2022.

authoritarianism to democracy, elite interests melded with local authorities and institutions.[34] Decentralization and local self-determination have encouraged local political leaders to be more daring with their state predation by co-opting state structures to fulfill their own interests and build patronage networks.[35] Along this line, teacher recruitment also embodies these patronage ties and clientelism, as teaching positions are often distributed by political leaders to their supporters following local elections.[36] There were even cases in which teachers themselves have been observed to organize political support for local leaders who are standing for elections.[37] These trends imply that teaching positions in civil service have become a currency in politics, particularly to build patronage networks to win public offices, rather than to improve teaching quality.

Conflicting political interests in the central government and decentralized decision-making at the regional level have made efforts to enact reforms addressing poor teacher quality an uphill battle. Policymakers seeking to make changes need to consider these dynamics and determine realistic policy goals at an appropriate level of government. Taking these factors into account, RISE Programme Indonesia partnered with a number of local governments across Indonesia to tackle the learning crisis. This strategy to engage with local educational authorities was a conscious decision, since local governments were endowed with significant authority over education policies beyond teacher recruitment. With politics on the table, aside from defining the scope of intended change and how this change would interact with the rest of the education system, efforts to reform education policies are also a matter of seeking the right "champions" at different levels of governance, working closely with them to ensure buy-in.

Improving Learning Processes

When faced with policy challenges, the instinctive response is often to create new programs. While this can be beneficial in addressing policy gaps, in Indonesia where overlapping regulations and underutilized programs already exist, adding more initiatives may not be the best solution.

[34] Aspinall, 2010.
[35] Aspinall, 2014; Berenschot, 2018.
[36] Pierskalla and Sacks, 2020.
[37] Rosser and Fahmi, 2018.

Recognizing this, RISE Programme Indonesia took a different approach. Instead of prescribing solutions, it partnered with local governments to evaluate existing policies, resources, and institutional arrangements to identify opportunities for reform. This bottom-up approach contrasts with the more common top-down models, which often dictate solutions to problems rather than engaging local stakeholders in the process.

One of the biggest challenges in Indonesia's education system is the tension between centralized teacher recruitment policies and persistent gaps in teacher quality at the local level. To address this, RISE Programme Indonesia established "Learning Laboratories" in collaboration with local governments. These laboratories served as testing grounds for education reforms, allowing policymakers and researchers to identify problems, experiment with interventions, and measure their impact. Successful interventions could then be adopted and scaled by the government.

Between 2015 and 2023, RISE Programme Indonesia ran four Learning Laboratories—three at the district level and one at the provincial level. One example is Kebumen District in Central Java, where RISE conducted a study on parental involvement in learning. By working directly with regional education agencies, researchers engaged with real-world challenges, tested solutions with practical policy implications, and shared the costs of interventions. In turn, local governments benefited from data-driven insights, tested reform strategies, and strengthened their capacity to improve education service delivery.

The RISE Programme research team aimed to improve student learning within existing institutional constraints, such as limited district resources and regulatory frameworks. In collaboration with the Kebumen District Government, researchers designed and piloted an intervention focused on increasing parental involvement in education—a factor known to shape children's learning outcomes and experiences.[38] The study sought to determine whether local governments could enhance parental engagement using existing resources and whether this, in turn, could lead to measurable learning improvements.[39] This focus on parental involvement emerged from a series of in-depth diagnostics that identified key constraints in Kebumen's education system. By working within the capabilities of the education office and school staff, researchers ensured that the intervention was both feasible

[38] Todd and Wolpin, 2007; Houtenville and Conway, 2008.
[39] Tresnatri et al., 2022.

and well-received by local stakeholders. The collaborative design process increased government buy-in while keeping the intervention low-cost and scalable for potential replication elsewhere.

The study facilitated direct communication between parents and teachers across 65 control schools and 65 treatment schools, involving 500+ teachers, 5,000 students, and their parents. Results showed that parents in treatment schools spent more time engaging with their children, interacted more with teachers, and invested more in their children's education. The intervention successfully strengthened parental agency and fostered a more supportive home learning environment. Encouraged by these findings, the Kebumen District Government planned to expand the program to all 120,000 primary school students. However, such collaborations between scholars and policymakers are not always straightforward, which highlights the challenges of sustaining evidence-based interventions in practice.

Indonesia's geographic diversity presents challenges in policy implementation while also exacerbating regional inequalities. Remote areas, which are harder to reach and costly to supervise, often struggle with poor teacher accountability, such as high absenteeism, leading to lower education quality. To address these issues, RISE Programme Indonesia collaborated with the East Nusa Tenggara and West Kalimantan governments to test interventions aimed at improving teacher accountability.[40]

Between October 2016 and March 2018, the study was conducted in 270 schools across five districts—two in East Nusa Tenggara and three in West Kalimantan. RISE Programme Indonesia partnered with TNP2K, the Ministry of Education and Culture, and district governments to implement the intervention. The research team selected districts from the central government's list of disadvantaged regions, balancing cost and feasibility considerations before assigning schools to control and treatment groups. In treatment schools, researchers helped communities establish joint commitments between schools and local stakeholders to enhance education quality. Teacher-specific scorecards were introduced, monitored by a newly formed user committee, which evaluated and shared teacher performance results. Some schools also installed time-stamped cameras to track teacher attendance, and teachers became eligible for allowances tied to positive evaluations, recorded attendance, or both. As expected, all measures effectively increased teachers' teaching hours.

[40] Gaduh et al., 2020.

These promising findings suggest that similar interventions could be applied in other remote, infrastructure-poor regions. However, educational inequality is not confined to rural areas. In urban settings, students from disadvantaged backgrounds struggle to access top schools, reflecting systemic inequities in Indonesia's school admission system.

Indonesia's school admission system limits access to quality public junior secondary schools for lower-income students. Public schools generally outperform private ones due to better resources, trained teachers, and stronger student selection[41]. Graduates of public junior secondary schools score higher on the Grade 9 national exam, yet these schools serve only about 70% of students nationwide. Admission is based on Grade 6 national exam scores, leaving those who don't qualify with no choice but to attend private schools. Since high-performing students are more likely to come from wealthier families, they have better chances of securing public school seats. Meanwhile, lower-performing students—often from poor backgrounds—must pay for low-quality private education, as high-quality private schools remain financially out of reach. This system deepens educational inequality, disproportionately disadvantaging poor and low-performing students.

Thus, in 2018, RISE Programme Indonesia partnered with the Yogyakarta municipal government to study the impact of school zoning in 46 state and private junior secondary schools. The policy, introduced nationally in 2017, prioritizes students living near public schools for admission, aiming to promote equal access to quality education. However, Indonesia's decentralized system has allowed local governments to tailor implementation. The study found that while zoning increased low-performing student enrollment in public schools, many did not attend the best schools available to them. This was not due to a failure of the policy itself but rather because students self-sorted into lower-quality public schools.

When researchers and governments collaborate effectively, they can drive meaningful improvements in education—from diagnosing systemic issues to designing interventions that enhance learning. Insights from one region can inform solutions elsewhere, and successful programs can be scaled or replicated. However, not all partnerships endure. Some, like the collaboration in Way Kanan district during the COVID-19 pandemic, faltered when disruptions to in-person learning derailed research efforts. Effective partnerships require mutual commitment both from researchers and government

[41] Berkhout and Tresnatri, 2020a; 2020b.

officials, but even when promising initiatives take shape at the local level, their long-term sustainability is not guaranteed.

A key factor in strengthening these collaborations is ensuring that government counterparts have a stake in the process. In RISE Programme Indonesia's studies, for example, local governments funded the research while the team provided expertise, fostering a sense of ownership and increasing the likelihood of sustained implementation. Yet even with this structure, not all governments opted to continue the interventions, underscoring the persistent challenge of translating research into lasting policy change.

Political shifts often determine whether initiatives survive. In Way Kanan, a change in leadership led to waning commitment, ultimately dissolving the project. Similarly in Kebumen, a successful program to improve parental participation in education was discontinued in 2022 due to budget constraints, despite initial enthusiasm and positive results. These cases highlight a broader reality: even well-designed, evidence-based programs struggle to take root without sustained political will and financial support.

Formalizing programs and good practices into regulations is one way to achieve sustainability. However, advocating for regulatory reforms is often an uphill battle that not only takes a long time but also requires one to build a coalition with many stakeholders. Researchers are unfortunately often poorly equipped to handle these tasks. Despite the Ministry of Education's endorsement at the highest government levels in Indonesia, eventually many of educational decisions fell under the purview of local governments.

Reforming a Fragmented System

Education is an important driver for economic growth.[42] It is expected to endow students with a set of knowledge, skills, competencies, and abilities that improve their productivity in the labor market. Education can also help facilitate innovation and technological adoption that augment one's productivity. For education to translate into productivity, however, learning has to actually take place.

Indonesia has expanded access to education, improved school infrastructure, and increased enrollment rates over the years. However, student

[42] Hanushek and Woessmann, 2008; Barro, 2013.

learning outcomes remain below expectations, highlighting a gap between access and learning attainment. Allocating 20% of the national budget to education signifies a shift toward quality improvement. Yet, without strategic reforms and better coordination between central and regional governments, fragmented policies may hinder meaningful progress.

For reformers aiming to improve Indonesia's education system, two key considerations are crucial. First, they must define the scope of change and engage the appropriate level of government. Identifying the right decision makers and stakeholders is essential for ensuring that reforms are feasible and effectively implemented. Second, even with a clear reform strategy, broader political dynamics must be considered. Policies do not operate in isolation—they interact with various levels of government, interest groups, and existing regulations. Reform efforts must anticipate these complexities to ensure long-term success.

The sustainability of RISE-supported programs varied across regions. Some areas embraced long-term reforms, such as Jakarta, which replaced Way Kanan as RISE's Learning Lab in 2020 and partnered with RISE to reform teacher training and evaluation systems. Others, like Kebumen, struggled to continue the programs due to funding constraints. These mixed outcomes highlight a broader reality in Indonesian education reform: evidence-based policies can be effective, but their success depends on the commitment of politicians and bureaucrats to reform and institutional stability.

Though showing some promise, a bottom-up approach to problem solving still cannot solve a systemic issue. In the end, stagnating learning outcomes and poor teacher quality are merely symptoms of larger governance issues. What this means is that reform at a national scale is still needed.

Reforming National Education Policies

Indonesia's decentralization project set the stage for its education reform efforts after the democratic transition in 1998. This decentralization saw the devolution of much of the educational authority over the primary and secondary levels to sub-national governments. In principle, this policy was intended to grant greater authority to local governments who were thought to have better knowledge of the local policy context. This devolution, however, unleashed another challenge: a fragmented educational system in which authority over educational policymaking and implementation falls upon multiple actors. Policymakers seeking to improve learning could not ignore these political dynamics. Moreover, this decentralization means that policy reformers can no longer apply a one-size-fits-all approach toward education policy, given regional variations and the unique problems that each locality may face. This, however, does not mean that reform efforts should always be small- or medium-scale in nature, given heterogeneity across regions. While some reforms would be limited in scale, others could be implemented at the national level with a broader-ranging impact. The challenge is in determining the scope of any intended reforms and the stakeholders involved in both policy and implementation, as well as how policies at different levels and areas of governance interact with one another.

In 2022, the Ministry of Education and Culture introduced the National Education System Bill, aiming to streamline Indonesia's complex education laws. The bill sought to integrate and replace three existing laws governing education: the 2003 National Education System Law, the 2005 Teacher and Lecturer Law, and the 2012 Higher Education Law.[43] By consolidating these laws, the government aimed to eliminate bureaucratic bottlenecks, simplify rigid regulations, and improve both the education system's quality and teachers' welfare.

Currently, Indonesia's fragmented legal framework has led to misaligned regulations. A clear example is contract teacher recruitment and promotion, which operates differently at the central and regional levels, creating confusion and inefficiencies. Some regulations are too rigid, making it difficult to adapt policies based on evaluation and evolving socio-economic conditions. In other cases, policies fail to reflect shifts in political dynamics. A key example is teacher management. Under authoritarian rule, teacher promotions were often tied to loyalty to the regime, ensuring compliance rather than prioritizing teaching quality. However, in today's democratic system, the same structures have enabled political patronage, often at the expense of education quality. Without reform, these outdated frameworks risk perpetuating inefficiencies and preventing much-needed improvements in Indonesia's education system.

Indonesia's complex and restrictive education laws have often tied the government's hands, making meaningful reform difficult. With limited flexibility, both central and regional governments have frequently resorted to

[43] Dharmawan, 2022.

finding loopholes in existing regulations just to implement policy changes. However, these workarounds rarely produce lasting impact, as they operate within a rigid framework that does not support true innovation. The National Education System Bill aims to streamline and harmonize regulations, allowing education authorities at all levels to pursue reform with greater flexibility and to lead meaningful improvements in the system.

Beyond structural reforms, the bill also seeks to revamp teacher administration. One key issue is the Teacher Professional Education course, which has been a prerequisite for salary increases rather than a tool for enhancing teaching quality. This has shifted the focus of professional development toward financial gains rather than improving competence. The proposed bill seeks to redefine the course as a teaching license rather than a condition for financial benefits. This change would enable the government to create a more effective incentive structure, one that prioritizes professional growth and teaching excellence over bureaucratic requirements.

Reform in these areas echoes RISE Programme Indonesia's research findings. Although RISE was closely engaged with the Ministry of Education and Culture at the national level, the Ministry's limited scope of authority in several reform areas constrained its ability to enact systemic reforms. Furthermore, with few resources to advocate for legislative changes, researchers often had to rely on good faith that evidence from their research would somehow be considered by key policymakers. Despite questions of reform sustainability in its Learning Laboratory areas, knowledge from these studies remains valid. Though the road to the bill's legislation may still be long, its draft has shown promise that evidence from research is being considered. Beyond the need to account for political-economy dynamics and the various scopes of reform, another lesson to be learned from this story is that the path from evidence to policymaking within this process may not always be linear. Along the way, reformers—such as those in the RISE Programme—need to secure the support of local governments, which are key to the delivery of education services as well as their commitment to sustainable reform.

6

When Healthcare Is a Right: Taking the Right Steps

In a country as vast as Indonesia, turning the vision of universal healthcare into reality is no easy task. While recognizing healthcare as a basic human right in the year 2000 was a pivotal step forward, building a system that delivers on that promise has been far more challenging. Inequities in healthcare infrastructure persist, with modern hospitals concentrated in cities while rural areas remain underserved. At the same time, Indonesia's healthcare system has long been centered on treating illness rather than preventing it, often overlooking the vital role of early intervention. Over the past two decades, Indonesia has made impressive strides—from establishing a universal healthcare system to improving many health indicators. Yet even these successes reveal how much work remains. For one, achieving truly universal healthcare requires not just extending coverage or ensuring the scheme's sustainability, but also transforming the system to focus on prevention, equity, and quality. The journey is far from over, and the challenges are as vast as the nation itself.

Since 2000, Indonesia's health expenditure per capita has grown by more than 756%, from USD 15.54 to USD 132.96 two decades later.[1] This increase in spending has been accompanied by significant improvements across a range of indicators. For instance, the infant mortality rate was halved from 41 to 20 per 1,000 live births, and life expectancy at birth rose from 66 to 71 before the outbreak of the COVID-19 pandemic in 2019. Over the same period, Indonesia also established a health insurance system attaining near-universal coverage, with over 80% of the country's 270 million citizens registered by 2020.[2] This made Indonesia's JKN the world's largest single-payer health insurance system by 2021 due to its extensive coverage.[3] Despite all these developments, Indonesia still spends relatively little on health, or

[1] WHO, 2023.
[2] National Social Security Council. 2024.
[3] Maulana et al., 2022.

Evidence and the Politics of Reform. Sudarno Sumarto, Oxford University Press.
 DOI: 10.1093/9780197831717.003.0007

Table 6.1 Healthcare Financing Indicators in Select ASEAN Countries (2020)

	Indonesia	Malaysia	Singapore	Vietnam	Thailand
Current health expenditure (CHE) per capita in current USD PPP*	414.83	1122.76	5827.57	516.18	773.99
Current health expenditure as % of GDP	3.41	4.12	6.05	4.68	4.36
Domestic general government health expenditure (GGHE-D) as % CHE	55.05	52.75	52.41	45.11	70.36

USD PPP = United States Dollar.
Source: World Health Organization 2026.

about 3.4% of its GDP in 2020—compared to the average of 5.7% of GDP in upper-middle-income countries.[4] Additionally, although government health spending as a share of health expenditure per capita more than doubled from 23.7% in 2010 to 55.5% in 2020, this figure remains lower than in other ASEAN countries (Table 6.1). While these figures indicate progress, there is still much to do to improve healthcare in Indonesia.

In discussions of development, it is common to use health indicators such as infant mortality rate, vaccination rate, access to healthcare facilities, or life expectancy to denote progress. However, beyond these measures lies the recognition of healthcare as a human right and its manifestation in policy. This recognition implies a legal obligation for the state to guarantee universal access to quality health services and address the root causes of health disparities, including poverty, stigma, and discrimination.

Within two and a half decades, Indonesia has installed one of the world's largest single-payer healthcare systems. While democratic processes contributed to the recognition of health as a fundamental right, significant legal and technical work went into establishing the JKN and ensuring its sustainability. Covering nearly all of Indonesia's 275 million people by 2023, the

[4] WHO, 2022.

healthcare system continues to face supply-side challenges. These include underfinancing, a shortage of primary care providers and hospitals, limited access to quality medications in rural areas, and overall inaccessibility and inequity of care. Expanding JKN's coverage must be accompanied by improvements in service quality.

Although state-provided healthcare has been around since the Suharto era, Indonesia's transition to democracy in 1998 was also followed with a push to recognize health as a fundamental human right. In 2000, the country's People's Consultative Assembly passed the second amendment to the constitution, enshrining health as a human right and establishing the state's responsibility to provide healthcare. This led to the 2004 legislation of the National Social Security System, laying the groundwork for a public healthcare system. A decade later, the government implemented the law by rolling out the JKN—the country's universal healthcare system. The JKN covers comprehensive medical care, defined as medically necessary healthcare, in both public and private primary healthcare providers in its network with no co-payment or cost-sharing.

Healthcare's recognition as a right shortly after 1998 might give the impression that healthcare in Indonesia progressed due to democracy. However, that is just part of the story. While democratic competition became a driver for the legislation in 2004, the fact that it took a decade to fully establish the JKN and another decade until it attained universal coverage suggests that the political dynamics at play are more complex. Despite the legal mandate for public healthcare, between 2004 and 2014 the Yudhoyono administration was faced with a fiscal crunch caused by rising fuel-subsidy costs (see Chapter 2), which redirected the administration's focus toward the squeeze in the government's fiscal space. However, in 2010 a lawsuit was filed against the government by civil society coalitions. The lawsuit alleged that the government had neglected the mandate of the constitution by not providing public healthcare. Thus, the government rushed to pass Law No. 24 on the Social Security Administrative Body, which Yudhoyono finally signed in 2011. At the same time, the administration prepared a roadmap to actually implement the JKN after it was drafted. Yet, only in 2014 was the JKN rolled out. It was, however, the country's decentralization policy enacted in the early 2000s that eventually hastened the advance of the JKN once it was installed, as it made local governments key actors in Indonesia's JKN expansion.

Beyond the issue of human rights, the JKN is crucial from a welfare development perspective as it seeks to prevent catastrophic health spending. Inadequate financial protection can lead to financial hardship due to out-of-pocket health spending and financial barriers to access healthcare. In some cases, a person can fall into poverty due to healthcare spending. In other cases, families may delay seeking care due to costs associated with healthcare and only seek care once the illness gets more severe and thus more expensive or difficult to cure. The consequences of an illness are even more dire when experienced by a family's breadwinner. Sickness—and especially prolonged or debilitating illness—might prohibit them from working and earning a living for their family. As an insurance scheme, the JKN seeks to reduce an individual's out-of-pocket health spending.

While the intent to provide coverage is one thing, the JKN's implementation and quality of care is another matter. Despite JKN's near-universal coverage, reports of patients being denied care, or experiencing differential treatment in comparison to paying patients, persist. Moreover, by 2020, around 11% of individuals registered in the JKN were considered "inactive." This means that their dues were unpaid, preventing them from benefiting from the JKN. By 2023, this inactivity rate nearly doubled to 20% of JKN's registered members. Valid concerns over the scheme's sustainability include worries that only those who need care are paying into the system, and that they stop paying once they don't need it anymore.

Beyond problems with the JKN's implementation, there are issues of illness prevention and health-promotion activities, such as immunization to support JKN as a curative measure, which have not been optimized. Between 2019 and 2021, Indonesia's full vaccination coverage dropped from 83% to 81%.[5] Part of the problem was the COVID-19 pandemic, which took a significant toll on routine immunization services for children throughout the country due to supply chain disruptions, movement restrictions that limited vaccination activities, and a lack of available health workers.

This chapter tells the story of the tension between Indonesia's lofty ambitions to secure health as a constitutional right and the challenges of translating this right into effective social policies. It explores the interplay between normative ideals and practical realities, as well as the political dynamics of regime changes, democratic competition, and decentralization that shape healthcare provision in Indonesia.

[5] WHO, 2023.

The Politics of Well-being

The development of Indonesia's public healthcare system is deeply intertwined with the country's social security policies, which were linked to employment and labor protections. Both healthcare and social security policies aim to ensure the well-being of Indonesia's population, but they serve different purposes. Social assistance programs are typically designed to improve recipients' welfare levels and are usually targeted to those in poverty or economic vulnerability. Meanwhile, healthcare provisions and work-related social security provisions seek to prevent a sudden and dramatic fall in well-being level, such as natural a disaster, job loss, or debilitating illness. Unlike social assistance, which is means-tested, social security usually requires contributions from beneficiaries but is available to all citizens, regardless of income. When Indonesia formally recognized healthcare as a right, the political landscape of public health provisions shifted, eventually leading to the creation of one of the largest universal healthcare systems in the world.

Indonesia's social security system dates back to 1947, when it was first introduced as healthcare insurance for blue-collar workers (see Table 6.2). At the time, healthcare was considered a privilege tied to formal employment rather than a universal right. Regulated by the Ministry of Labor, benefits received by workers included healthcare services, maternity care, and financial support during illness or death. By the 1960s, these benefits were extended to include workers' spouses and children.

With Suharto's rise to power in 1964, the Ministry of Labor was restructured into the Department of Manpower, further reinforcing the state's role in protecting workers' rights, ensuring workplace safety, and providing assistance for employees and their dependents. This shift led to the establishment of Perum ASTEK in 1977, a state-owned corporation tasked with administering social security for non-civil servants and non-military workers. In 1984, a presidential decree expanded Perum ASTEK's mandate, introducing healthcare insurance, old-age benefits, and severance pay into its programs. While the Ministry of Manpower regulated contribution rates and benefit types, the administration of healthcare services and financial management was jointly overseen by both the Minister of Manpower and the Minister of Health. Meanwhile, healthcare for civil servants and military personnel followed a separate trajectory. In 1968, the government established BPDPK to manage their healthcare benefits, and by 1984, this responsibility was transferred

Table 6.2 Social Insurance Managers in Indonesia

Category	1947	1968	1977	1984	1992	2005	2008	2011
Non-Civil Servant and Non-Military-Affiliated workers	Limited Liability Company (PT) JAMSOSTEK		Public Company (Perum) ASTEK		Limited Liability Company (PT) JAMSOSTEK			BPJS-Ketenagakerjaan and BPJS-Kesehatan
Civil Servants an Military Officers		Executing Agency of Healt Maintenance Funds (Badan Penyelenggara Dana Pemeliharaan Kesehatan, BPDPK)		Public Company (Perum) Husada Bhakti	Limited Liability Company (PT) ASKES			
People in Poverty						*ASKESKIN*	*JAMKESMAS*	BPJS- Kesehatan

Note: Text in italic denotes program name.

to Perum Husada Bhakti, a public corporation dedicated to administering health services for government employees and the armed forces.

In 1992, the parliament passed a law on social insurance for workers, which made it compulsory for companies with at least 10 workers to allocate money for pension, work accident coverage, death coverage, and healthcare under the JAMSOSTEK insurance plan. The law also led to the transformation of Perum ASTEK to PT JAMSOSTEK, which assumed authority over the JAMSOSTEK schemes. Similarly, the Perum Husada Bhakti was also restructured into PT ASKES. At the same time, the two agencies' transformation into corporations meant that beyond services provisions, PT JAMSOSTEK and PT ASKES also became profit-seeking entities.

Although the state remained the majority shareholder for both firms, the pursuit of profit gradually took precedence over the original missions of PT JAMSOSTEK and PT ASKES to provide public service, with a portion of profits being channeled back into the national budget. As a for-profit company, PT JAMSOSTEK derived its income through the contributions of its subscribers minus its costs and taxes. The remaining profits were distributed to shareholders as dividends. During the 1990s and early 2000s, revenue from social security investments became an important source of the state budget, which conflicted with the principle of prioritizing the right to social security. In 2000, JAMSOSTEK paid IDR 110 billion in dividends and IDR 3 billion in corporate taxes to the Ministry of Finance. The Ministry of Finance then reallocated part of these funds for social projects, such as building low-rent houses and hospitals in 2001.[6] Moreover, between 1992 and 2000, JAMSOSTEK experienced low benefit take-up rates, which allowed the company to retain more revenue. Coupled with the state's role as the largest shareholder (despite not contributing financially), the state rather than JAMSOSTEK's subscribers became the primary beneficiary of the company's profits.

The lack of financial transparency, along with the shift toward profit-making, raised concerns about JAMSOSTEK's operations. Beyond questions about who truly benefited from the scheme, corruption that had long plagued Suharto's governance also ran deep in Indonesia's social insurance agencies and persisted after his fall. Following Indonesia's transition to democracy, politicians were navigating uncharted waters. With the economy devastated by the 1997–1998 financial crisis and the high costs of elections,

[6] ILO, 2002.

illegal campaign funding from sources such as PT JAMSOSTEK became an attractive option for politicians and political parties. The social security scheme provided political incumbents and bureaucrats affiliated with these agencies access to liquid funds for political ends. This made it clear that JAMSOSTEK's independence from state interests needed to be protected, and that public oversight of the social security funds was essential.

Despite concerns over financial transparency, political momentum for social reforms was growing. In 1999, Indonesia held its first truly democratic elections in nearly 45 years, with the PDI-P party, led by Megawati Soekarnoputri, emerging victorious on a platform that emphasized greater equity. The following year, parliament amended the 1945 constitution to include the right to receive medical services. Two years later, another amendment reinforced the state's responsibility to provide health services and develop a comprehensive social security system for all citizens.

To advance these reforms, Megawati, then serving as vice president, established a working group in April 2002 tasked with drafting a social security law. The initial draft envisioned merging all state-owned insurance firms into a single, non-profit trust fund operating as the sole payer. However, this proposal faced strong opposition. The directors of the existing insurance firms resisted losing their lucrative operations and feared the restructuring would expose their financial dealings to public scrutiny. Employers were also concerned that mandatory participation in the new system would drive up costs, as they would no longer be able to opt out of state-run schemes. Some private-sector employees and labor unions objected to the bill, worrying that the new contributions would shift the financial burden onto workers and reduce benefits. They also feared that workers' premiums might be used to subsidize services for the poor, further diminishing their own coverage.[7] After undergoing 56 revisions, the bill was finally submitted to parliament in January 2004.

With the PDI-P party holding a majority in the state's legislative body, the National Social Security Law could be passed in 2004. On October 19, 2004, President Megawati Soekarnoputri signed Law No. 40/2004 on the national social security system. Under the law, healthcare, work accident, old-age, and death benefits are guaranteed for all Indonesian citizens. These programs are to be funded through social insurance schemes and compulsory savings. By law, the government is obliged to pay healthcare contributions

[7] Wisnu, 2007; Thabrany, 2008; Marzoeki et al., 2014.

for those unable to pay. Thus, to provide healthcare for the poor, the government appointed the PT ASKES, which was a state-owned enterprise that provided healthcare insurance for civil servants, retired civil servants and military servicemen, veterans, independence pioneers, and their families. Services for the poor are covered through government contribution from the state's budget in the ASKESKIN scheme, which provides health insurance for people in poverty. Moreover, the law also states that the existing social security services carriers, which were PT JAMSOSTEK, PT ASKES, PT TASPEN, and PT ASABRI,[8] should operate under the coordination of the DJSN—a national board in charge of social security governance.

Indonesia's constitution guarantees every citizen the right to social security, ensuring they can meet basic needs for a decent life. It also mandates the state to provide comprehensive social protection. However, when the social security law was passed in 2004, it lacked a clear roadmap for implementation. When Megawati Soekarnoputri lost the presidential election that year, her successor, Susilo Bambang Yudhoyono, inherited the difficult task of turning the law into a functioning system. This proved far more challenging than anticipated, particularly because social security agencies remained deeply tied to the state. Bureaucrats and politicians, with vested interests in maintaining the status quo, resisted change.

Beyond political resistance, the reform also faced strong opposition from both business owners and workers. The passage of the 2003 Labor Law had already imposed strict regulations on employers, including minimum wage requirements and costly severance payments. Many businesses saw Indonesia's labor environment as increasingly expensive, and the new social security law only added to their concerns. It required employers to contribute to workers' insurance, pensions, and old-age savings, further increasing operational costs.

Workers, on the other hand, were skeptical of the reform, fearing it was merely a way to deduct money from their wages without offering meaningful benefits. They also faced indirect consequences: as businesses sought to offset rising costs, many employers resorted to layoffs, pay cuts, or the growing practice of contract hiring. These pressures brought workers and employers,

[8] PT TASPEN (*Perseroran Terbatas Dana Tabungan dan Asuransi Pegawai Negeri*), or the Public Servant Savings and Insurance Fund Corporation, is a state-owned enterprise that provides old-age savings insurance and pension funds for civil servants and state officials. Meanwhile, PT ASABRI (*Asuransi Sosial Angkatan Bersenjata Republik Indonesia*), or the Social Insurance for the Armed Forces of the Republic of Indonesia Corporation, provides similar benefits to military servicemen, members of the police forces, as well as civil servants under the Ministry of Defense and police forces.

who usually stood on opposite sides of labor disputes, together in opposition to the reform.

Further complicating matters was the financial uncertainty surrounding Indonesia's existing social security agencies. Concerns arose over the government's outstanding liabilities in the schemes for civil servants and military officers, as well as doubts about the financial health of PT ASKES, the state-run healthcare insurer. In particular, the sustainability of ASKESKIN, a health insurance scheme for the poor under PT ASKES, was questioned. The program relied on government funding, which in turn depended on the budget saved from reduced fuel subsidies. When the government cut fuel subsidies in 2005 (see Chapter 2), some of the savings were redirected to fund ASKESKIN. However, given Indonesia's vulnerability to global oil price fluctuations, many feared that subsidy reductions might be reversed in the future and force paying members of PT ASKES to bear the costs of free healthcare services.

With these financial uncertainties and strong resistance from both employers and workers, efforts to consolidate all social security schemes under the DJSN stalled. The proposed increase in contribution rates faced backlash, and broader reforms struggled to gain traction. As a result, much of the effort to implement the 2004 Social Security Law remained at the national level.

President Susilo Bambang Yudhoyono's inauguration in 2004 further put the agenda on hold. As the social security law had been initiated by Megawati and her PDI-P party, the Yudhoyono administration saw social security as a partisan agenda and did not prioritize the law's implementation early in his administration. Further pushing the issue aside were fiscal pressures from the costly fuel subsidies that drew the administration's attention away from issues of social security for all and toward transfer programs for the poorest citizens in the country (see Chapter 2). However, subsequent needs to cut back on fuel subsidies eventually pushed Yudhoyono's administration to expand healthcare provisions to the poor.

After years of poor administration that delayed reimbursements to healthcare providers, as well as complaints of poor quality of services, the Ministry of Health took over provider payment for the ASKESKIN scheme from PT ASKES in 2008, which was then renamed JAMKESMAS. Yet JAMKESMAS was not without its shortfalls. For one, its non-standard approach to identifying beneficiaries led to complaints about the accuracy of its targeting and "leakages" to local elites' families and colleagues who were neither poor nor vulnerable. By 2009, JAMKESMAS reached only 33% of the people it was targeting.[9] Additionally, a lack of public awareness about the program meant there were fewer participants than there should have been. The inequality of access to quality health services, especially in rural and remote areas, also meant that program beneficiaries underutilized its benefits. Moreover, at the time, JAMKESMAS' contributions were set without proper accounting procedures and had not been revised since 2008. With JAMKESMAS's limited reach, local governments play a large role in expanding healthcare access at the regional level, especially to those in poverty.

The decentralization law passed in 2001 saw the devolution of authority over a range of matters from the central government to regional governments. Within this decentralized government framework, the healthcare sector emerged as one of the areas under the authority of both the central government and district or municipal governments. In the newly decentralized system, the expectation was that regions with higher fiscal capability would be able to finance the majority of their healthcare needs with only a marginal contribution from the central government.

With the inauguration of JAMKESMAS in 2008, the central government actively pushed local governments to provide health coverage for the poor and near-poor who were not yet covered by the JAMKESMAS. Hence local governments rolled out a range of social assistance coverage under the JAMKESDA scheme, an extension of the JAMKESMAS scheme at the regional level.[10] Between 2008 and 2012, the number of district-level JAMKESDA schemes grew from around 60 to at least 245.[11] Some districts even offered program benefits that far exceeded the national standards offered by JAMKESMAS. In Aceh province, for instance, every citizen was entitled to free inpatient care. Moreover, the scheme even covered treatment overseas in some cases. At that time, the provision of health services through JAMKESDA was often tied to electoral ends as local politicians vying for regional leadership positions promised better and broader coverage.

Despite progress, two decades after the decentralization policy was rolled out, factors such as different fiscal capacities, competing policy priorities, and variations in regional leaders' capacity significantly influenced the

[9] Data from Indonesia Statistics' National Socio-economic Survey (SUSENAS) 2009.
[10] Agustina et al., 2019; Pisani et al., 2017.
[11] Aspinall, 2014a.

extent of decentralization's success in improving health outcomes.[12] Within this period, a substantial number of regions remained dependent upon financial allocations from the central government to sustain their healthcare sectors. Consequently, some local governments still consider the Ministry of Health as the primary source of financial support, providing healthcare personnel, essential medical equipment, pharmaceuticals, and vaccines. If anything, the decentralization process resulted in a disjuncture between health financing and service delivery due to poor coordination between the central and regional governments.

In 2008, progress was made toward implementing the 2004 Social Security Law beyond subsidized healthcare for those in poverty. The Yudhoyono administration established the National Social Security Council (DJSN) to outline the law's details, but progress remained slow, prompting frustration among parliamentarians and civil society groups. While the DJSN had drafted a new law, the government was reluctant to move forward, leading PDI-P legislators to take charge. Adding pressure, the KAJS—a broad coalition of labor and citizen organizations—staged demonstrations, lobbied both parliament and the executive branch, and even sued the president for failing to implement the law.[13] In June 2010, the court ruled in KAJS's favor, intensifying political momentum. Under this pressure, parliament passed the Social Security Administering Agency Law in November 2011, replacing four social security corporations with non-profit public trust fund bodies. BPJS Kesehatan, built upon PT ASKES, was designated to manage health insurance, while BPJS-TK, evolving from PT JAMSOSTEK, was tasked with overseeing workers' social security schemes.

In 2012, the DJSN, TNP2K, and other key ministries and agencies developed a roadmap to launch BPJS Kesehatan by January 1, 2014. The transition needed to be systematic, well-coordinated, and aligned with both the 2004 Social Security Law and the 2011 BPJS Law to ensure that social health insurance would be accessible to all Indonesians. A series of regulatory measures were introduced to integrate participants from various existing schemes, which included ASKES (for civil servants), JAMSOSTEK (for private-sector workers), healthcare programs for the armed forces and national police, and JAMKESMAS (for low-income populations), under BPJS Kesehatan's

[12] Erlangga and Shi, 2014; Nikijuluw, 2021.
[13] Wisnu, 2007.

administration. This newly unified social health insurance program was called the JKN.

Additionally, all participants under regional JAMKESDA schemes were scheduled to be transferred to the JKN scheme under BPJS Kesehatan by the end of 2016. The plan also required employers to register their workers and their families to ensure that no employees were left without coverage, while self-employed workers were expected to enroll gradually between 2014 and 2019. With this phased approach, Indonesia aimed to achieve universal health coverage by the end of 2019.

When the JKN was finally launched at the start of 2014, the total number of participants managed by BPJS Kesehatan was 116 million, or about 45% of the country's population then. However, experience from other countries demonstrates that providing universal coverage is not as easy as it seems. A particular challenge, for instance, is in reaching out to certain segments (mainly the non-waged or informal sector) of the population. In Indonesia, where a large proportion of the population works in the informal sector, reaching out to these workers posed a challenge to the BPJS Kesehatan. In fact, covering informal-sector workers was not the government's only issue. At that time, many regular wage earners were not even registered as JKN participants, let alone informal-sector workers. Poor program visibility meant that a lot of formal-sector workers did not realize that they needed to make regular contributions to benefit from the JKN. Moreover, many people did not fully understand the insurance's benefits and were reluctant to pay their monthly dues.

Another major challenge in launching JKN was integrating the diverse local JAMKESDA schemes into a unified national system. The complexity stemmed from the fact that JAMKESDA programs varied widely across regions—not just in management style, payment methods, and contribution sizes, but also in the benefits they provided and the people they covered. In most cases, local schemes insured those who were not covered by JAMKESMAS, the national health assistance program at the time. However, some local governments took a different approach, covering their entire population regardless of JAMKESMAS eligibility.

Adding to the difficulty was the lack of reliable participant data. Many local databases contained errors, with inconsistent name and address formats, partly because most JAMKESDA schemes had open membership. Unlike structured national programs, these schemes allowed participants to enroll and leave at will, making it hard to maintain accurate records. Some local administrators even granted healthcare access to individuals who presented a poverty statement—a letter from local authorities certifying that they were poor—regardless of whether they were listed as official participants. This lack of standardized enrollment made the transition to JKN particularly challenging. By the time JKN was launched, only 5.9 million out of the 31.86 million people enrolled in local JAMKESDA programs had been successfully integrated into the Ministry of Health's central payment systems, underscoring the scale of the administrative hurdles the government faced.

The evolution of Indonesia's public healthcare system is a testament to the country's shifting political priorities and its ongoing struggle to provide equitable healthcare access for all citizens. Initially tied to formal employment and labor protections, healthcare was once a privilege afforded to the few. Over the decades, Indonesia transformed its healthcare system, culminating in the establishment of one of the world's largest universal healthcare programs. However, this transformation was neither straightforward nor without resistance, as competing interests slowed the path to reform.

Indonesia's journey toward universal healthcare reflects the complexity of implementing large-scale social reform in a diverse and decentralized country. While the passage of the 2004 Social Security Law and the subsequent launch of JKN in 2014 were major milestones, the ongoing challenges of integrating regional schemes, covering informal-sector workers, and ensuring financial sustainability highlight that the work is far from finished. However, legal frameworks and administrative efforts alone cannot ensure the success of a healthcare system. The ability to deliver services hinges upon the quality of healthcare infrastructure and resources throughout the nation. Addressing these technical issues is crucial for ensuring that the promise of universal healthcare translates into effective, accessible care for all citizens.

Ensuring the JKN's Sustainability

Ten years after its establishment, it has become apparent that the JKN remains a work in progress. The regulations that launched the JKN laid a solid foundation, but their implementation on the ground depends on local stakeholders. Although progress has been made in designing Indonesia's social security institutions, critical details like increasing JKN participation and ensuring compliance have been largely left to be addressed in practice.

Table 6.3 Health Financing Indicators in Indonesia

Indonesia	2000	2004	2010	2020
Current health expenditure per capita, per capita in current USD PPP*	94.36	132.57	235.29	415.63
Current health expenditure as % of GDP	2	2	3	3
Domestic general government health expenditure (GGHE-D) as % CHE	30	35	24	55
Out-of-pocket spending % of health spending (OOPS%CHE)	45	46	61	32
Priority to health (GGHE-D%GGE)	4	4	4	10

*USD PPP = United States Dollar.
Source: World Health Organization, 2024.

Additionally, concerns about the financial sustainability of the JKN and the need to improve its overall uptake rate remain pressing.

JKN's expansion is intended to reduce the disparity in healthcare access that favors the rich. It does so by weakening the relationship between healthcare service utilization and a household's economic status. Indeed, between 2000 and 2020 the ratio of out-of-pocket spending—or the share of healthcare costs borne by individuals over their total healthcare spending—had fallen from 45% to 32%[14] (Table 6.3). Moreover, household members with JKN membership are far less likely than the uninsured to pay out of pocket for healthcare, and they pay less in general even with out-of-pocket fees.[15] Despite its contributions to equating access to healthcare, the JKN's sustainability remains a challenge.

The 2004 law recognizing healthcare as a right led the government to subsidize JKN contributions for individuals in poverty, while requiring others to pay their monthly premiums. This subsidy, which replaced the dissolved ASKESKIN program, was specifically designed for those in poverty. By 2023, 51.2% of JKN's members received government subsidies. With around 10% of the country's population living under the national poverty line, what the

[14] WHO, 2024.
[15] Maulana et al., 2022.

government is subsidizing through the national and regional budget is well above the share of people living in poverty—assuming that none of the poor are excluded. At the same time, there are also concerns that taking people off the subsidy recipient list will increase payment non-compliance rates that could hurt the BPJS Kesehatan's cash flow and liquidity in the short run.

The sustainability of the JKN hinges on payment compliance, particularly from non-poor informal workers. While the government can enroll and collect JKN contribution from formal-sector workers through their employers, informal workers, who make up around 60% of the workforce in Indonesia, are less likely to enroll and comply with the JKN's terms by paying their contribution in a timely manner. Although the government can use the Unified Database (see Chapter 3) to identify and enroll low-income individuals and provide them with subsidized JKN payments, the same cannot be done to reach out to non-poor workers in the informal sector who are not listed in the database. Moreover, their work in the informal sector means that their incomes are not directly observed by the government like formal-sector workers. This makes enrolling them and enforcing payment challenging. Additionally, if only the least healthy individuals are registered as JKN members—given that they are the ones with the most incentive to comply with the JKN's payment scheme—BPJS Kesehatan would face a higher claims ratio, which would threaten the sustainability of the JKN fund. To ensure the JKN's viability, the government must ensure that healthy individuals and informal-sector workers pay their dues regularly.

Before the launch of BPJS Kesehatan in 2014, the government envisioned achieving universal health coverage by 2019. To accelerate this goal, President Susilo Bambang Yudhoyono signed a Presidential Regulation in 2013, reinforcing JKN's mandatory enrollment for all Indonesian citizens as mandated by law. By the end of Yudhoyono's term in 2014, JKN had already covered 52.1% of the population—a significant milestone for a country of nearly 260 million people at the time. However, the path forward was challenging. Beyond expanding coverage to all citizens by 2019, the incoming Joko Widodo administration also had to address JKN's financial burden, as 71.3% of its members were subsidized. In response, Widodo reaffirmed the government's commitment to universal coverage by issuing a Presidential Regulation in 2015, which integrated JKN expansion into the country's medium-term development plan and made it a key priority for his administration.

While some have argued for making the JKN entirely free for all citizens through government funding, the situation is more complex. First, the government's difficulty in effectively collecting taxes limits its fiscal capacity to support a fully government-funded universal program. Second, funding the JKN solely through the national budget would expose it to political forces and uncertainties, undermining its role as a stable social insurance program meant to provide reliable coverage. Finally, there are also concerns about free-riding, where individuals might exploit the system without contributing. Requiring personal contributions not only protects JKN from political influence and deters free-riding but also positions members as stakeholders with a vested interest in the program's governance. By having the power to withhold contributions, members can hold BPJS accountable and ensure its effective operation.

By December 2019, JKN enrollment had reached approximately 224.2 million people, covering 83.6% of Indonesia's population (see Table 6.4). Of these, only 88.8 million—or 39.6%—were independent members who did not receive subsidies. However, payment compliance within this segment stood at just 79.4%, meaning that only around 79.53 million individuals made regular monthly contributions. This shortfall in premium payments has been a key factor in BPJS Kesehatan's ongoing financial deficits, as contributions have struggled to cover claims and operational costs. Since its launch in 2014, BPJS Kesehatan has consistently operated at a deficit, peaking at IDR 17.04 trillion in 2019.

In recent years, the government has attempted to reduce the number of subsidized JKN members by reclassifying them as "non-formal sector workers." At the same time, formal-sector workers who have missed payments for three consecutive months have also been moved into this category. As a result, the share of JKN members classified as "non-formal sector workers" more than doubled between 2022 and 2023, leading to an increase in the proportion of inactive JKN members from 17.8% to 20.1% despite record-high membership coverage. Most of these inactive members were those reclassified during this period. While these reclassifications may improve the program's optics, they do little to ensure the sustainability of JKN's coverage. Instead, concrete policies are needed to improve compliance and reduce the number of inactive members.

One key challenge is that the non-poor informal sector workers who constitute about 30% of Indonesia's workforce must register individually and make monthly premium payments. Enrollment is often cumbersome,

Table 6.4 JKN Membership Statistics (2014–2023)

Year	Number of Registered Members	Share of Population Registered (%)	Inactive Member Ratio (%)	Share of Subsidized Members (%)	Share of Non-Subsidized Members (%)	Ratio of Membership by Segment					Share of Inactive members
						Central Government Subsidized (%)	Regional Government Subsidized (%)	Formal Sector Workers (%)	Non-Formal Sector Workers (%)	Non-Workers (%)	
2014	13,34,23,653	52.1	n/a	71.3	28.7	64.8	6.6	18.2	6.8	3.7	n/a
2015	15,67,90,287	60.5	n/a	63.1	36.9	56.0	7.1	24.1	9.5	3.2	n/a
2016	17,19,39,254	66.5	5.9	61.9	38.1	53.0	9.0	23.9	11.2	2.9	5.9%
2017	18,79,82,949	71.8	7.1	59.9	40.1	49.1	10.8	23.9	13.5	2.7	7.1%
2018	20,80,54,199	78.5	9.4	58.6	41.4	44.3	14.4	24.0	14.9	2.5	8.8%
2019	22,41,49,019	83.6	9.0	60.4	39.6	43.1	17.3	23.9	13.5	2.2	9.0%
2020	22,24,61,906	82.6	11.1	59.7	40.3	43.4	16.3	24.8	13.7	1.8	11.1%
2021	23,57,19,262	80.9	20.7	58.9	54.5	41.0	17.8	25.5	13.1	1.9	20.7%
2022	24,87,71,083	89.8	17.8	61.0	39.0	44.6	16.4	24.9	12.4	1.7	17.8%
2023	26,73,11,566	96.0	20.1	51.9	48.1	36.2	15.7	20.0	26.1	2.0	20.1%

Source: National Social Security Council, 2024.

requiring families to apply in person at a district office or online through JKN's website, submit multiple identity documents, and provide bank and tax information. Furthermore, membership retention remains an issue, as individuals can enroll at any time throughout the year, creating an incentive to delay signing up until they need medical care and drop coverage once they recover. While penalties exist for lapses in coverage, they have not been effective in preventing this pattern.

To address these challenges, interventions that reduce costs or improve awareness of benefits can encourage higher enrollment and retention. Because the value of health insurance is often difficult to assess before purchasing, allowing individuals to experience coverage firsthand may positively influence future participation. Trust in the administering institutions also plays a critical role in enrollment decisions. Between 2015 and 2018, I worked alongside researchers from the Abdul Latif Jameel Poverty Action Lab (J-PAL) in close collaboration with BPJS, BAPPENAS, TNP2K, and the KSP to evaluate how different incentives and information campaigns could improve JKN enrollment and retention among non-poor informal workers.[16]

The study involved 5,996 households from two major cities in Indonesia and tested various interventions to increase JKN enrollment rates. The findings revealed that temporary subsidies effectively boosted enrollment and retention without additional costs to the government. However, many households that attempted to enroll failed to complete the process. Additional information alone had no impact, suggesting that lack of awareness was not the primary barrier to enrollment. Instead, the most common challenge reported was difficulty in providing official identification documents, with fewer than one-fifth of households that tried to enroll successfully completing registration.

In 2016, these findings informed discussions at BAPPENAS and BPJS Kesehatan regarding JKN's pricing strategy. As a result, the government decided against raising premiums between 2016 and 2019. However, long-term results highlighted ongoing challenges in maintaining JKN's financial sustainability. In October 2019, the Ministry of Finance increased premiums for non-subsidized JKN members, who accounted for roughly 40% of total membership. Following this adjustment, BPJS Kesehatan recorded surpluses of IDR 45.3 trillion in 2020 and IDR 44.45 trillion in 2021 (see Figure 6.1).

[16] Banerjee et al., 2021.

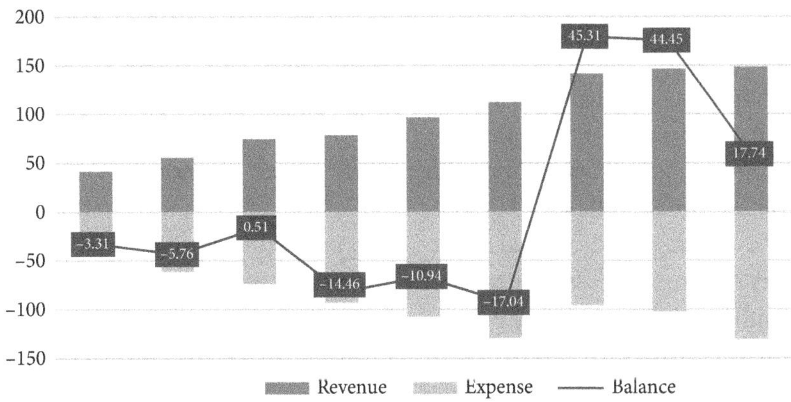

Figure 6.1 Surplus/Deficit of BPJS-Kesehatan in IDR Trillion
Source: BPJS Kesehatan, multiple years.

These surpluses, however, were largely due to reduced healthcare utilization during the COVID-19 pandemic. As JKN utilization rebounded post-pandemic, concerns arose about the potential impact on BPJS Kesehatan's financial position. By 2022, the surplus had declined to IDR 17.7 trillion and was projected to continue decreasing, raising questions about the program's long-term fiscal health.

To alleviate the burdens on JKN, the government must reduce its reliance on curative measures and shift toward preventive and promotive health strategies, as it did between 1988 and 1993. During that period, Indonesia transitioned from a treatment-focused approach to one that prioritized disease prevention and health promotion. Initiatives such as the Clean and Healthy Lifestyle (*Perilaku Hidup Bersih dan Sehat*) campaign helped prevent communicable diseases and encouraged healthier living, while the Family with Toddler Development (*Bina Keluarga Balita*) program supported families in providing adequate care for young children. These efforts significantly improved public health outcomes, including an increase in the percentage of children aged 12–23 months vaccinated against measles from 51% to 68% and a reduction in infant mortality from 67 to 55 per 1,000 live births.[17]

Local primary care facilities, known as *puskesmas*, and integrated healthcare units, or *posyandu*, played a crucial role in these achievements.

[17] WHO, 2024.

While *puskesmas* primarily focused on curative care, *posyandu* emphasized preventive and promotive measures, making them vital components of Indonesia's public health strategy. Their success in past public health efforts underscores their importance in reaching local communities and their potential to strengthen the government's approach to disease prevention and health promotion today.

Additionally, JKN's tiered service today means that patients are required to visit a primary care service facility and consult a doctor at that particular healthcare facility. Primary care is available at *puskesmas* and private clinics. If the patient's health issues cannot be solved at this service level, they will be referred to a more advanced service facility, such as a hospital. This suggests that underfunding primary care units can result in poor-quality care and in patients bypassing primary health care to access more costly hospital care.

To ensure JKN's sustainability, beyond improving member compliance with contribution payments, the Ministry of Health must also prioritize basic preventive and promotive health services, particularly at the primary care level. Despite their importance, the budget allocation for preventive and promotive measures remains limited, with only around 26% of the Ministry of Health's budget dedicated to these interventions between 2015 and 2017 compared to 61% for curative measures, including JKN subsidies.[18] Moving forward, activities such as community health development, disease prevention and control, and health services development must take center stage in Indonesia's public health strategy. These efforts will be crucial for balancing the system and securing long-term health outcomes for the population.

Addressing Healthcare Supply Issues

The JKN tells only part of the Indonesian healthcare system's story. While the expansion of the JKN helped to tackle healthcare demand issues, healthcare supply issues—or the quality and spread of healthcare personnel and health infrastructure—are another matter. While the JKN's expansion addressed demand-side issues such as access to healthcare, supply-side challenges—namely the availability and quality of healthcare personnel and infrastructure—remain significant. Focusing solely on the JKN as a demand-side fix will have limited impact if supply-side issues, which are

[18] Saputri et al., 2024.

essential for delivering high-quality healthcare services, are not addressed in tandem.

Despite attempts to improve health outcomes, including the introduction of JKN, Indonesia's vital health statistics still lag behind those of neighboring countries. For instance, life expectancy in Indonesia by 2022 was 68 years, while the figure was 76 and 80 in Malaysia and Thailand respectively.[19] Likewise, maternal and child mortality are still high, especially among those in poverty. Child mortality rates in the poorest 20% of households in the country, for instance, are three times higher than those in the 20% richest households, who have better access to skilled birth attendants.[20] Child mortality rates are highest in rural areas and among young mothers, with significant geographic disparities. For instance, child mortality rates in West Sulawesi, Maluku, and West Nusa Tenggara provinces are more than four times higher than those in Central Java and Yogyakarta. Indeed, while healthcare needs tend to be concentrated among the poor, access to healthcare is concentrated among the more affluent. Moreover, if all financial barriers were eliminated, access to healthcare might still be unequal due to other factors, such as lack of health knowledge and awareness, the unbalanced distribution of health infrastructure, and the varying progress of infrastructure development in different areas.[21] Thus, aside from broadening JKN's coverage, there is still much to do on the healthcare supply end to improve access to and quality of healthcare services.

Indeed, regardless of JKN coverage, if not equally tackled these supply-side problems will still lead to gaps in health outcomes. For instance, with a population of more than 270 million, according to the World Health Organization, Indonesia needs at least 270,000 doctors or one physician per 1,000 persons. However, by 2021 Indonesia only had some 0.65 physicians per 1000 people, which was still below the WHO's standard.[22] At this rate, Indonesia's doctor-to-patient ratio was far below Malaysia's 2.28:1000 and Thailand's 0.93:1000. Moreover, there are concerns over the disproportionate role that the JKN plays within Indonesia's public health system as a curative measure, while not enough attention is given to preventive and promotive aspects of healthcare such as providing prenatal care for mothers and healthy lifestyle promotional campaigns.

[19] World Bank, 2024.
[20] UNICEF, 2020.
[21] Shresta, 2021.
[22] WHO, 2023.

A study exploring the asymmetry in access to various health services in Indonesia found that access to outpatient care at primary care facilities is pro-poor.[23] In other words, those in poverty are more likely to access health services than prior to JKN's rollout. In contrast, access to outpatient and inpatient treatments at private clinics and at hospitals is biased toward the rich. Meanwhile, access to inpatient care in public hospitals is pro-poor in urban areas but pro-rich in rural areas. After the JKN was rolled out, the study found that access gaps between poorer and richer groups are smaller than prior to JKN, especially for outpatient care at private clinics, which is consistent with the fact that the JKN expanded healthcare access to the private sector. Moreover, the degree of inequality in access for private clinics post-JKN is more than halved from its pre-JKN level. This reduction in access gap is driven by changes in individuals' health-seeking activities. In particular, in the JKN era the growing number of insured persons and their propensity to use health services is higher. Furthermore, household economic positions have weaker influence over access to care. This is due to JKN's role in preventing the need for individuals to pay a large sum of money when they are seeking care. Yet the study also found that there remains a gap in access to healthcare facilities between urban and rural areas. This suggests that specific rural programs might be needed to ensure access to care for those in poverty in these areas.

By the end of 2023, BPJS Kesehatan's network included more than 23,250 primary care units, 3,095 hospitals and advanced care units, and 5,432 pharmacies and optical services nationwide.[24] This marked an improvement from 2017, when the network comprised 20,664 primary care units, 2,069 hospitals and advanced care units, and 3,074 pharmacies and optical services. However, these overall figures obscure critical challenges, such as the ratio of primary care units to JKN members. In 2017, there were 11 primary care units per 100,000 JKN members, but by the end of 2023, this had declined to 8.7. This suggests that while JKN membership has grown, the expansion of primary clinics partnering with BPJS Kesehatan has not kept pace. Furthermore, disparities in healthcare access across regions, particularly between rural and urban areas, highlight the need for more equitable distribution of healthcare facilities.

[23] Johar et al., 2018.
[24] National Social Security Council, 2024.

Table 6.5 Health Personnel and Hospital Beds per 1000 People Availability in Southeast Asia, 2016

	Physicians	Nurses and midwives	Hospital beds
Indonesia	0.4	2.1*	1
Cambodia	0.2*	0.7	0.9
Lao PDR	0.4	1.3	1.5*
Malaysia	1.6	4.1	1.6
Philippines	1.3*	4.7*	1*
Thailand	0.4	2.7	2.1*
Vietnam	0.8	1.5	2.6*

Note: *Not available in 2010: physicians in Philippines 2010, Cambodia, 2014, Indonesia 2017, hospital beds in Thailand, 2010, Philippines, 2014, Vietnam 2014, Lao PDR 2015; nurses and midwives in Indonesia 2017, Philippines 2017.
Source: World Bank, 2024.

Universal health coverage requires adequate healthcare infrastructure on the supply side. Although insurance coverage has expanded, healthcare infrastructure development has lagged behind. Scarcity and uneven distribution of health personnel, along with suboptimal service performance, have long affected the Indonesian healthcare system.[25] Indonesia falls behind other ASEAN countries in areas like physician-to-population ratio, nurse and midwife availability, and hospital bed provision (Table 6.5). Unequal distribution of healthcare resources continues to be a critical issue in Indonesia.

In 2016, 25% of *puskesmas*, predominantly located in rural and remote areas, operated without the presence of medical doctors.[26] Disparities in healthcare quality, particularly in rural and remote areas, also contributed to the underutilization of previous health insurance programs such as ASKESKIN and JAMKESMAS.[27] Furthermore, there is a prevailing skepticism toward *puskemas* and a stigma that they are only for the poor, which has resulted in a reluctance among the population to visit *puskesmas*. This results in longer waiting times at hospitals.[28]

To address these challenges, the government introduced Regulation No. 47/2021, aimed at improving the quality and equity of JKN implementation. The regulation sought to resolve issues such as the uneven distribution

[25] Rokx et al., 2009; Heywood and Choi, 2010.
[26] Harimurti et al., 2013.
[27] TNP2K, 2015.
[28] Erlangga and Shi, 2014; Mboi, 2015.

of healthcare professionals, shortages in both the quantity and quality of health workers, inadequate hospital bed capacity, and inefficiencies in the referral system. One of its key measures was the standardization of hospital bed capacity, scheduled to be implemented between 2023 and 2025. However, concerns have been raised about the financial burden this may place on private hospitals as they work to meet the new standards.[29]

More recently, the enactment of the Omnibus Law on Health (Law No. 17/2023) is expected to strengthen Indonesia's healthcare system, particularly on the supply side, to support universal health coverage. According to the Ministry of Health, the law introduces several key reforms, including shifting the focus from treatment to disease prevention and health promotion, expanding access to healthcare services, encouraging domestic self-sufficiency in the health industry, and strengthening the health system's resilience against disasters. It also aims to enhance efficiency and transparency in health financing, address healthcare worker shortages by simplifying licensing procedures, improve protections for healthcare workers, and integrate health information systems using the latest technology. The law is envisioned to improve access, quality, and fairness in Indonesia's healthcare system. However, achieving these goals will require better coordination among all stakeholders to truly uphold healthcare as a right. A clear division of responsibilities between BPJS Kesehatan and the Ministry of Health—particularly regarding funding, administration, and governance—will be crucial. Additionally, local governments must play a well-defined role in ensuring effective healthcare service delivery.

As Indonesia continues its journey toward universal healthcare, the path remains fraught with challenges and opportunities. The JKN, a landmark achievement in the country's commitment to healthcare as a fundamental right, has undeniably expanded access and improved many health indicators. Yet, achieving the ideal of universal and equitable healthcare requires more than just expanding coverage. It demands a concerted effort to address systemic inequities, improve service quality, and foster a culture of preventive care.

[29] PERSI, 2024.

Despite the impressive strides made, the disparities in healthcare access—between urban and rural areas, rich and poor, and across different regions—underscore the need for ongoing reform. The financial and administrative hurdles that have emerged highlight the complexities of sustaining such a vast system. As we have seen, the challenges of underfinancing, inadequate primary care, and varying levels of service quality are critical areas that need attention.

The story of Indonesia's healthcare evolution is a testament to both the progress made and the distance still to be covered. The journey from vision to reality has been marked by significant achievements, but also by the sobering reminder that the task of ensuring true universal healthcare is never complete. To truly honor the right to health, Indonesia must not only build on its successes but also tackle the persistent issues that hinder its healthcare system from fully meeting the needs of all its citizens. As the nation forges ahead, the quest for equity, quality, and sustainability will remain central to its healthcare narrative.

7

Localizing Power

A Reflection of Indonesia's Decentralization Project and Development at the Village Level

In Indonesia, rural poverty levels have long been higher than urban poverty levels, underscoring the geographic nature of deprivation and the limitations of one-size-fits-all poverty alleviation strategies (see Figure 7.1). While the gap between rural and urban poverty rates narrowed between 2013 and 2023, progress has not been enough to address the country's "last mile" challenge in lifting the poorest of the poor out of extreme poverty. The roots of rural and urban poverty differ, requiring distinct solutions tailored to local conditions. Yet, despite strong evidence supporting bottom-up development, Indonesia has struggled to fully embrace this model. Rather than empowering communities to drive their own development, the country has instead moved toward political recentralization, consolidating decision making at higher levels of government rather than where it may be most effective.

While social protection programs are needed to improve the village population's well-being, this alone may not be sufficient. First, most workers in rural areas are engaged in the agricultural sector, which generally has lower productivity than any other sector in the economy. Moreover, the agricultural sector is also mainly comprised of informal labor. In 2022, 73.79% of workers in rural areas were engaged in the informal sector.[1] For informal workers, job security is not guaranteed, and they lack employment benefits such as health or work accident insurance, or pensions. While it is true that for short-term poverty metrics, direct cash transfers are the much better option, they do nothing for the productive base or market access for people in poverty. The village population's heightened vulnerability, lower productivity, and limited market access suggest that people in rural areas may need a different set of social protection programs from those living in urban areas. With agriculture being the base of rural economy, investments that

[1] SAKERNAS, August 2023.

Evidence and the Politics of Reform. Sudarno Sumarto, Oxford University Press.
 DOI: 10.1093/9780197831717.003.0008

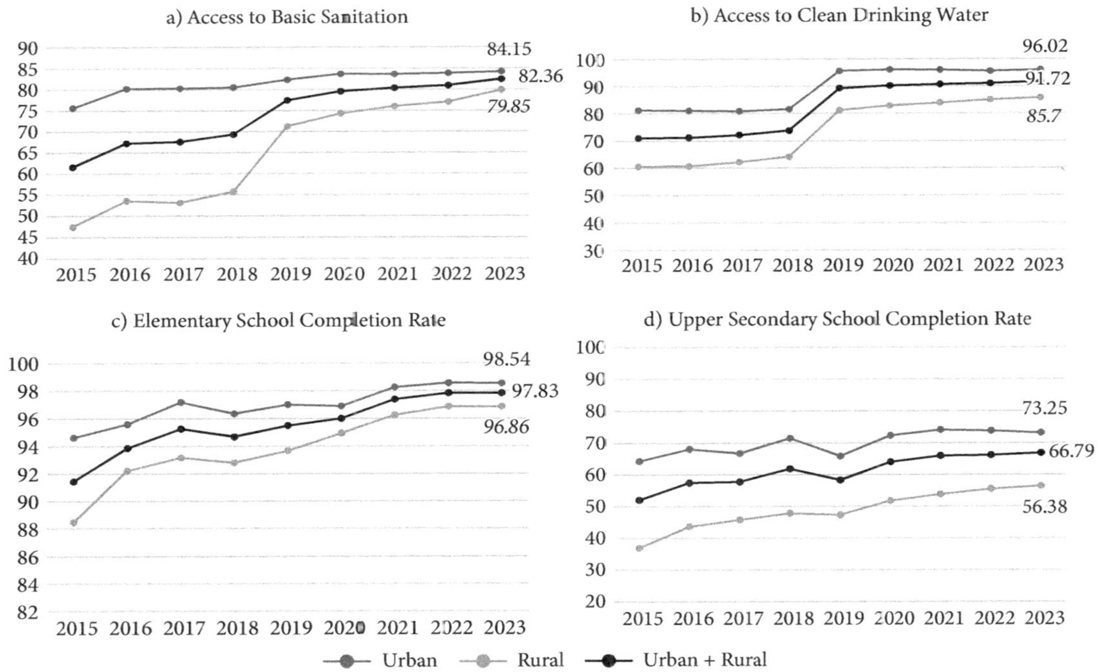

Figure 7.1 Urban and Rural Developmental Indicators

Source: Statistics Indonesia, multiple years.

could improve productivity, such as infrastructure and services provisions, as opposed to cash handouts, may have a more enduring impact.

Beyond specific social protection provisions, people in rural areas also face poor infrastructural development and gaps in the delivery of basic services when compared to those living in urban areas. For instance, despite an expansion of universal health coverage, gaps remain in access to healthcare facilities and healthcare output between urban and rural populations (see Figure 6.1 and Chapter 6). In 2023, more than 20% of rural residents did not have access to basic sanitation, while the figure was a bit less than 16% for urban residents.[2] A similar gap can also be found in access to clean drinking water, where nearly 15% of rural residents were deprived of clean drinking water as opposed to just 4% of urban residents. In terms of education, though elementary school completion rates have converged between urban and rural citizens, there is a sizeable gap in upper secondary school completion rates. In 2023, just a bit more than half of rural residents have completed upper secondary school compared to nearly three-quarters of urban residents.

Despite progress in poverty alleviation and in reforming the country's social protection system since Indonesia's transition to democracy, the urban–rural gap in access and development indicators persists. This gap suggests a need for a tailored approach to development and welfare policy formulation. In this spirit, Indonesia legislated the Village Law in 2014, which mandated the devolution of government powers to the village level. This law is a continuation of Indonesia's decentralization project from the early 2000s, which saw the devolution of power from the central government to regional governments in most areas of governance except a few, such as foreign policy, safety, law, and monetary and fiscal policy.[3] Intended to improve the ability of local governments to respond to local conditions, Indonesia's decentralization project has been heralded as a landmark policy for advancing development. First, it endowed local governments with the ability to adopt locally appropriate regulations and to experiment with policies that would advance development and welfare. Moreover, it also let local governments spend central government transfers in ways deemed suitable for local needs.

[2] All figures are calculated using multiple year data of the National Socio-economic Survey collected by Statistics Indonesia.

[3] See Brodjonegoro, 2009; Seymour and Turner, 2002.

In the same spirit of decentralization, Indonesia's House of Representatives passed the Village Law (Law No. 6/2014) in January 2014, granting villages greater autonomy and significantly increasing their budgets. As part of this initiative, the central government launched the Village Fund in 2015, directing funds to nearly 75,000 villages nationwide. The fund was intended to support village-led development, including poverty alleviation, community empowerment, infrastructure projects, public services, and village-owned enterprises. By granting villages control over their own development, the policy aimed to strengthen democratic institutions, improve accountability, and foster closer ties between the state and local communities. Ultimately, it was expected to reduce regional disparities and ensure more equitable access to services across Indonesia.

Nearly a decade later, however, the impact of the Village Fund remains mixed. Rural poverty persists, and the gap between urban and rural areas has not significantly narrowed (Figure 7.2). Beyond high rural poverty rates, Indonesia also struggles with "poverty pockets"—regions where both the proportion and absolute number of people in poverty remain alarmingly high. For instance, in 2023, Papua's poverty rate stood at 26.03%, nearly three times the national average. Such stark inequalities continue to hamper progress in poverty reduction.

Persistent poverty of this kind is often described as the "last mile" challenge—the hardest phase in eradicating poverty, where the remaining barriers are often the most entrenched. While the Village Fund alone cannot solve structural issues beyond a village's control, such as poor road connectivity that limits farmers' access to urban markets, it should at least help address local problems that national and regional policies might overlook. After all, solving last-mile challenges at the village level is only possible when progress has been made across all the earlier "miles" at higher levels of governance.

Between 2018 and 2022, the Village Fund averaged IDR 68.1 trillion (approximately USD 4.2 billion) annually, distributed among nearly 75,000 villages across Indonesia. Each village received around IDR 1 billion per year, making up a significant portion—about 57%—of village revenues in 2022.[4] In principle, the transfer to villages should allow for local government and community participation from the bottom up in a way that

[4] Statistics Indonesia, 2024. "Statistik Keuangan Pemerintah Desa 2022 dan 2023." Jakarta: Badan Pusat Statistik.

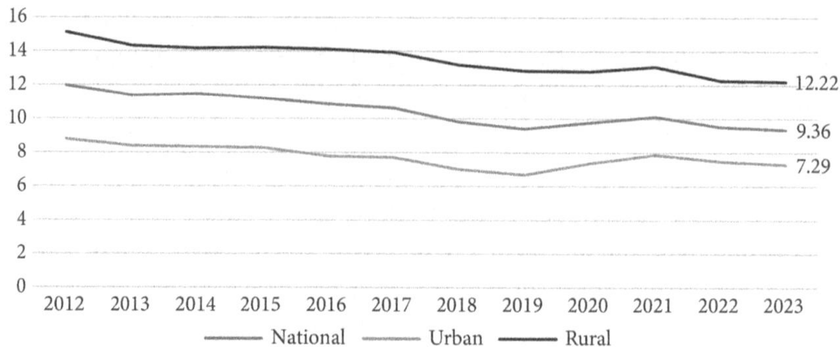

Figure 7.2 Indonesia's National, Urban, and Rural Poverty Rate (2012–2023)
Source: Statistics Indonesia, various years.

leverages local knowledge to drive development. However, in practice, the level of community participation or level of economic growth still varies between villages.

Some villages have seen tangible progress, while others continue to struggle with weak community participation and stagnant economic growth. A key concern is accountability: in 2023, Indonesia Corruption Watch identified 187 cases of alleged corruption related to the fund, the highest of any government-sector spending. While this might seem like a small number of cases given that there are around 75,000 villages across the country, this number under-represents the true extent of the problem, as many cases fly under the radar due to a lack of transparency. Meanwhile, others attribute this to endogenous factors unique to each locality and variation in local natural resource endowment.[5] Yet, declaring the policy a failure outright would be neither accurate nor productive. Instead, it is essential to assess what Indonesia's village decentralization has done right and where it has fallen short in improving welfare outcomes. Understanding these nuances is key to refining the policy and ensuring that village autonomy translates into meaningful development.

A crucial issue here lies not in the lack of evidence but in the disconnect between knowledge and policy implementation. Research had already provided valuable insights, such as randomized controlled trials demonstrating effective ways to curb corruption in village governance, and infrastructure impact evaluations highlighting best practices for community-led

[5] Syukri et al., 2018.

construction.[6] Yet these findings were not systematically integrated into the Village Fund's rollout. Instead, the economic and political agendas were pursued separately: on the one hand, the Village Fund was expected to drive local economic growth, while on the other, the Ministry of Home Affairs used it to consolidate political support among village heads. This strategic unbundling happened largely outside the epistemic community's radar, either because experts were unaware, lacked access to decision-making spaces, or did not act on the warning signs. In the end, the failure was not just in policy design but in the breakdown of evidence translation. This case presents an example of how even well-intentioned reforms can drift off course when political incentives are not aligned with research-backed solutions. But while the Village Fund's implementation has been imperfect, the broader question remains: What role should villages play in Indonesia's decentralized development framework? Simply channeling funds to villages is not enough. Making them true frontiers for socio-economic development requires recognizing that, in post-1998 Indonesia, villages are not and should not be mere extensions of the central government's authority.

Instead, village governance must be acknowledged as an autonomous force in shaping local welfare. In the context of social protection provisions, this is particularly important given projected rising uncertainties and vulnerabilities that arise largely from climate change. In this regard, villages have an advantage of thinner bureaucracy and closer proximity to their inhabitants, both of which the central government is lacking. These factors are believed to allow local governments to provide public goods more efficiently than the central government.[7] Moreover, both factors lend villages the flexibility and adaptability to tackle emergent challenges and fill gaps that the central government is unable to fill, truly driving development from below.

While noble, these goals are at risk of being lofty at best. In practice, the Village Law's rollout was an example of an evidence-to-policy failure. Despite the program's passage, broad political support, and implementation, over time it highlighted the weakness of the "wise technocrat" model in implementing a development program. The policy was premised on the idea that subsidiarity in village governance, where local actors are empowered with resources and decision-making authority, would function as intended within a broader process of democratization. In theory,

[6] Torrens, 2005; Olken, 2007.
[7] Arends, 2020.

villages would take on roles traditionally played by higher levels of government, such as local negotiations, risk surveillance, and sanctioning, based on shared information. In reality, however, this assumption did not hold. At the end of the day, technocrats need to take into account a host of organizational and political variables that are key to a policy's successful implementation.

This case highlights how economic theory fell short in accounting for the political-economy conditions necessary for subsidiarity to work. The government of Indonesia and its knowledge partners largely overlooked these conditions, assuming that technical solutions could override political realities. This chapter examines the limits of evidence-based policymaking, not as a failure of data or analysis but as a cautionary tale about the risks of treating evidence as a neutral force that is divorced from the institutional and political contexts that shape its application.

Decentralizing Development

Consisting of around half of the country's citizens up until 2020, villages play an important role in Indonesia's development. Indonesia's transition to democracy in 1998, however, marked a major shift in villages' role in development as a part of a broader shift in approach to governance in Indonesia. The question that remains, however, is whether this new approach to development from the bottom up has succeeded in improving village welfare.

The end of President Suharto's 32-year autocratic rule in 1998 opened the door for more democratic and participatory governance. Politically, this led to the adoption of democratic elections, while in governance it took the form of decentralizing power to regional governments in the early 2000s. A decade later, the Village Law of 2014 extended this decentralization to the village level, ostensibly to empower villages to develop their potential and improve the welfare of their residents. However, in practice, the law tightened central control over village governance. While villages received substantial funding, much of it was earmarked for national priorities rather than local needs. At the same time, village heads were given greater administrative authority but were effectively integrated into the state apparatus, limiting their autonomy. Unlike regional governments, villages were not granted fiscal authority to levy taxes. Villages could have the authority to determine how their budgets were spent, and they generated their own revenue beyond intergovernmental transfers from central and regional governments. This decentralization thus represented a major shift in the village government's role from the Suharto era.

Under President Suharto's centralistic tendencies, villages represented an extension of the central government. This included implementing the central government's development policies at the local level. Law No. 5 of 1979 on Village Governance stated that the two pillars of Suharto's regime, which were economic development and national stability, could be achieved only if the central government was in control over the countryside by supervising village governments. With the passage of the 1979 law, village affairs were brought under the supervision and control of higher authorities. Moreover, the Department of Home Affairs also standardized village structures and assigned officers and village branches of state organizations to uphold order. This process dissolved traditional village governance structures along with its community institutions and traditional social security mechanisms.[8] The law clearly defined the subordinate nature of the village as "the lowest level of the government structure directly under the sub-district head," with the village head "positioned as the instrument of the central government, of the regional government and of the village government." In other words, village heads owed their power to higher authorities and could not do much without the approval of sub-districts and district governments. This also included financial matters. As a result of the total submission of the village heads, and thus the village population, there was no room for innovation from below or for aspirations that did not align with those of the higher authorities.[9]

At that time, village administrations acted as an extension of the central government, enforcing decrees and policies determined from above. A range of government agencies were present in villages, and various ministries set up programs and institutions in every locale. "Electricity Comes to the Village" (*Listrik Masuk Desa*), "The Military Comes to the Village" (*ABRI Masuk Desa*), "Television Comes to the Village" (*TV Masuk Desa*), "Student Community Service" (*Kuliah Kerja Nyata*), and other government programs incorporated the village into the Indonesian state.

Beyond a locus of infrastructural development, villages are also key to the regime's agenda in improving the country's human capital, especially in regard to public health. In the 1970s, Suharto's government introduced

[8] Antlöv, 2002.
[9] Antlöv, 2003.

community healthcare centers (*Puskesmas*) at the sub-district and village levels. In 1984, the government introduced Integrated Service Centers (*Posyandu*) to complement the *Puskesmas*. While the *Puskesmas* focuses on curative aspects of healthcare, the *Posyandu* revolves around promotive and preventive health efforts. Staffed with midwives and National Family Planning Agency (BKKBN) cadres, the *Posyandu* provided services as well as information and knowledge about community health, especially the health of mothers, babies, and toddlers. The presence of BKKBN personnel at the grassroots level helped to improve the sustainability of programs on the ground–such as birth control provisions, immunization campaigns, diarrhea prevention, and nutritional campaigns. Until 1993, more than 6,700 *Puskesmas* were constructed across the country. Between 1970 and 1993, infant mortality per 1,000 live births more than halved from 113 to 55.[10] Meanwhile, by the end of Suharto's rule in 1998, the rate of measles immunization for children between 12–23 months was as high as 77%, compared to just 13% in 1984.[11]

Given the developments during his rule, Suharto was dubbed the country's "Father of Development." At the same time, his centrally planned development programs stripped away the development authority and agency of village leaders, and the villagers by extension. While this mode of development worked at that time, it may not be the case today. First, Indonesia has transitioned away from autocracy to democracy, which would make central planning less likely to gain political support. Second, decentralization means that the central government's authorities—especially in terms of resource mobilization at the regional and village level—are more limited. Finally, on a more technical level, during Suharto's era the whole country had a low baseline on many development indicators. This made a standardized approach to development programs the most efficient method in that context. In contrast, today the government is faced with disparities in development outcomes and gaps in service provisions. The result of inaction—or failure to take an appropriate approach—has created an increasing gap between areas and groups left behind, and those reaping the benefits of socio-economic development in the past two and a half decades.

Two decades after the end of Suharto's New Order regime, Indonesia has made steady progress across many developmental indicators. It has managed

[10] World Bank, 2024.
[11] World Bank, 2024.

to more than halve its poverty rate since its peak during the 1998 Asian financial crisis. Much of this poverty reduction could be attributed to the country's robust growth in the two decades after the crisis and its social protection system. Indonesia's achievement in installing a comprehensive social protection system to guarantee its citizens' well-being, in particular, deserves appreciation. Work continues to be done to improve its programs (see Chapters 4–6), targeting system (see Chapter 3), and institutional framework (this chapter) to ensure that the government can more effectively eradicate poverty and improve the population's welfare. Yet these efforts tend to be focused at the central government level—insufficiently taking into account how central government policies interact with regional political-economic dynamics. Unequal welfare outcomes across regions reveal the limits of a one-size-fits-all approach to welfare policy and poverty alleviation. Lingering inequality that hampers progress in poverty alleviation suggests that there is a need to take a more tailored and flexible approach to social protection provisions. In finishing up "the last mile" in poverty alleviation, local governments need to be seen as the central government's equals rather than their subjects in development.

Driving Development from the Periphery

The Village Fund that was launched in 2015 represents the government's commitment to bottom-up development and its recognition of the village's authority. This approach to development is a shift away from a centralistic development model under Suharto's New Order regime that treated villages as peripheral subjects. In truth, the Village Fund is not the first example of a bottom-up approach to development but simply its latest form.

When a range of social protection programs were rolled out in the aftermath of the Asian financial crisis in 1998, the Indonesian government launched the KDP. The KDP was a community-based, demand-driven project funding initiative. At the time of the KDP's launch, corruption was widespread, and little of the state budget allocated for poverty alleviation actually reached the villages. Thus, to rebuild its credibility among the masses and to reduce poverty, the Indonesian government supported the formation and initiation of the KDP project with the World Bank's assistance—who also aided the government in other crisis-recovery social safety net programs. The KDP targeted the poorest sub-districts in the country and provided additional funds to the eastern island sub-districts hit hardest by El Niño. The program sought to empower communities to exercise control over their developmental decisions, from identification of their needs to the implementation of the project. The project also focused on gender equality and encouraged women to participate in planning and decision-making activities. Through the project, villagers were encouraged to voice their needs for infrastructure projects or small-scale economic activities in the form of proposals submitted to the *kecamatan*.[12] Decisions on planning, procurement, and management of funds were set to be made by villagers. Groups of villagers would plan projects within villages, which would then be proposed to the *kecamatan*. Two proposals would be selected for implementation every year, with one of them given to a women's group.

The KDP covered more than 30% of the rural *kecamatans* in the country. By the time it reached its third year in 2002, the project had been introduced to more than 21,000 villages in about 1000 *kecamatans* in most of the provinces of Indonesia.[13] Around 75% of the funds were used for village-level infrastructure, such as roads, bridges, water supply systems, and school repairs, while the remaining 25% was lent out to villager groups for working capital. Following its success, in its second iteration, KDP-II is estimated to have reached close to 20–30 million people, with 200 *kecamatans* added each year and 15,000 villages covered across the country. Since the KDP mainly aimed to ensure transparency and democracy in its operations, not only were villagers involved throughout the project from its inception to implementation, but also all transactions were carried out in public and information was disseminated by way of notice boards, posters, radio programs, and signboards. Additionally, since poverty alleviation was the project's secondary goal, it is notable that 78% of the loans lent out through the KDP were given to beneficiaries perceived to be poorer members of the communities, of which 38% were women.

In 2007 President Susilo Bambang Yudhoyono established PNPM Mandiri, which continued KDP's path in funding community-led programs as a part of the country's poverty-reduction agenda. Government decision makers designated PNPM as an integral part of the agenda because

[12] *Kecamatan* is a government administrative unit in Indonesia, right below regency/municipality—which delineates rural and urban areas—and province. Beneath *kecamatan* are villages/sub-districts, which are the smallest administrative units in Indonesia. *Kecamatan* consists of an average of 20–25 villages and approximately 100,000 inhabitants.

[13] Bhatnagar et al., 2003.

of demonstrated outputs, impacts on poverty, improved transparency and accountability, and widespread support from both communities and local governments. By 2009, the PNPM Mandiri had reached all provinces across the country. Between 2008 and 2011, the total value of financial transfers to communities had more than doubled to about USD 1.7 billion. PNPM's proliferation meant that the initiatives reached a broader set of beneficiaries and addressed the needs of many citizens across regions. However, challenges emerged, including inconsistent implementation and community confusion over program objectives and processes. Despite these hurdles, PNPM Mandiri became a model for grassroots development, proving that local participation could drive meaningful change. Recognizing its potential, the government integrated PNPM Mandiri into its broader strategy to accelerate poverty reduction, solidifying its role in Indonesia's development agenda.

In 2011, the Yudhoyono administration introduced a comprehensive poverty alleviation strategy, bringing together programs from various government ministries and agencies, including PNPM Mandiri. To improve coordination, the government had already issued Presidential Regulation 15 in 2010, mandating the creation of the TNP2K at the central level. Similar coordination teams were established at the provincial and district levels to streamline efforts nationwide. The new strategy categorized poverty-reduction initiatives into three clusters: family-based social assistance, community empowerment, and support for micro and small enterprises. PNPM Mandiri was placed under the second cluster, reinforcing its role in promoting grassroots participation in development.

Under Yudhoyono's presidency, community-based development became a permanent fixture of Indonesia's governance with the introduction of the Village Fund through the 2014 Village Law. This law transformed village development into an entitlement, providing direct block grants from the central government to villages. While it institutionalized grassroots development and ensured long-term funding, it also fundamentally changed the nature of the initiative. What had once been a community-driven process under KDP and PNPM Mandiri became more centralized, shifting toward a top-down government program rather than a locally led effort.

While the Village Fund aimed to carry forward the spirit of community empowerment and bottom-up development, its legal framework, program design, and funding mechanisms made it fundamentally different from its predecessors. The law embedded community-driven development within the state's bureaucratic structure, reflecting a broader effort to reconcile local participation with centralized governance. This shift is evident in the role of Village Fund Facilitators, who were once accountable to local communities under KDP and PNPM Mandiri but are now answerable only to the Ministry of Villages. Similarly, village leaders, instead of reporting to their communities, are required to report to the Ministry of Home Affairs. This further reinforced the state's oversight over what was originally intended as a grassroots initiative.

The transition from PNPM Mandiri to the Village Fund marked the breakdown of Indonesia's "wise technocrat" model of development. While research evidence had long supported Indonesia's bottom-up development model up until the PNPM Mandiri, its transformation into the Village Fund saw the model fundamentally reshaped through political and bureaucratic processes. This process ultimately shifted the program's structure. However, this change did not happen overnight.

The debate over the role of villages in Indonesia's governance first gained traction in 2005, when the government and parliament decided to revise Law No. 32/2004, which governed decentralization. This led to the drafting of three separate laws on regional governance, direct elections, and villages. As discussions on village governance progressed, an academic paper was commissioned to serve as the foundation for a new Village Law. At the same time, civil society organizations actively lobbied politicians to support the initiative.

By 2011, pressure from civil society and village officials intensified, pushing the Village Law onto the legislative agenda. In early 2012, President Yudhoyono formally requested the House of Representatives to begin deliberations, leading to the formation of a special committee. As discussions unfolded, political parties—particularly the opposition PDI-Perjuangan—took a keen interest in the bill, recognizing its potential impact on rural communities. With the 2014 presidential and legislative elections approaching, debates over the size of central government transfers to villages became a focal point of political negotiations. Concerned that prolonged discussions could delay the bill beyond the end of Yudhoyono's term, lawmakers reached a final agreement in December 2013. The Village Law was officially enacted in January 2014, cementing the transformation of Indonesia's community-driven development model into a formalized state program under the Village Fund.

The bill's discussion and legislation subjected the idea of decentralization to a political-economic force. As political parties in the House of

Representatives sought to represent village apparatus's interests for greater transfer allocations, the government was concerned over the viability of the transfers, given the state's fiscal space availability. After the Village Law's legislation, the technocratic idea of "bottom-up development through village empowerment" underwent a political-economic push-and-pull as a bill in the House of Representatives. Further complicating the translation of technocratic ideas into practice on the ground was how, after its legislation, the Village Law still needed to be spelled out into programs with operational rules. The task of translating the law to practices fell upon the Ministry of Home Affairs.

At this point, it became apparent that the Village Law's implementation was a political and bureaucratic project. Though its discussion and legislation began in the House of Representatives—mainly on the transfer formula—the law's implementation was then taken over by the Ministry of Home Affairs, which responded to a lobbying campaign by village heads. At the same time, TNP2K took its eye off the ball on the PNPM Mandiri program and its mandate to eradicate poverty through community empowerment. Although TNP2K had created a roadmap to ensure the sustainability of PNPM Mandiri and its complementarity with the government's larger poverty alleviation effort, it surrendered to allow politics to take over the program. While initially it was about the amount of central government transfers that villages were entitled to, as the details of the transfers were finalized it became clear that both the recipients of the transfers and those with the authority to determine spending guidelines would wield a lot of political power. While villages received transfers for the KDP and PNPM Mandiri to be disbursed to villagers, allowing village governments and villagers to be the locus of decision making for these programs, the Village Law replaced this system. Under the Village Law, the central government transfers funds to the regency or municipal government, which approves the village's budget plan before disbursing funds. Under this arrangement, villagers were effectively taken out of the equation. Though the Village Law mandated the Village Fund to prioritize village development projects, formal room for consultation with the villagers and their active participation in project determination was effectively removed.

Decades of treating villages as subjects of the central government's policies under Suharto's New Order regime have altered the fabric of villages. Under Suharto, village bureaucrats were installed as an extension of the state, making village leaders increasingly divorced from community interests and acting more as the central government's client.[14] Although democracy and Indonesia's *Reformasi* era brought about the devolution of power to local government units, the bureaucratic village structure remains unchanged. If anything, the Village Law and the Village Fund, dubbed as the central government's commitment to take a bottom-up approach to development, only cemented the absorption of village governments into government bureaucracy. Yet this did not occur without resistance from reformers. The Village Fund's predecessors took a more democratic approach to community development and empowerment—in the spirit of the recently democratizing country. Ultimately, a political, economic, and bureaucratic process that strengthened the program's legal standing and its sustainability also transformed its technocratic ideals into a clientelist network between the central government, district/municipal governments, and village apparatuses—and by extension the villagers. With these changes, and so little change to the village's bureaucratic structure from its Suharto-era reform, expecting technocratic participative governance models to magically work in driving development and poverty alleviation is simply unrealistic. Reverting the Village Law or amending it is a legal battle often beyond the reach of technocrats. At the same time, dismantling village bureaucracy to make way for village autonomy, as before the New Order era, is like trying to turn back time. While previously technocrats could dream of community empowerment programs, it has become painfully clear that averting their gaze when politics and bureaucracy had their hands on these ideals led to a ruinous end. Anyone seeking to reform anything needs to find ways that could make villages equals as the central government's partners in development and to break the patronage chain.

From Patronage to Partnership

Despite being a product of Indonesia's democratic reform, the Village Fund transfers were launched in a bureaucratic political arrangement that poorly rewarded democratic participation. Part of the problem with the Village Fund stems from the Village Law that serves as its foundation. After the Village Law was signed, the responsibilities for village development were divided up between the Ministry of Finance, the Ministry of Villages, and

[14] Antlöv, 2002.

the Ministry of Home Affairs. As a result, the law has fragmented support toward villages and laid the foundation for weak coordination, oversight, and accountability, which is reflected in how the Village Fund is run and governed a decade after its passage. With little that ties public participation and oversight to the Village Fund cash flow, local community empowerment remains just a concept. Instead of being accountable to community members, the nature of Village Fund transfers as entitlements transferred directly to village governments made it a fertile ground for New Order-style patronage to re-emerge. To ensure that the Village Fund can foster central and local government partnership in improving public welfare, incentives must be well-placed.

Up until 2019, the value of the Village Fund transfer varied by village and was calculated based on a fixed "base" allocation as well as variable "affirmative" and "formula" components. The affirmative allocations were determined by whether the village was characterized as "underdeveloped" and if this was coupled with high poverty. Meanwhile, the formula allocations were determined by the village's population size, area, geographic difficulty index, and poverty level—which was given the greatest weight in the formula allocations calculation. In 2019, 72%, 3%, and 25% of the Village Fund transfers made up the base, affirmative, and formula allocations respectively. With a lack of accountability linking the transfer's amount and how the transfers were actually spent, the Village Fund more closely resembled an entitlement.

Indeed, there is a mismatch between who granted the funds, who should benefit from it, and to whom villages should demonstrate accountability. Although the villagers were intended as the Village Fund's beneficiaries, its nature as an intergovernmental transfer made it fundamentally different from the KDP or PNPM Mandiri. As the KDP and PNPM Mandiri were explicitly branded as community empowerment programs with village community members as the programs' beneficiaries, both programs channeled funds directly to villagers. Aside from engaging villagers at all stages of development projects, they also ensured that beneficiaries received the full amount of transfers and assumed accountability. In contrast, since the Village Fund is an intergovernmental transfer, it directs funds from the central government to village governments. This transfer is intended to be used for village development projects—be it implemented by village governments or villagers. Although the Village Fund's continuity was better secured once it was formalized as a government program under the mandate of law, this process formed a bureaucratic structure that disempowered citizens. By leaving less room for communities to take part in fund management and demanding accountability over transfer usage, the program lost much of its ability to empower communities when compared to its predecessors. Thus, in 2020, the Ministry of Finance introduced the "performance" component to the Village Fund transfers to alleviate the issue.

The Village Fund's performance component is calculated based on how village governments manage village budgets and Village Fund transfers, as well as the Village Fund transfers' output and the villages' developmental progress. This allocation is expected to incentivize village governments to use the budget efficiently and effectively for development. Though it was a welcome development, its share over the total Village Fund transfers may not be sufficient to warrant the desired effect. By 2020, the ratio of allocations was amended, with the base and affirmative allocations reduced to 69% and 1.5% respectively, while the formula and performance allocations increased to 28% and 1.5% respectively. For the Village Fund to truly foster development, its disbursement needs to have better linkage with performance. Beyond that, the community's role in project development, implementation, and oversight needs to be integrated into the Village Fund's structure.

The Village Fund's adoption into the bureaucracy with all its budgetary and governing constraints meant that the central government could have some instrument to control the Village Fund's use. This can be used to foster intergovernmental partnership in the implementation of the central government's development agenda. Although by law the central government has no authority over the Village Fund's use (such as earmarking funds for specific uses dictated by the central government), the performance allocations can be used to incentivize the adoption of good practice. Villages' reduced bureaucracy and proximity to communities, particularly when compared to the central government, can be leveraged to create programs that can quickly respond to emergent issues. In fact, the Village Fund's use for disaster mitigation was not unheard-of.

During the COVID-19 pandemic, extraordinary conditions allowed the central government to request villages to use the Village Fund for an emergency cash transfers scheme. Through the Minister of Villages, Development Disadvantaged Regions, and Transmigration's regulation, all villages were asked to reallocate 25%–35% of their annual Village Fund budget for the 2020 fiscal year to fund the transfer. Though placing financial pressures on villages with ongoing programs, the severity of the pandemic's economic impact pushed villages to adopt the scheme. The scheme targeted households who had not yet received any assistance from the central government, with priorities given to female-headed households, persons with disability, and elderly persons. The village head facilitated the village representative body (BPD) in conducting a special village meeting (*Musyawarah Desa*) by inviting community representatives to determine the candidates for receiving the village fund cash assistance (BLT-*Dana Desa*).

Initially, village governments sorted out prospective recipient families using the Family Hope Program and Program Sembako regular transfer program beneficiary list obtained from the district government.[15] Later, village governments and volunteers collected potential program beneficiary data through house visits. Meanwhile, other villages opted to directly visit the residents' homes. Selecting potential BLT-DD recipients was not a simple process, because the existing program beneficiary lists had a lot of errors. Thus, beyond listing new beneficiaries for the Village Fund Cash Transfer scheme, villages also updated the existing beneficiary lists.

By the end of 2020, 71,065 villages or 95% villages across Indonesia had disbursed Village Fund Cash Transfers. Out of all the program's beneficiaries, 2,341,750 families, or 31% of all transfer beneficiary families, were female-headed households. The program continued all the way to 2021, with some villages keeping the scheme up until 2022. Such a scheme demonstrated how a bottom-up approach can complement the government's top-down efforts in providing social protection for its citizens. Moreover, the policy has encouraged villages to demonstrate their ability to efficiently and effectively manage a social assistance program under time pressure. This also demonstrated a potential avenue in developing a social protection system governance model that mixes a top-down and bottom-up approach for improved benefit delivery.

It is clear that villages can assist in program targeting through potential beneficiary identification. Local knowledge in particular is well-suited to complement top-down survey sweep methods to collect potential beneficiary data (see Chapter 3). These methods tend to be slower to respond to changes in an individual's life and welfare levels, which impact their benefit eligibility criteria. Villages are in a good place to assist the central government in providing coverage where it has not been provided and to

[15] Kurniawan, 2020.

update program beneficiary databases. Since the task of data updating falls upon social workers at the district or municipality level, who often lack the resources and time to do so, decentralized data updating at the village level can help spread data-updating costs and make the process more efficient. Yet the road ahead is rocky.

In 2024, the country's House of Representatives passed an amendment to Law No. 6/2014 on Villages, which immediately came into effect. Political commentators and the media have highlighted how the amendment accommodated the subjective interests of village government officials. First, the amendment increased the length of a village head's term substantially, from six to eight years for a maximum of two terms. Moreover, the law also permitted current village heads who have not finished their second term to run again in the coming elections. This, coupled with their authority over most village affairs—including budget and planning—as well as little oversight and room for villagers to hold village heads accountable, caused the amendment to raise concerns of moral hazard.

At the start of 2025, newly elected President Prabowo Subianto launched the *Koperasi Merah-Putih* (Merah Putih Village Cooperative) program under the Ministry of Villages and Development of Disadvantaged Regions. This initiative aims to foster village self-reliance and improve community welfare. By strengthening cooperatives at the village level, the program envisions a more effective management of local resources, ultimately increasing incomes and enhancing the quality of life in rural communities.

The strategy for developing the *Koperasi Merah-Putih* involves both establishing new cooperatives and revitalizing existing ones, financed through a combination of Village Fund transfers and loans from state-owned banks. A key feature of the program is inter-village cooperation, particularly in infrastructure development. By collectively investing in warehouses for storing agricultural and cooperative-managed products, villages can reduce business operations costs and operate more efficiently. This approach is intended to build a more resilient and sustainable local economy. To further empower villages, the government has also proposed to increase the Village Fund budget while reducing earmarked activities, allowing greater flexibility in fund allocation based on local needs. Additionally, the government also planned to improve logistics and transportation networks aimed at enhancing market access for village products, strengthening rural economies, and fostering broader economic integration. In theory, these measures position the *Koperasi Merah-Putih* as a catalyst for village-level economic development. Yet Indonesia's history with community-driven development highlights key challenges that may resurface in the *Koperasi Merah-Putih* initiative.

While the program nominally includes community participation in its early discussions, the extent to which villagers can meaningfully influence decision making remains unclear. In practice, the central government has already predetermined much of how funds and resources will be used, limiting local autonomy. This raises concerns about whether communities have any real agency beyond formal consultations. Furthermore, the program's implementation lacks clarity on where and how communities can engage beyond the planning stage. For instance, it remains uncertain whether villagers will have a role in the construction of warehouses or their long-term management. The blanket mandate to build warehouses in villages across the country assumes a one-size-fits-all approach to rural economic participation, disregarding variations in local economies and priorities. Not all villages require the same infrastructure, and imposing a uniform model may not align with their specific needs.

By implementing a one-size-fits-all infrastructure development policy over local engagement, *Koperasi Merah-Putih* risks sidelining grassroots participation and diminishing village agency. A highly centralized approach, even when framed as bottom-up development, can ultimately restrict the very empowerment it seeks to achieve. This raises a fundamental question: does *Koperasi Merah-Putih* genuinely strengthen village independence, or does it merely reassert central control under the guise of community-driven development?

Though Indonesia seeks to move away from a centralistic village governance model that fosters patronage, changes to village governance under democracy have yet to close the gap between urban and rural areas across many developmental indicators. Though the Village Fund represents the central government's commitment to rural area development through a decentralized approach, it still does not address the central government's responsibilities to play its part in village development. To put it simply, the central government cannot throw money to villages and call it a day. Poor village infrastructure such as electricity, roads, and internet coverage, as well as insufficient basic services like schools and healthcare facilities, indicates a nationwide issue that needs to be solved, beyond a single village. Moving forward means that central and local governments need to identify different problems and their scopes, then seek to complement one another in providing services to village residents. This way, village-led bottom-up approaches to development and service provisions can complement the central government's top-down approach. At the same time, for a bottom-up approach to truly work, there need to be changes to village governance to better align cash flows with accountability mechanisms and community empowerment.

8

Weathering the Storm

Indonesian Social Policy amid the COVID-19 Pandemic

After seven deaths and hundreds of new COVID-19 cases daily, on March 17, 2020, the Indonesian National Board for Disaster Management declared an emergency period. Three days later, President Joko Widodo shifted the government's budgetary priorities toward COVID-19 mitigation efforts. By the end of March, the number of daily active cases had already reached more than 1,000 and the president enacted a large-scale social restriction policy in major cities across the country. When the government enacted mobility restrictions intended to slow down the virus's spread, the policy essentially halted the country's economic engine. The Indonesian economy slid from 5.06% growth in the first quarter of the previous year to 2.97% in the first quarter of 2020.[1] This fall continued in the second quarter of 2020 as GDP growth dipped below zero. And, after three quarters of negative growth, Indonesia officially fell into recession. Indonesian economic growth only turned positive in the second quarter of 2021.[2]

With the economy taking such a hit, various institutions expected the worst for Indonesia's poverty numbers (see Table 8.1). The Asian Development Bank placed its lower estimate for Indonesia's poverty rate growth at a minimum of 2.5% and its highest estimate at as much as a 3.4% increase. This estimation was echoed by others, such as The World Bank, who projected that Indonesia's poverty rate would increase by at least 1.9% up to 3.0%. Defying these projections, Indonesia's poverty rate peaked at 10.2% in September 2020 from 9.2% in September 2019, or a modest 1.0% increase compared to the projections (Figure 8.1). This figure gradually declined subsequently and returned to its pre-pandemic number by September 2021. Many attributed Indonesia's achievement to how it mobilized its social protection system during the pandemic.[3]

[1] Statistics Indonesia, 2021a.
[2] Statistics Indonesia, 2021b.
[3] Suryahadi, Al Izzati, and Yumna, 2021.

Evidence and the Politics of Reform. Sudarno Sumarto, Oxford University Press.
© Sudarno Sumarto (2026). DOI: 10.1093/9780197831717.003.0009

Table 8.1 Various Estimates of the Poverty Impact of COVID-19

Source	Lower Estimate	Upper Estimate
Suryahadi, Izzati, and Suryadarma (2020)	0.50% +1.3 million new poor	7.30% +20.0 million new poor
Ministry of Finance	0.40% +1.2 million new poor	1.40% +3.8 million new poor
Asian Development Bank	2.50% +7.1 million new poor	3.40% +9.7 million new poor
Yusuf (2020)	0.90% +2.5 million new poor	1.30% +3.6 million new poor
World Bank	1.90% +5.5 million new poor	3.00% +8.5 million new poor
The National Team for the Acceleration of Poverty Reduction (TNP2K)	2.20% +6.0 million new poor	4.20% +11.2 million new poor

COVID-19 = coronavirus disease.
Sources: Suryahadi, Izzati, and Suryadarma, 2020; Kacaribu, 2020; Asian Development Bank, 2020; Yusuf, 2020; World Bank, 2020; TNP2K, 2020.

When the pandemic hit, Indonesia was in a better position than its last major shock in 1998 during the Asian financial crisis. Prior to the COVID-19 pandemic, Indonesia already had a functioning social protection system infrastructure. Despite its shortfalls, this welfare infrastructure could be mobilized to dampen the pandemic's impact on the poor. While the 1998 crisis mainly impacted the poor, what was different this time was that the crisis's reach had extended beyond the poor. As economic uncertainty and labor vulnerability rose, citizens at every income level—except the richest 25%—experienced negative expenditure growth between March 2020 and September 2020 (Figure 8.2). With the pandemic's widespread economic impact, the government saw the need to expand social assistance beyond the poor by mobilizing its social protection system and expanding its coverage for crisis mitigation at a scale never seen before. However, the pre-COVID-19 social protection system was designed for a stable Indonesia: it was not built to withstand a sudden shock, and even an increase in poverty rate as small as 1.0% meant that there were around 1.2 million new poor.

Prior to the pandemic, Indonesia's social protection system mainly consisted of social assistance programs designed to alleviate poverty. To target program beneficiaries, the government used the *Data Terpadu*

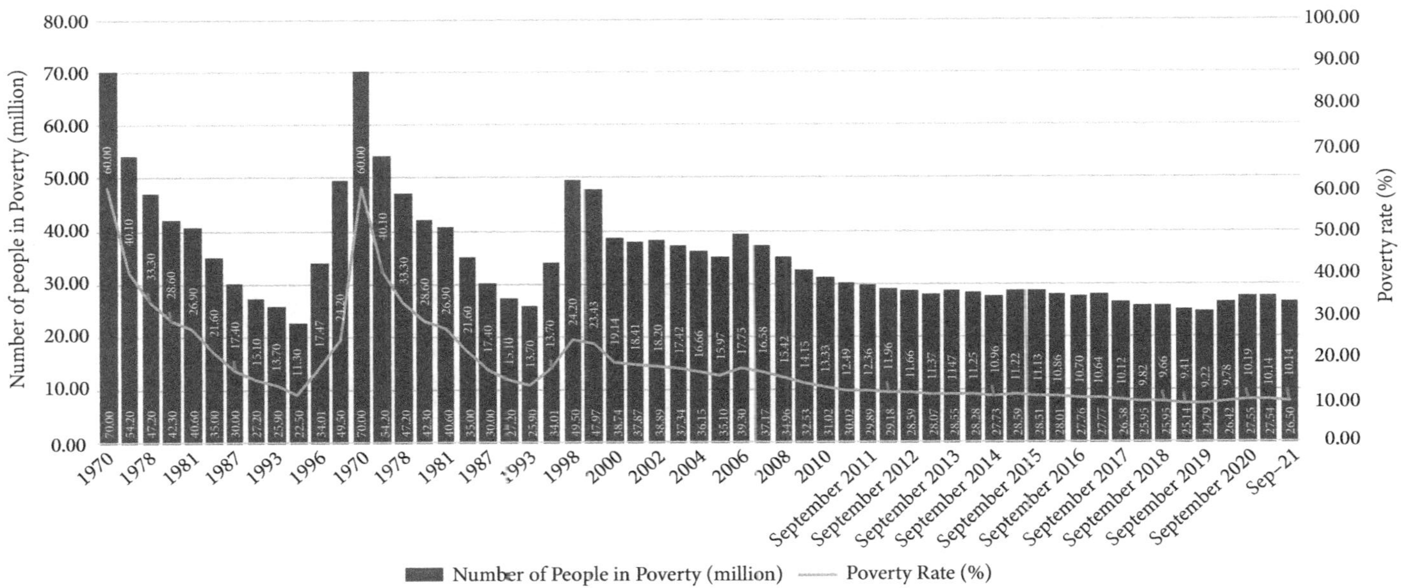

Figure 8.1 Poverty Rate in Indonesia (1980 to September 2021)

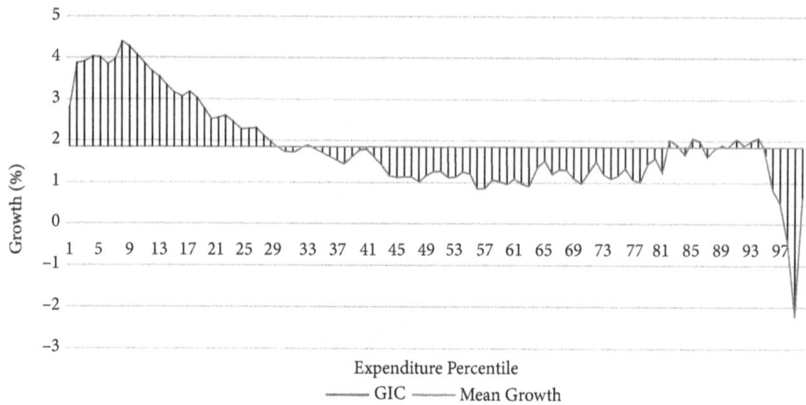

Figure 8.2 Growth Incidence Curve (GIC): Average Expenditure Per Capita Per Month for Every Expenditure Percentile (March–September 2021)
Source: Susenas March and September 2021.

Kesejahteraan Sosial (DTKS). As a targeting instrument, the DTKS was designed to list the name, address, and socio-economic status of the country's poorest 40% families. Prior to the pandemic in 2019, this amounted to more than 52 million people spread across more than 8,000 islands across the country. When the pandemic hit, the government was able to increase the value and coverage for existing programs to reach everyone in the DTKS database. However, this design practically left the middle class outside its scope. The reason the middle class became such an issue during the pandemic is that millions of people right above the poverty line were suddenly pushed below it, while the rest experienced a fall in their welfare level measured by a drop in their expenditure as seen in Figure 8.2. Additionally, since the DTKS had seen its last large-scale data updating in 2015, when it was used to target program beneficiaries during the pandemic it could not fully reflect people's moves in and out of poverty since then. The suddenness of the pandemic overwhelmed the Indonesian social protection system.

To its credit, the Indonesian government did a total reversal away from its obsession with inclusion error and instead focused upon avoiding large-scale exclusion errors.[4] This involved a lot of innovations, including the launch of

[4] "Inclusion" and "exclusion" errors are metrics that the Indonesian government use to evaluate transfers or program targeting accuracy. The former refers to people that are wrongly included in program beneficiary list, while the latter refers to those wrongly excluded from beneficiary lists despite their eligibility. These errors are usually evaluated through Statistics Indonesia's sample surveys that are conducted twice annually each March and September.

new programs like *Kartu Prakerja* and income subsidies, community-based targeting, and the use of Village Fund community development transfers for emergency social safety nets, among many others. These new innovations and expansions to existing programs were partly enabled by the government's dramatically increased budget for social programs. Prior to the pandemic, budget for social assistance amounted to IDR 134.26 T, or 0.85% of the GDP. As a response to the pandemic, this amount was increased to IDR 220.4 T or 1.40% of the GDP. Despite this nearly doubled budget and the Indonesian government's relative success in mitigating the pandemic's socio-economic impact, since the system was meant for a stable Indonesia its ability to cushion the citizens' fall was limited. Aside from excluding people as program beneficiaries, existing welfare infrastructure was not designed to handle a sudden welfare shock like the pandemic.

Although the Indonesian social protection system played an extensive role in providing a social safety net for the population during the crisis, there are many lessons to be learned from our experience with COVID-19. Indeed, there is still much to improve. This chapter lays out how the Indonesian government mobilized its resources through the country's social welfare system to cushion the pandemic's socio-economic impact. We also evaluate the extent of the government's success in making its social protection system a key instrument in its crisis mitigation strategy. Finally, we reflect upon the lessons learned from the pandemic, particularly on how Indonesia can build a social protection system that better protects its citizens from vulnerabilities and future storms.

Mobilizing Indonesia's Social Protection System as a Shock-Absorbent Strategy

The COVID-19 pandemic was not the first time that the Indonesian government mobilized the country's social protection system to serve as a social safety net that could absorb shock to its citizens' welfare. This system has been mobilized under different circumstances to varying degrees of success, albeit still operating as separate programs instead of a unified system in its early days. By the time the COVID-19 pandemic hit, Indonesia already had a range of regular transfers for the poor and a universal healthcare scheme that, despite its limitations, made Indonesia better prepared to face the crisis when compared to other countries at its development level.

The 1997–1998 Asian financial crisis was the first time Indonesia mobilized its welfare system as a social safety net. In the aftermath of that financial crisis, the government implemented several programs dubbed the Social Safety Net (*Jaring Pengaman Sosial,* JPS). At that time, the government launched the JPS to ensure food security, promote school enrollment, provide healthcare, create jobs through labor-intensive efforts, and empower communities through block grants. With a lack of permanent transfers to the poor prior to the crisis, it is remarkable that more than half of all poor households in the country reported to have benefited from the government's rice subsidies program.[5] This achievement was impressive, since developing countries like Indonesia do not usually have adequate social protection measures and suffered as welfare shocks like a financial crisis hit.

Following the crisis, the Indonesian social protection system continued to serve as shock-absorbent mechanism. However, what is different after the 1997–1998 Asian financial crisis is that the government began to actively mobilize the system to both absorb shock caused by external pressures like a crisis and shock resulting from government policy changes. During the 2008 global financial crisis, the Indonesian government once again deployed the safety net. However, given that the crisis mainly hit the more affluent citizens, the government focused efforts on shielding the Indonesian financial system from the impact of the crisis at the macroeconomic level rather than relying extensively on the social protection system as it did in 1998. It was during global oil price shocks that the government used the system extensively.

Between 2003 and July 2008, oil prices steadily rose, reaching $100/bbl in late 2007 from around $20–$30/bbl in 2003. Amidst the rising oil prices, Indonesia turned from a net oil exporter to a net oil importer in 2004. With fuel subsidies reaching as much as 24% of the government's expenditure at that time, the Susilo Bambang Yudhoyono administration resorted to scaling back the subsidies. When the administration raised oil prices in the following year, they also launched a temporary cash transfer using fiscal savings created by the subsidy cutbacks to dampen the effect of the policy change on the poor. The government provided nearly 19 million of the poorest households in the country with quarterly transfers to compensate for the increased oil price.[6]

[5] Sumarto et al., 2001.
[6] Bazzi, Sumarto, and Suryahadi, 2015.

Under time pressures to quickly disburse the transfers, the government listed potential program beneficiaries within two months through Statistics Indonesia's household survey. Through the survey, the government sought to identify poor households that would be entitled to the transfers. This household database is what would later be widely known as the Unified Database, which was the country's early attempt at a social registry that could support the outreach, registration, and determination of potential eligibility for social programs. In addition to the cash transfers, the government also introduced a school transfers program dubbed the Schools Operational Assistance (*Bantuan Operasi Sekolah*, BOS) and expanded the existing free healthcare for the poor program (*Jaminan Kesehatan Masyarakat,* Jamkesmas). When another significant fuel price hike occurred in 2008, this increase was also accompanied by a compensation package, as in the last major price hike. On this occasion, data collected from the 2005 survey became a part of the framework for the government to once more conduct a survey and distribute unconditional cash transfers.

Fuel prices were set to be increased again in 2011. As in previous price hikes, the government also planned to roll out another set of transfers for the poor that would have been the hardest hit by the changes. Using household data from the 2010 Census that updated the country's national population data more comprehensively than the previous sample surveys, the government updated data entries collected in 2005 and 2008 for targeting purposes. Although the government canceled the plans to raise fuel prices in 2011, household data that was collected and used to select transfer beneficiaries then was used to target beneficiaries for other more permanent programs, such as the Family Hope Program conditional cash transfer, the Raskin food assistance, *Bantuan Siswa Miskin* educational aid, and the Jamkesmas health aid.[7]

Between 2005 and 2011, the beneficiary list used to determine eligibility for the ad hoc social safety net programs transformed into a Unified Database that was used to target beneficiaries for a number of the government's flagship social transfers. Coupled with the transformation of many ad hoc transfers into more permanent programs, this shift represented an attempt to integrate disparate social programs into a welfare system. Thus, when the COVID-19 pandemic hit in 2020, the Indonesian government

[7] TNP2K, 2019.

already had a social protection system that could be fashioned into an ad hoc social safety net.

It is, however, important to distinguish between the two, especially in the context of a welfare shock. While a social protection system encompasses the entirety of the welfare system, which consists of some kind of targeting mechanism, programs, legal bases, and regulations to give it some legitimacy, the social safety net is more specific. The social safety net refers to programs and mechanisms that could be triggered to dampen the impact of a welfare shock, such as the death of the breadwinner in the family, or covariate shocks like failed crops or a natural disaster whose impact is community-wide. However, the term *social safety net* itself has been criticized for conflating social safety *nets* and social safety *ropes*, which were two related but different things.

Sumarto, Suryahadi, and Pritchett (2001) contend that safety nets are programs that guarantee against a fall past an *absolute level,* which is usually the poverty line. On the other hand, safety ropes are those that guarantee against a fall no more than a certain *distance*. While those at the bottom of the welfare ladder may get reassurances from the safety net, those more well-off are at the risk of falling deeper, only to be caught once they are at the very bottom. They contend that while safety nets concern *poverty*, safety ropes are related to risk *mitigation* that reduces vulnerability. This mitigation mechanism is important in the face of shocks, whether people are pushed below a certain threshold or not. However, it is also important to note that social safety ropes are distinct from social insurance like JKN or BPJS-TK that rely on its member contributions.

In 2020, as the COVID-19 pandemic's economic impact swept through the population, the social safety net that the Indonesian government implemented resembled one implemented during the 1997–1998 crisis. However, adjustments were made as the impact of the crisis extended to the middle class that was not previously covered by the social protection system. To do so, in 2020 the government employed both safety net and safety rope programs. While the former was intended for the poor and near-poor, the latter was intended for the more well-off citizens and the poor who were missed out by the safety net programs. In total, around 50% of the country's 270 million population benefited from at least one of the government's transfers and subsidies programs designed to mitigate the impact of the COVID-19 pandemic.

The next section looks at the government's initial attempt to roll out a social safety net at a scale never before seen in the history of the Indonesian welfare system. This dramatic expansion was made possible through the National Economic Recovery Plan (PEN) 2020, which was an emergency budget legislated through the Government Regulation No. 23/2020 on the Implementation of the National Economic Recovery Program. PEN 2020 was intended to fund a series of activities that would reduce the impact of COVID-19 on the economy. Thus, in addition to addressing the health crisis, the government also funded efforts to mitigate the decline of economic activities, especially in the informal sector, which employed 56.50% of Indonesia's workers prior to the pandemic on February 2020, and rose to 59.62% on February 2021 following COVID-19 as people lost their jobs in the formal sector (Statistics Indonesia, 2020, 2021), reflecting the population's increased vulnerability.

The National Economic Recovery Plan (PEN) 2020: Breaking the Fall

In April 2020, following the recognition of COVID-19's potentially catastrophic impact, the government rolled out a Rp700 trillion PEN 2020 (Table 8.2). This equates to roughly more than $50 billion. PEN was a series of programs designed to tackle the health emergency and dampen the impact of COVID-19 on the Indonesian economy. While 14% of PEN 2020 was allocated to health programs, 38% of it was earmarked to fund the social protection system, while the rest (48%) was allotted for micro, small, and medium-sized enterprise (MSME) assistance, corporate financing, as well as ministries/agencies and local government support activities. Additionally, out of the funds allocated for health programs, Rp4.1 trillion (6.5% of the PEN health program allocation) was budgeted to subsidize the poor and vulnerable population's National Health Insurance (JKN) premium. Although only 38% of PEN 2020 was budgeted for social protection, its share amounted to 42% of the actual PEN 2020 spending by December 2020 (Table 8.3).

Throughout 2020, social assistance measures in the PEN became the primary means for the government to support the poor and vulnerable population. In the first quarter of 2020, gross domestic product (GDP) fell by

Table 8.2 National Economic Recovery Plan (PEN) 2020 Budget (IDR billion)

Health	**63.51**	**Economy**	**579.78**
COVID-19 handling	42.52	MSMEs (interest subsidies tax subsidies)	112.44
Healthcare staff incentives	9.55	Social protection	220.39
Death compensation	0.60	Corporate financing	60.73
JKN premium subsidies	4.11	Sectoral ministries/government agencies and local government	66.59
COVID-19 Task Force	3.22	Business incentives (tax breaks)	56.12
Tax incentives	4.05		

COVID-19 = coronavirus disease; JKN = Jaminan Kesehatan Nasional (National Health Insurance); MSMEs = micro, small, and medium-sized enterprises; PEN = National Economic Recovery Plan.
Source: Ministry of Finance (2021).

2.97% from a growth rate of 5.07% in 2019. This drop reflected an economic slowdown across various economic indicators, including sluggish growth in the business sector that employed millions of Indonesians. The Ministry of Manpower (2020) revealed that workers in both the formal and informal sectors were impacted by layoffs and reduced hours. From February to August 2020, unemployment rose from 4.94% to 7.07% (Statistics Indonesia, 2020). What followed was a decline in household consumption and an increase in their likelihood of falling into poverty.

At that time, the Indonesian government recognized that rather than tax incentives, increasing spending for social assistance was the appropriate policy response to the pandemic. Amidst an economic slowdown, tax revenues from commercial and business activities plummeted, which would have made tax incentives ineffective as an engine of growth. On the other hand, social assistance could increase household demand and accelerate economic recovery. Maintaining household consumption was key to slowing down Indonesia's economic contraction, particularly since it comprised 56.81% of the country's total GDP as of March 2019.[8] To mobilize social assistance as a catalyst for economic recovery, the government focused on two things: first, the timely provision and distribution of social assistance; and second, the expansion of social assistance to the middle class.

[8] Calculated using the March 2019 National Socio-economic Survey.

Table 8.3 National Economic Recovery Plan (PEN) 2020 Audited Spending (IDR billion)

Health	**62.67**	**MSME**	**112.26**	**Corporate Incentives**	**58.38**
COVID-19 handling	41.77	Interest Subsidies	2.81	Income tax borne by the government	1.72
Healthcare worker incentives	8.83	Fund placement (including corporate fund placement)	66.75	Import income tax exemption	14
Vaccination handling	0.63	MSME credit guarantee	2.09	Deduction of income tax installments	20.63
COVID-19 Task Force	3.21	Final MSME income taxes borne by the government	0.67	Preliminary VAT refund	7.57
JKN premium subsidies	4.12	Investment financing for the MSME fund management	1.29	Deductions in corporate income tax rates	12.68
Health tax incentives	4.05	Grant for Micro Enterprises (Bantuan President Produktif Usaha Mikro, BPUM)	28.65	Exemption from minimum requirements and from electricity subscription fees	1.69
Death compensation	0.06			Entry fees borne by the government	0.09

continued

Table 8.3 *continued*

Social Protection	**216.59**	**Government Ministry/Agencies and Local Government**	**65.22**
PKH and PKH Rice Assistance	41.94	Cash for Work	19.79
Program Sembako	43.89	Housing Incentives	0.48
Banpres	7.09	Tourism	2.9
Cash Transfers	32.6	Regional Incentives Fund for economic recovery	4.96
Kartu Prakerja	18.25	Physical special allocation fund reserves	7.29
Electricity Subsidies	11.45	Regional Loan	18.76
BLT-DD	23.74	Islamic Boarding School Assistance	2.61
Wage Subsidies	29.48	PEN funding (Ministry of Public Works and Housing)	1.48
Income Support for Contract Teachers (Ministry of Education)	2.94	Workforce pandemic mitigation initiatives	0.53
Income Support for Contract Teachers (Ministry of Religious Affairs)	1.13	Investment opportunity map (The National Investment Coordination Board)	0.08
Internet Quota Subsidies (Ministry of Education)	3.83	Cleric certification and religious civil organization assistance	0.04
Internet Quota Subsidies (Ministry of Religious Affairs)	0.23	Fertilizer Subsidy	3.14
		PEN public communication (The Ministry of Communication and Information)	0.32
		PEN funding (The Ministry of Agrarian Affairs and Spatial Planning/National Land Agency)	0.05
		Certification for Domestic Component Level (Tingkat Komponen Dalam Negeri, TKD)	0.01

Banpres = Bantuan Presiden (Presidential Assistance); BLT-DD = Bantuan Langsung Tunai—Dana Desa (Village Fund Cash Transfers); BST = Bantuan Sosial Tunai (Cash Transfers); COVID-19 = coronavirus disease; JKN = Jaminan Kesehatan Nasional (National Health Insurance); MSMEs = micro, small, and medium-sized enterprises; PEN = National Economic Recovery Plan; PKH = Program Keluarga Harapan (Family Hope Program); VAT = Value-Added Tax
Source: Ministry of Finance (2021).

For the former, the government utilized the distribution channels and disbursement mechanisms of existing social programs. For instance, the government used the existing beneficiary eligibility data and distribution channel of various regular transfer programs like the Program Sembako food voucher. This saw an increase of Program Sembako's benefit value from Rp150,000 to Rp200,000 for six months in 2020 and its expansion from 15.2 million to 20.0 million beneficiary families. The Family Hope Program (*Program Keluarga Harapan*, PKH) saw a similar expansion in coverage—from 9.2 million to 10.0 million beneficiary families—as well as a 25% increase in the value of its transfers for recipients. Meanwhile, the electricity subsidy program was expanded to reach an additional 500,000 households and 1.3 million business subscribers on top of the existing 31.1 million beneficiary families.

In the expansion of both Program Sembako and PKH, the DTKS played a central role in targeting beneficiary families. Under normal circumstances, the existing social assistance programs would reach the poorest 40% of households in Indonesia with the aid of the DTKS. However, the DTKS was last updated in 2015 and is no longer updated. Moreover, the pandemic's impact also stretched beyond the poor. Simply increasing the value of regular transfers would not have been sufficient, since it would still leave many people vulnerable to the pandemic's impact.

With movement restrictions during the pandemic, those holding service and manual labor jobs who did not have the privilege of working remotely were more adversely affected, as they were prone to layoffs or salary cuts. Statistics Indonesia (2020) found that the ratio of people working in the informal sector who lacked work insurance and a pension fund membership went up by 4.59% from August 2019 to August 2020. One reason for this could be women's increased participation in informal labor to supplement falling family incomes. A survey by the SMERU Research Institute[9] found, however, that out of all the people switching jobs amidst the pandemic, half of them moved to the informal sector. This suggests that the increase in informal labor might have been related to a general shift from formal to informal labor rather than simply women entering the labor market and taking up informal work. With the pandemic's widespread economic impact, the government saw the need to expand social assistance beyond the poor.

[9] SMERU et al., 2020.

To both expand social assistance to the middle class and cover the bottom 40% that were missed by the DTKS, the government launched several ad hoc programs in response to the pandemic. These programs were mainly targeted at poor and vulnerable productive-aged individuals and those living in urban areas most impacted by movement restrictions. Of the 1,125,600 people pushed into poverty from March to September 2020, almost 78% (or 876,500 people) of them were located in urban areas.[10] As a part of the 2020 PEN, the government launched the Banpres in-kind food assistance program for 1.9 million poor and vulnerable households in the Greater Jakarta area. Meanwhile, for those in urban areas outside Greater Jakarta, the government launched the Cash Transfers (*Bantuan Sosial Tunai,* BST) program for 9 million low-income families. Moreover, the government also had to resort to alternative measures to reach new beneficiaries, as reliance on the DTKS was insufficient.

To disburse the benefits of these new programs, the government partnered with several state-owned enterprises. For instance, it used Program Sembako's distribution channel and replicated its disbursement mechanism. Under normal circumstances, state-owned banks have the mandate to issue debit cards and top up food vouchers for Program Sembako recipients. In response to COVID-19, state-owned banks were authorized to transfer cash to their account holders who were listed as eligible beneficiaries. Recognizing that not all potential beneficiaries had bank accounts, the government partnered with Pos Indonesia, the national postal company. Until 2017, Pos Indonesia was the government's partner in benefit disbursement for a host of regular social assistance programs. Beneficiary families had to obtain a benefit eligibility card from their local postal service and cash out their transfers there. Changes in the disbursement mechanism for regular transfers saw Pos Indonesia's role scaled back to distributing disaster relief on an ad hoc basis as was during the COVID-19 pandemic.

Another transfer that the government provided for families was the electricity subsidies program. When compared to Banpres and BST, providing electricity subsidies could be considered more feasible since data for potential beneficiaries was already available. Since the National Electricity Company (*Perusahaan Listrik Negara*, PLN) had a list of electricity subscribers, the Indonesian government could easily use this data to administer electricity subsidies during the pandemic. Free electricity bills were supplied for

[10] Statistics Indonesia, 2020b

24 million households who were 450VA electricity subscribers, while a 50% discount on electricity bills were provided for seven million households who were 900VA electricity subscribers. Only those registered in the DTKS were considered eligible to receive this discount. Compared to other COVID-19 response social programs, this electricity discount performed relatively well in targeting beneficiaries since it had the privilege of a pre-existing beneficiary database and relatively simple delivery mechanisms. Initially planned for three months from April to June 2020, this program was later extended to nine months between April and December 2020.

Besides utilizing existing distribution channels, the government recognized that with a projected fall in tax revenue and increased spending for the 2020 PEN, it had to tap into other funding sources to expand social assistance coverage. Although not hit as hard as urban areas, rural areas were also impacted by COVID-19. Reduced remittances from workers in urban areas could negatively impact rural farmers' ability to purchase farming input. Meanwhile, the return to villages of urban workers who lost their jobs could lead to social tension as competition for work in rural areas tightened.[11] When the government found that it was already cash-strapped in its ability to offer protection to the rural population, the Dana Desa (Village Fund) grant became a viable solution.

The Village Fund is an annual grant that the Indonesia central government has provided to villages across Indonesia since 2015. The Village Fund grant was designed to improve community participation in development. By law, local governments have the discretion to spend the grant so long as the money is spent on activities that empower villagers and improve their welfare. As a response to the pandemic, in March 2020 the central government issued a Government Regulation in Lieu of Law that mandated local governments to prioritize the Village Fund for the BLT-DD cash transfer and COVID-19 mitigation programs.[12] Local village governments were tasked with identifying poor households eligible to receive BLT-DD, with priority given to female-headed households and those with older adults or people with disabilities. In practice, village authorities partnered with local COVID-19 task forces and other civil society organizations in villages to identify potential beneficiaries. By doing so, the government managed to shift some of the financial liabilities arising from the assistance program and

[11] Asmanto, Maulana, and Jutarto, 2020; Asmanto, Dewi, et al., 2020.

[12] Asmanto, Maulana, and Jutarto, 2020; Asmanto, Hidayat, et al., 2020; Asmanto, Dewi, et al., 2020.

delegated the task of beneficiary identification and benefit disbursement to local governments.

By December 2020, BLT-DD covered 8 million households in 74,311 villages or 99.14% of Indonesia's 74,953 villages.[13] Of all BLT-DD's beneficiary households, 2,341,750 families or 31% were female-headed households. Additionally, a rapid assessment of the Village Fund grant found that an increase in grants received was related to an increase in the economic activity of villages during the pandemic.[14] This suggests that the Village Fund might have attained its objective of spurring economic growth in villages. However, the same study also noted that this link between the grant and economic activity was stronger in Java and less so in less developed areas of the country. This raises a concern about the possible emergence of a new dimension for socio-economic disparity across regions in Indonesia, as well as the Village Fund's role in attenuating this phenomenon.

Aside from programs aimed at families, the government also launched several initiatives targeted at individuals. In addition to fully subsidizing the JKN premium for 96.4 million subscribers listed in the DTKS, the government also partly subsidized the premium for citizens holding a Class III JKN membership. To support vulnerable workers, the government launched an income-support program for JKN Employment Insurance (BPJS-TK) holders. This assistance was given to 15.7 million workers in the private sector and non-permanent civil servants with salaries under Rp5 million who were registered as active BPJS-TK subscribers. Additionally, a new program dubbed the Wage Subsidies Program (*Bantuan Subsidi Upah*, BSU) was launched to expand social protection coverage to lower middle-income workers. In targeting BSU beneficiaries, the government utilized an existing database of BPJS-TK members to identify workers whose salary fell below a certain eligibility threshold. By the end of 2020, the program covered 12.4 million workers and 2.6 million teachers.

To further support vulnerable productive-aged individuals, the government launched *Kartu Prakerja* in April 2020. Kartu Prakerja was initially designed as a re-skilling and entrepreneurship training program aimed at job seekers, workers who had lost their jobs, and workers who needed general re-skilling. It also included people working in the MSME sector. However,

[13] Coordinating Ministry for Human Development and Cultural Affairs, 2020.
[14] Dartanto et al., 2021.

it soon came under intense public criticism in the mass media, since the program would not have been effective amidst an economic slowdown and contracting job market.[15] Additionally, the Indonesian Corruption Eradication Commission called for an evaluation of Kartu Prakerja because of alleged mismanagement.[16] In response to the criticism, the government soon transformed Kartu Prakerja into a hybrid between a re-skilling and an income-support program. As of December 2020, Kartu Prakerja had 5.5 million individual beneficiaries—with 82% of them unemployed at the time of the training. Of those beneficiaries holding employment at the time of the training, 78% were in the informal sector. By excluding people in the DTKS who were already covered as Program Sembako recipients—along with offering JKN Class III premium discounts to families beyond the DTKS—the government attempted to broaden the benefit coverage beyond those in the poorest 40% of families.

Beyond supporting productive-aged individuals, with the COVID-19 pandemic causing school closures and forcing teaching activities online, the government also launched transfers in the education sector. Since this distance learning required internet-based digital platforms, families needed to spend more on internet expenses amidst the economic pressures from the COVID-19 pandemic. Hence, the government launched the Internet Quota Assistance for students from preschool to university, as well as their teaching instructors. Through this program, free internet credits were given out. In 2020, 60.1 million people benefited from the program between September and December 2020.

The extensive coverage of the welfare programs rolled out by the government in the 2020 PEN played a key role in slowing down Indonesia's economic contraction amidst a global shock. In 2020, Indonesia managed to keep its GDP contraction at −2.07%, which was well below the global average of −3.50% and the emerging market and developing economies' average of −2.45%.[17] Despite this success, the government could not afford to be complacent—particularly given that high spending on stimulus and aid, combined with low tax revenue as in the 2020 PEN, was untenable in the long run. With the pandemic still ongoing beyond 2020, the government had to "restart the economic engine" and prevent lasting damage.

[15] Assariy, 2020; Rizal, 2020.
[16] Komisi Pemberantasan Korupsi, 2020.
[17] International Monetary Fund, 2020.

The PEN 2021: A Way to Recovery

As the pandemic extended beyond 2020, the Indonesian government continued many social protection programs under PEN 2020 while discontinuing the rest. This decision was in line with PEN 2021's focus on economic recovery and a vaccine rollout in hopes for a swift return to normalcy. Thus, PEN 2021's budget was scaled back for social assistance and social safety nets and increased for business stimulus, which also included micro, small, and medium enterprise and corporate support programs. In this budget, social protection amounted to 23% of the budget—which was nearly half of its ratio under PEN 2020—while MSME and corporate support and health amounted to 26% and 25% of the budget respectively (Table 8.4). This budget reflected the government's priorities to support businesses and push for widespread vaccination as the country's recovery strategy.

Considering the moderately successful COVID-19 containment and the slowly improving economic conditions by the end of 2020, the government was optimistic about recovery in 2021. In 2021, the government's primary strategy for accelerating socio-economic recovery focused on continuing intensified health measures, mobilizing social protection systems in response to the pandemic's dynamics, and ensuring business continuity. To do so, the PEN program was continued in 2021 to accelerate economic recovery.

As the citizens were faced with slow economic growth during the COVID-19 pandemic, the government launched several incentives and programs to accelerate their economic recovery. Indonesian MSMEs account for nearly 97% of domestic employment and 56% of total business investment in the country.[18] Given the large amount of vulnerable labor working in the MSME sector, the government has provided a range of support for MSMEs since 2020. These support programs include the postponement of credit repayment installments, credit restructuring, incentives for interest subsidies, and the government taking the role of guarantor for MSMEs seeking financing. For MSMEs that were already liable to pay taxes, the government provided tax deductions. Finally, for MSMEs that were not yet eligible to access financing, the government provided opportunities for them to receive a Micro Business Productive Assistance (*Bantuan Produktif Usaha Mikro*, BPUM)

[18] Ministry of Co-operatives and SMEs, 2018.

Table 8.4 National Economic Recovery Plan (PEN) 2021 Budget (IDR billion)

Health	**176.32**	**Business incentives**	**58.47**
Diagnostics for testing and tracing	9.91	Income tax borne by the government	5.78
Therapeutics for care, self-isolation, healthcare personnel incentives, and medications	61.94	Final income tax for MSMEs borne by the government	0.84
Vaccination for herd immunity	58.18	Sales tax on vehicles borne by the government	2.99
Laboratory research on COVID-19 vaccination	0.67	Import duties borne by the government	0.49
COVID-19 Task Force	0.53	Income tax on housing borne by the government	4.62
Communication and campaign for health and safety protocol and vaccination	1.18	Import income tax exemption	13.08
JKN premium subsidies	2.43	Deduction of income tax installments	19.71
Healthcare and laboratory supplies	1.3	Preliminary VAT refund	4.43
Health tax incentives	18.61	Decrease in corporate income tax rates	6.53
Regular vaccination backup	3.71	VAT not collected for the ease of import for export purposes	0.004
Other health measures to strengthen local COVID-19 handling	14.86		
Budget for preventive programs	3		

Social protection system	**157.41**	**Priority programs**	**122.42**	**MSME and corporate support**	**184.83**
PKH for 10 million beneficiary families	28.71	Ministry/ Government Agency Labor-Intensive Program	27.33	Interest subsidy for MSME credit for 17.8 million MSMEs	31.95
Program Sembako (Food Voucher) for 18.8 million beneficiary families	45.12	Tourism (ecotourism and human resources training)	8.66	Grant for 12.8 million businesses valued at Rp1.2 million	15.36

continued

Table 8.4 *continued*

Social protection system	**157.41**	**Priority programs**	**122.42**	**MSME and corporate support**	**184.83**
Cash transfer for 10 million beneficiary families valued at Rp300,000 month	12	Food security (food estate and irrigation)	47.1	MSME and corporation guarantee fees	8.51
Kartu Prakerja (Pre-Employment Card)	20	Information technology (social registry updating)	16.55	MSME Rp62 trillion guarantee fees for guaranteed credit targets	4.76
Electricity subsidy for 31.4 million households	5.64	Industrial estate for the development of strategic areas	11.22	Corporate Rp66 trillion guarantee fees for guaranteed credit targets	3.75
Village fund cash transfer for 8 million beneficiary families valued at Rp300,000 month	14.4	Local loan facilities	10	Loss limit guarantee for MSMEs and Corporations	2
Internet credit subsidies, 20 GB (kindergarten), 35 GB (elementary–high school), 50 GB (university)	7.79	Other priority programs (local loan interest subsidies)	1.47	Exemption from administrative checks, burden fees, and subscriptions for a 3-month extension (January–March)	1.27
Insurance subsidies (Job Creation Act No. 11/2020)	1.55			Equity for six state-owned enterprises, Indonesian Export Financing Institution, and Sovereign Wealth Fund	58.76
Cash assistance reserve	22.2			Funds for bank credit restructuring	66.99

COVID-19 = coronavirus disease; GB = gigabyte; JKN = *Jaminan Kesehatan Nasional* (National Health Insurance); MSMEs = micro, small, and medium-sized enterprises; PKH = *Program Keluarga Harapan* (Family Hope Program) cash transfer; VAT = value-added tax
Source: Ministry of Finance (2021).

grant that could be utilized for business capital. These programs designed to support MSMEs were continued under the 2021 PEN.

In addition to supporting MSMEs, the government was working to accelerate spending to boost economic growth through job creation. Labor-intensive programs that were able to employ vulnerable and poor people were the main pillars in this effort. In the 2021 PEN, various ministries and state agencies proposed a host of programs valued at up to Rp123.8 trillion. This included labor-intensive programs under the Ministry of Public Works and Public Housing, the Ministry of Transportation, the Ministry of Agriculture, the Ministry of Energy and Mineral Resources, and the Ministry of Marine Affairs and Fisheries. Furthermore, the Ministry of Village Development of Disadvantaged Regions and Transmigration had also shifted the priority of the use of Village Funds from BLT-DD to finance the Labor-Intensive Village Grant (*Padat Karya Tunai Desa,* PKTD) focused on job creation. This program mix reflected a shift in the PEN's strategic direction, from dampening the impact of the crisis by maintaining household consumption levels to hastening economic recovery by fostering productivity.

Although several social protection programs were continued to protect the poorest 40% of households beyond 2020, additional programs related to COVID-19 were phased out. Aside from regular transfers, such as PKH and Program Sembako, only four programs launched in 2020 continued in 2021, which were BST, Electricity Subsidies, Internet Quota Assistance, and BLT-DD. While Kartu Prakerja was continued, its program design was gradually reverted to its full-training form instead of a hybrid between training and social assistance. To ensure a smooth recovery, the government continued to provide BST for four months and the Electricity Subsidies for nine months. Additionally, the Internet Quota Assistance was still offered for the first semester of the school year in 2021. The BLT-DD was also still provided with a more modest target of 11 million families, as many of its beneficiaries were covered under the BST program in 2021. In 2022, the Village Fund was returned to its original design, which reserves local governments the right to decide how funds are used for village development programs instead of having to allocate a part of it to fund BLT-DD.

Despite expectations for recovery in 2021, the pandemic proved to be persistent. In July 2021, the Delta variant broke, which resulted in a severe second COVID-19 wave in the country. To respond to Delta's emergence, the government implemented another social restriction in July 2021, which came with an expectation of another welfare shock similar to the previous year's mobility restrictions. To mitigate this shock, the government provided a top-up of 10 kg rice to 28.8 million Program Sembako and BST beneficiaries between July and August 2021. Additionally, the duration of the BST, Electricity Subsidies, and the Internet Quota Assistance were also extended until the end of the year, while Kartu Prakerja was expanded to cover an additional 336,000 beneficiaries beyond the existing 5.6 million beneficiaries. The government also continued the Wage Subsidy program for 8.4 million workers in regions facing government mandated mobility restrictions. However, instead of a continued transfer, under PEN 2021 the program was a one-time transfer. Finally, to accelerate the disbursement of BLT-DD, the government relaxed the program's targeting criteria and gave more authority to village governments to determine eligible benefit recipients.

Due to the expanded social protection as a response to the second COVID-19 wave, the actual PEN 2021 spending for COVID-19 ballooned from IDR 122.42 T to IDR 186.64 T, reflecting an increase of approximately 52.5% (see Table 8.5). On the other hand, spending for MSME and corporate support fell below its budgeted amount by 12%. Part of the issue with poor budget realization was that programs for MSMEs under the PEN were mainly cost-deferral in nature and could only be accessed by MSMEs who already received loans from banks and were already paying taxes. In other words, these assistance programs could only be accessed by formally registered MSMEs, despite the fact that informal micro businesses were more numerous. Aside from their largely informal nature, micro businesses are usually formed by low-income families as a subsistence mechanism.[19] Where low-income families faced difficulties to generate income in both formal and informal markets, they would resort to government assistance to survive, especially during the pandemic. This further highlights the importance of the social protection system in normal times, and more so amidst welfare shocks.

Lessons Learned from Indonesia's COVID-19 Response

During the pandemic, Indonesia managed to defy predictions on the severity of its poverty rate growth. A study by Suryahadi, Al Izzati, and Yumna (2021) estimated growth incidence curves—defined as per capita household

[19] Syarifah, 2022.

Table 8.5 National Economic Recovery Plan (PEN) 2021 Spending (IDR billion)

Health	**214.96**	**Social Protection**	**186.64**	**Business Incentives**	**62.83**
Diagnostics for testing and tracing	4.5	PKH	28.31	Income tax borne by the government	5.16
Therapeutic	87	Program Sembako	48.69	Final income tax for MSMEs borne by the government	1.42
Vaccination	57.75	BST	17.46	Sales tax on vehicles borne by the government	3.46
Research and Communication	1.17	Kartu Prakerja	21.2	Import duties borne by the government	0.49
Mobility Restrictions	0.79	Electricity Subsidy	5.64	Income tax on housing borne by the government	3.31
COVID-19 Laboratory Facilities	1.6	BLT-DD	28.8	Import income tax exemption	13.35
JKN premium subsidies	2.43	Internet Credit Assistance	8.53	Deduction of income tax installments	20.49
Health Related Transfers to Villages	32.61	Work Insurance Subsidies (Jaminan Kehilangan Pekerjaan, JKP)	1.55	Preliminary VAT refund	6.48
Health tax incentives	20.85	In-Kind Rice Assistance	22.2	Deductions in corporate income tax rates	6.53
The Indonesian Disaster Management Board	1.99	Mobility Restrictions Related Food Assistance	7.08	VAT not collected for the ease of import for export purposes	0.004

continued

Table 8.5 *continued*

Health	**214.96**	**Social Protection**	**186.64**	**Business Incentives**	**62.83**
Tracing	3.3	Wage Subsidies	8.8	VAT borne by the government outlet rent	1.18
		Educational Assistance	3.14	Final income tax for constructions services	0.07
				Government borne tax carry over from 2020	0.88

Priority Programs	**117.94**	**MSME and Corporate Support**	**162.4**
Cash for work	37.37	Interest subsidy for MSME credit	42.17
Tourism (ecotourism and human resources training)	7.67	Grant for micro enterprises (Bantuan Presiden Produktif Usaha Mikro, BPUM)	15.36
Food security (food estate and irrigation)	33.1	Loss limit guarantee for MSMEs and Corporations	2
Information technology (social registry updating)	16.66	Exemption from administrative checks, burden fees, and subscription fees	2.11
Industrial estate	10.54	Equity for six state-owned enterprises	63.66
Creative economy support	2.4	Street vendor assistance	1.2
Regional loan facilities	10	Loan services fee for MSME and corporations	5.66
Other priority programs (local loan interest subsidies)	1.47		

BLT-DD = Bantuan Langsung Tunai—Dana Desa (Village Fund Cash Transfers); BST = Bantuan Sosial Tunai (Cash Transfers); COVID-19 = coronavirus disease; JKN = Jaminan Kesehatan Nasional (National Health Insurance); MSMEs = micro, small, and medium-sized enterprises; PEN = National Economic Recovery Plan; PKH = Program Keluarga Harapan (Family Hope Program); VAT = Value-Added Tax

Source: Ministry of Finance (2021).

expenditure between September 2019 and September 2020—for each percentile of the expenditure distribution. The study found that without the benefits from the government's social protection programs, expenditure growth would have been lower. This was especially true for households at the lower end of the expenditure levels. Wright et al.'s (2021) findings using a micro-simulation method also corroborated this finding. Overall, these reports find that social protection programs were able to limit the increase of poverty rate in Indonesia. Yet there is still room for improvement if Indonesia is to fully be prepared to weather future storms, such as crises, pandemics, disasters, or other inevitable events.

Although the Indonesian welfare system has been used to moderate shocks on a number of occasions since the 1997–1998 Asian financial crisis, even until it was mobilized as a COVID-19 pandemic mitigation strategy in 2020, it remained largely ad hoc in nature. Since shocks like natural disasters, economic crises, or pandemics are bound to happen again in the future, Indonesia needs to institutionalize social safety net and rope programs under its social protection system. While the regular social assistance and contributory social insurance elements of the Indonesian social protection system are largely legitimized by various laws and regulations, the social safety nets and ropes are largely ad hoc and only rolled out once the need arises. What this means is that there are no regulations on what they entail, when they can be activated, and who is responsible for implementing them, nor are there clearly defined budgetary plans. As a result, it may take a while for programs to kick in and reach their intended targets. These issues defeat the programs' purpose in timely mitigating unexpected shocks. Moreover, with a lack of clearly delineated budget structures or regulations, social safety nets could be politicized at the government's whim. For instance, early in the pandemic, the Banpres assistance was criticized for prominently featuring the presidential office's logo, which raised concerns about whether the assistance was a political move. Worsening matters, the Ministry of Social Affairs, at that time in charge of COVID-19 assistance, was found to be involved in graft.

Another repercussion of the lack of regulatory framework for the Indonesian social protection system for disaster mitigation was also a lack of suitable infrastructure to respond to sudden shocks on a large share of the population. Many regular programs existed prior to COVID-19, such as PKH and Program Sembako, and their infrastructure could be mobilized during the pandemic—but scaling up the programs proved to be the more challenging task. As the PKH and Program Sembako used the DTKS for targeting, their ability to be scaled up hinged upon the DTKS's quality as their targeting instrument. However, the DTKS was last updated at a large scale in 2015, and thus in 2020 no longer reflected people's moves in and out of poverty. An analysis conducted by TNP2K of the February 2019 DTKS data found that 93% of the entries in the DTKS had not been updated since 2015.[20] Moreover, the pandemic had pushed many below the poverty line, further compromising the DTKS's accuracy. As a result, in March 2021 only 36.59% of the poorest 40% families received either Program Sembako or PKH.[21] Thus, local governments needed to rely on alternative targeting mechanisms, such as community targeting and social worker mobilization under time pressures. These pressures strained local governments' resources and jeopardized many people's health and safety amidst a global pandemic.

Although through PEN 2020 and PEN 2021 the government expanded the coverage of the Indonesian social protection system beyond the poor, such coverage for the middle class was intended to be temporary. To ensure that the Indonesian social protection system is prepared to take on sudden shocks in the future, a social registry that contains not only the poor is needed. Social registries are information systems that could support the outreach, intake, registration, and determination of potential eligibility for one or more social programs, usually in the form of a database. This would in practice be similar to the already existing DTKS, but it would have a much broader coverage, dynamic data updating mechanism, and possibly interoperability with other government databases that could not only help keep the entries up to date but also expand the database's usability beyond a handful of social programs. Coverage beyond the poorest 40% of families in the country would cover not just the poor but also the middle class. This would help ensure that safety nets or ropes could be quickly and accurately deployed in times of need.

Aside from the much-needed coverage for the middle class, some vulnerable populations were still overlooked in the design and implementation of the Indonesian social protection system. With reduced physical capacity, the ability of people with disabilities and the elderly to generate income is diminished. Thus, it was not surprising that by 2018, the highest rates of poverty were among people over 60, and even higher among people over 80.[22] Due to

[20] Data analysis conducted by TNP2K on August 2021 using data from the Ministry of Social Affairs' Center for Data and Information.

[21] Analyzed using the March 2021 National Socio-economic Survey.

[22] TNP2K, 2018.

their higher tendency to fall into poverty, the elderly should be prioritized by the social protection system. Similarly, the lives of people with disabilities are challenging given the high costs of care and medical services. Moreover, if their caregivers need to give up work or reduce their working hours, this may result in a diminished income for the household. Despite these challenges, most people with disabilities have very limited access to social assistance programs, and during the pandemic they were not yet prioritized to receive benefits. Although the elderly and people with disabilities received benefits through regular PKH and Program Sembako, the two programs' efficacy in supporting these populations was limited due to benefit sufficiency issues. To make sure the Indonesian social protection system is inclusive, it should ensure that no one is left behind. This makes accurate data more pressing, as it is key not only for identifying low-income households deemed eligible for program benefits but also marginalized people who are facing heightened risks and vulnerabilities.

Beyond issues with data, benefit sufficiency was also an issue. Assuming that the benefit incidence of the social assistance program in each income group did not change since March 2019, the proportion of assistance received by the poorest 10% of households would, on average, account for 11.35% of their total household expenditure. This proportion decreases as families move up the welfare ladder. However, in general, the value of assistance being offered by the government has not been proportionally distributed. An analysis found that families receiving COVID-19 ad hoc assistance programs in the form of the BST and electricity discount had a greater proportion of their expenditure covered by government assistance than the less well-off families receiving regular assistance such as PKH and Program Sembako.[23] On average, the more well-off families entitled to ad hoc assistance received aid that amounted to 21.30% of their monthly household expenses. Meanwhile, the less well-off households receiving regular programs—such as PKH, Smart Indonesia Program (PIP) school assistance, Program Sembako, and the electricity discount—received benefits that only covered 16.95% of their total monthly expenditure. Consequently, this raises a concern of fairness in benefit disbursement in the 2020 PEN.

Finally, an expansion of the Indonesian social system would imply an increased level of investment. In 2020, Indonesia's total expenditure on social protection—excluding health—amounted to 1.3% of the GDP.

[23] Asmanto, Hidayat, et al., 2020.

This included expenditure on services and transfers provided to individual persons and households and expenditure on services provided on a collective basis.[24] This figure is much lower when compared to other countries in the Asia Pacific region that spent on average 7.5% of their GDP on social protection. However, an increase in social welfare spending needs to be done carefully.

Moving forward, Indonesia needs to shift from broad-based and regressive subsidies, such as fuel subsidies, toward more targeted social programs. Targeted programs are not only more efficient but also align with the principles of justice, ensuring that only those in need benefit from these programs while the more well-off contribute more to the system—either through taxes or premiums. Finally, a shift toward more targeted programs also means that the government could free up more fiscal space to invest in a more sustainable and equitable social protection system. This investment needs to be combined with more effective and efficient program implementation through improved program management, accurate program targeting, broad social protection coverage, as well as rigorous program monitoring and evaluation to identify further areas for improvement.

Weathering Future Storms

Indonesia's social protection system has proven to be critical in cushioning the impact of the COVID-19 pandemic on people's welfare. The extensive breadth and coverage of the welfare programs rolled out by the Indonesian government in both the 2020 and 2021 PEN played a key role in keeping Indonesia's poverty rate down. Despite this success, the Indonesian government cannot afford to be too complacent, particularly given that high spending on stimulus and aid combined with low tax revenue, as in the 2020 PEN, is untenable in the long run. With the pandemic still ongoing beyond 2020, the Indonesian government launched PEN 2021 to hasten economic recovery. In PEN 2021, many programs that previously covered the middle class were scaled back. However, as the pandemic has shown, like the poor, the middle class are also prone to experiencing welfare shocks but are lacking social safety ropes that could break their fall. This raises a question on how Indonesia could build back the economy with a strong social protection

[24] ILO, 2022.

system as its foundation. Furthermore, this social protection system needs to be one that is prepared to take on more sudden and widespread shocks like the COVID-19 pandemic. In short, the COVID-19 pandemic has amplified the need for a robust social protection system to protect the people not just under normal circumstances, but also in crisis.

Over the years, Indonesia has built a social protection system infrastructure. Moreover, since the 1997–1998 Asian financial crisis, Indonesia has mobilized its social protection system to cushion both externally triggered welfare shocks and internal welfare shocks due to policy changes. Thus, when the pandemic hit, the Indonesian government could swiftly mobilize this infrastructure and learn from its past experience to expand existing programs and launch new programs to mitigate COVID-19's socio-economic impact. Although an increase in the country's poverty rate could be limited, COVID-19 has revealed cracks in the Indonesian social protection system. From insufficient coverage, poor data quality that hampered targeting accuracy, to issues with social inclusion. Indonesia still has a long way to go. There is still much for Indonesia to do in building a social protection system that can truly protect the country's citizens from welfare shocks.

9

Redrawing the Poverty Line

Poverty has long been a central political issue in Indonesia, but how it is measured and what officially counts as poverty has often been overlooked. The 1997–1998 Asian financial crisis, which catapulted the poverty rate from 17.47% in 1996 to 24.2% in 1998, eroded public trust in the government. In the years that followed, poverty alleviation became a rallying cry for politicians seeking popular support. Yet, amid these debates, the construction of the poverty line—how poverty itself was defined and counted—remained largely absent from policy discussions. This chapter explores how the choice of where to draw the poverty line shapes our understanding of poverty and, in turn, the policies designed to address it.

In response to the crisis, Indonesia introduced social safety net programs such as subsidized rice, educational block grants, and healthcare, which laid the groundwork for future social assistance. Social protection spending grew significantly in the following decades, peaking at 30% of government spending between 2012 and 2014 before fuel subsidies were scaled back due to their regressive nature (see Chapter 2). From 2015 to 2022, social protection allocations averaged 19.5% of the central government's budget, shifting focus from broad energy subsidies to targeted assistance for the poor and vulnerable. While energy subsidies resurged after the COVID-19 pandemic, reforms aimed to direct them toward those most in need. Throughout these shifts, the poverty rate became the primary benchmark for justifying social protection spending, shaping both budget priorities and policy design. Yet, while debates over spending and policy are frequent in public and political discourse, the question of how poverty itself is measured remains largely overlooked.

Statistics Indonesia is the key government agency mandated to calculate poverty numbers and collect various socio-economic figures. It first calculated the poverty rate under Suharto's authoritarian government. Poverty numbers were first released in 1984 to cover the years 1976–1981 using the

Evidence and the Politics of Reform. Sudarno Sumarto, Oxford University Press.
 DOI: 10.1093/9780197831717.003.0010

National Socio-economic Survey.[1] Since then, poverty numbers have been calculated using the same survey every three years. Although poverty numbers had always been calculated at the provincial, urban, rural, and eventually national levels, Statistics Indonesia only began officially publishing the provincial poverty figures in 1993.

With a highly bureaucratic and non-partisan government agency shouldering the mandate to calculate the poverty numbers, the technical aspects of how these numbers are calculated rarely feature in public discussions or popular political discourse. Indonesian law prescribes "bureaucratic neutrality," which refers to how civil servants—including those within Statistics Indonesia—must prioritize public service provisions that remain insulated from political forces. Bureaucratic neutrality is important to ensure that the government can provide services to the citizens effectively and efficiently. Although the law still does not guarantee bureaucratic neutrality, since many bureaucratic positions are occupied by officials or appointees from the ruling party, Statistics Indonesia's highly technical work, as well as its specific scope of work, have so far insulated its role from political appointments. Moreover, although the mass media often reports on the trend of poverty numbers as a proxy for the government's policy success or to gauge the economic climate, these discussions rarely get technical. This changed when President Joko Widodo set a goal to eliminate extreme poverty by the end of his term in 2024, and technical discussions of the poverty line entered the public discourse for a brief moment.

In 2021, Indonesia's extreme poverty rate, as calculated by the World Bank, stood at 2.16%—far lower than the national poverty rate of 10.14% reported by Statistics Indonesia.[2] This stark contrast sparked public debate, with media, opposition parties, and the public questioning the reliability of Statistics Indonesia's methodology. At its core, the discrepancy stemmed from differences in purpose and approach. The World Bank's poverty line is designed for cross-country comparisons, relying on purchasing power parity (PPP) adjustments, which come with well-documented limitations—including

[1] Sutanto and Avenzora, 1999.

[2] The World Bank's International Poverty Line Project calculates a global extreme poverty line that allows for a poverty rate comparison across time and place. Although the World Bank came up with different poverty lines following an update to their calculation method in 2018, the Government of Indonesia referred to the World Bank's poverty line calculated with the 2015 method. Using the 2015 method, the World Bank calculated poverty lines at different thresholds with the "extreme poverty line" referring to the poverty line at \$1.9 purchasing power parity (PPP) with 2011 as a base year.

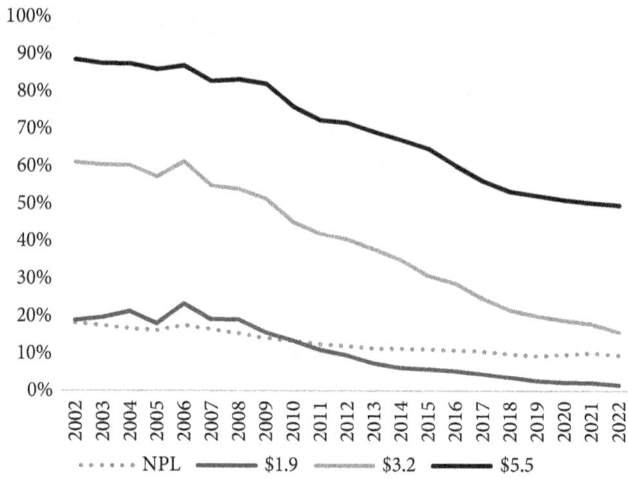

Figure 9.1 Poverty Headcount Rates Using $1.90, $3.20, and $5.50 per-day 2011 PPP and the Indonesian National Poverty Line (NPL)

Note: The World Bank calculates poverty lines at different thresholds. Extreme poverty refers to the poverty line at $1.9 purchasing power parity (PPP) with 2011 as a base year. Although the World Bank came up with different poverty lines following an update to their calculation method in 2018, the Government of Indonesia referred to the World Bank's poverty line calculated with the 2015 method.

Source: Statistics Indonesia, 2023; World Bank, 2022.

price distortions and differences in consumption patterns across countries. In contrast, Statistics Indonesia defines poverty based on the cost of meeting basic needs within the country, making it more relevant for national policy decisions. Even the World Bank itself acknowledges that domestic poverty lines are more appropriate for tracking poverty within a country.[3] Within policymaking circles, this debate was not new. For years, questions have been raised about whether Indonesia's poverty measurement fully captures economic hardship, particularly since World Bank estimates have declined more steeply than official national figures (see Figure 9.1). As part of this ongoing discussion, I have contributed in my capacity as chairman of the Indonesian Statistical Community Forum (FMS), an independent body of scholars who provide input to Statistics Indonesia.

Within the two decades between 2002 and 2022, using the World Bank's calculation method, Indonesia's extreme poverty rate fell from 18.99% to 1.52%, a 17.47 percentage points decrease. However, within the same period,

[3] World Bank, 2022.

the national poverty rate fell from 18.20% to 9.54% using Statistics Indonesia's poverty line. This was a mere 8.66 percentage points fall, or nearly half the decrease when using the World Bank's method. While the World Bank's poverty lines have shown a more dramatic change in poverty over time, Statistics Indonesia's poverty line made it seem -as though not much happened to the poverty rate within the same time span. This was, however, not the first time that policymakers and scholars had noticed these trends.

In 2007, BAPPENAS, Indonesia's national development planning agency, described poverty reduction like chasing a kite—no matter how fast one runs, the kite always stays just out of reach. This reflects a fundamental challenge: the way poverty is measured affects how progress is seen. The World Bank, for instance, sets a single poverty line for global comparisons, using a standard based on the poorest countries and adjusting for differences in living costs across nations. This method ensures consistency but has its flaws, as it relies on international price comparisons that may not fully reflect the reality of poor households, especially in rural areas. In contrast, Statistics Indonesia defines poverty based on what households in Indonesia actually need to meet basic living standards. This makes it more relevant for national policymaking but also means the poverty line shifts over time as people's spending habits change. As a result, even when incomes rise, the poverty line may also rise, making it feel like poverty reduction is a moving target. For BAPPENAS, this raised concerns about whether poverty could ever truly be "solved" or if the **goalpost** would always keep shifting.

BAPPENAS's criticism in 2007 sparked a debate about how Indonesia measures poverty, drawing in Statistics Indonesia and the FMS. The World Bank soon joined the discussion, organizing workshops to explore possible updates to the poverty calculation method. By 2017, the push for reform gained international support. Scholars like the late Martin Ravallion endorsed the effort, and the Australian government provided financial and technical assistance through its Knowledge Sector Initiative, which aimed to improve the use of research in policymaking. The conversation continued until 2021, when BAPPENAS took a major step by drafting an academic paper to support a bill proposing changes to Statistics Indonesia's poverty measurement. This was the closest the debate had come to shaping actual legislation. However, as the country was still recovering from the COVID-19 pandemic and budget priorities shifted, the plan was put on hold.

The 14 years between 2007, when discussions about revising Indonesia's poverty line first began, and 2021, when the plan was set aside, were marked by periods of progress and stagnation. While the idea had strong backing from multilateral organizations, academics, and key government bodies like BAPPENAS and TNP2K, the political will to push the change through was often lacking. Ultimately, how poverty is measured is a deliberate choice by the state—one that carries real policy consequences. Different actors had different visions of how poverty should be "seen," and that ongoing tension often stood in the way of reform.

The Mechanics of "Seeing" Poverty

Determining the poverty rate and counting the number of people in poverty may seem simple. It entails drawing a "poverty line" where people above it are considered non-poor and people below it are considered poor. However, this simplicity is deceptive, as determining where to draw the line is a delicate task. This is especially true since the way we compute the poverty line has implications on policymaking.

Defining a poverty line reduces a complex social reality into a single number, making it easier for the government to design policies and allocate budgets. Despite its importance, the process of setting these standards often goes unquestioned. Even if we agree that the poverty line should be based on the cost of meeting basic nutritional needs and essential non-food items, difficult questions remain: What level of nutrition is considered adequate? Which goods and services should be included? There is no single correct answer, as poverty is a deeply complex issue. However, any method for measuring it should be grounded in the realities of those experiencing poverty, internally consistent, based on a well-reasoned social standard, estimated using a sufficiently large sample, and calculated with statistical rigor.[4]

Statistics Indonesia estimates poverty using data from the National Socioeconomic Survey, a nationally representative sample survey conducted since 1963. The survey consists of a core questionnaire, which is asked in every round, and additional modules that vary over time.[5] In the early years, the core survey included only five questions: four on demographics and one on education. However, in 1992, Statistics Indonesia expanded it to

[4] Pradhan et al., 2001.
[5] Priebe, 2014.

include questions on household consumption, enabling the agency to track poverty levels more consistently and publish poverty figures after each survey round.[6]

Statistics Indonesia takes an expenditure approach to calculating poverty. This means that the poverty rate is calculated using the amount of money people spend to fulfill basic needs. To determine this, it sets a poverty line, which is the minimum amount of money required for daily living, by calculating the cost of a "basket" of essential goods and services. Households whose spending falls below this threshold are considered to be living in poverty. This poverty line consists of two components: a food basket and a non-food basket. The food basket includes 52 items, ranging from staples like rice and protein to snacks and ready-made meals. These items are selected to meet a daily intake of 2,100 calories per person, a standard set by Indonesia's 1998 National Workshop on Food and Nutrition.[7] This calorie threshold represents the minimum energy required for an individual to maintain basic physical activity. Beyond food, the poverty line also accounts for other necessities through the non-food basket, which includes essential expenses such as schooling, clothing, and transportation. These non-food components reflect the broader costs of living and ensure that poverty measurement captures not just survival needs but also the basic requirements for social and economic participation. By incorporating both food and non-food expenses, this approach aims to provide a more comprehensive picture of poverty in Indonesia.

To determine the poverty line, Statistics Indonesia examines the spending patterns of a reference population which includes the 20% of people living just above a temporary poverty threshold. This threshold is updated each year to account for inflation. While this method ensures the poverty line reflects real-life consumption patterns, it also means that the poverty line shifts over time as the reference population changes. As a result, poverty rates calculated using this approach are not always directly comparable year to year. This is why Indonesia's poverty measure is described as "weakly absolute," which adapts to economic conditions rather than being based on a fixed standard.

[6] Statistics Indonesia usually runs two National Socio-economic Survey rounds annually in March and September. Although run twice a year, its September sample is much smaller than its March sample. Although poverty rates could then be determined twice annually, the poverty line is calculated using its March survey results.

[7] Adji et al., 2020.

Indonesia's approach to calculating poverty has faced several criticisms, particularly regarding its consistency and accuracy. A well-designed poverty measure should allow for comparisons over time (temporal consistency) and across regions (spatial consistency), but Indonesia's method struggles with both. The reference population used to determine the poverty line changes frequently, making it difficult to track poverty trends over time. At the same time, using average commodity prices to set regional poverty lines can distort comparisons between provinces. To address these issues, Statistics Indonesia could use median prices instead of averages to reduce distortions from extreme price fluctuations. Additionally, rather than adjusting the consumption bundle every year, adopting a fixed set of goods and services from a base year could enhance stability and comparability.

Another challenge is whether the survey sample is large enough to produce reliable poverty estimates. Unlike many countries that use a single national poverty line, Indonesia has 76 different poverty lines: one for urban and rural areas in each of its 38 provinces. The complexity doesn't stop there: each of Indonesia's 520+ districts and municipalities also has its own poverty threshold. While this level of detail captures regional differences, it comes at the cost of consistency and precision. The more poverty lines there are, the harder it is to ensure reliable comparisons. The small sample sizes in some areas make matters worse, as certain commodities may not be widely consumed in every region, further complicating calculations. Even with 345,000 surveyed households in the March round of the National Socio-economic Survey, the sample may still be too small to generate robust estimates across all regions.

Beyond sample size, the poverty line itself needs to better reflect how the poor actually live. Currently, Statistics Indonesia selects a reference group that includes people who live above the poverty line, rather than focusing on the poor and near-poor. This skews the poverty calculation, making it less representative. Additionally, the items that make up the food and non-food baskets need updating. Since 1998, Indonesia's consumption patterns have changed significantly (see Table 9.1). The share of food in household spending has dropped by 12 percentage points, while ready-made food consumption has increased by 11 percentage points. At the same time, grain consumption has declined, yet the poverty calculation still relies heavily on outdated assumptions. Even tobacco is counted as part of food expenditure, despite contributing nothing to actual nutrition. Meanwhile, the non-food basket is based on a 2004 survey and no longer reflects modern necessities.

Table 9.1 Average Expenditure Per Capita Per Month (1998 and 2019)

Category	1998	2019	Change (%)
Food:			
- Grains	15.61	5.57	−10.04
- Tubers	1.00	0.51	−0.49
- Fish	5.51	3.89	−1.62
- Meat	3.67	2.13	−1.54
- Eggs and milk	3.74	2.78	−0.96
- Vegetables	4.09	3.25	−0.84
- Beans and nuts	2.60	0.97	−1.63
- Fruits	2.80	2.36	−0.44
- Oil and fat	3.52	1.13	−2.39
- Drinks	3.74	1.44	−2.3
- Spices	1.94	0.93	−1.01
- Others	1.48	0.86	−0.62
- Ready-made food	6.19	17.26	11.07
- Tobacco and betel	5.38	6.05	0.67
Total Food	61.33	49.14	−12.14
Non-Food:			
- Housing	18.42	25.49	7.07
- Other goods and services	12.00	12.40	0.4
- Clothing, shoes, and head covering	4.29	3.03	−1.26
- Durable goods	3.17	5.04	1.87
Taxes and insurance	1.16	3.01	1.85
- Ceremonial expenses	1.45	1.89	0.44
Total Non-Food	38.67	50.86	10.37

Source: Statistics Indonesia (1998, 2019).

Items such as LPG for cooking and mobile phone credit, which are both essential today, are missing. A major revision is long overdue.

Lastly, statistical robustness requires more careful methodological choices. One way to ensure consistency is by following the Laspeyres index, which tracks price changes based on a fixed set of goods from a base year. This prevents the poverty line from shifting due to changing consumption patterns, making it easier to compare across time. But methodology alone isn't enough—survey design also matters. Right now, Statistics Indonesia conducts the National Socio-economic Survey twice a year, in March and September, with the March round using a larger sample. However, the sample size is still too small to fully capture shifts in spending patterns. A better solution would be to conduct the survey once a year but with a significantly larger sample, improving the accuracy and representativeness of Indonesia's poverty estimates. By addressing these issues, Indonesia can build a poverty measurement system that is more consistent, more representative, and more reliable—ensuring that policies are based on an accurate understanding of who is truly in need.

The way poverty is measured is not just a technical exercise, as it shapes how the state perceives poverty, understands welfare, and ultimately designs policies. Methodological choices in poverty calculations determine who is classified as poor, how the effectiveness of social programs is assessed, and how resources are allocated. As such, refining Indonesia's poverty measurement is not just about statistical accuracy but about ensuring that government policies genuinely improve the lives of those in need. Indonesia's current approach to calculating poverty has four major policy consequences.

First, because poverty is measured using a reference group that includes households who are not actually poor, the impact of government programs and interventions may be inaccurately assessed. This means that even if an anti-poverty program succeeds in lifting people out of hardship, the official poverty figures might not fully reflect these gains. Second, several methodological issues—such as a small sample size, a reference group that is not fully representative of the poor, and a non-food poverty line that does not accurately reflect real consumption patterns—make it difficult to craft effective poverty alleviation strategies. If the poverty line fails to capture the true cost of basic needs, programs designed to support the poor might not be well-targeted, leading to either under-coverage or inefficiencies in social spending. Third, the weakly absolute nature of Indonesia's poverty measure can lead to an underestimation of poverty reduction efforts. This is evident in comparisons with the World Bank's absolute poverty measure, which often shows a faster decline in poverty rates. As a result, Indonesia's current approach may fail to fully recognize the progress made by government initiatives, potentially influencing policy decisions based on an overly conservative estimate of poverty reduction.

Finally, poverty statistics play a crucial role in budget planning, influencing how local government transfers and ministry budgets are allocated. If poverty numbers are biased due to methodological inconsistencies, resources may not be directed to the areas that need them most. Inaccurate poverty estimates can lead to misallocation of funds, in which some regions receive insufficient support while others are overfunded relative to their actual needs. These consequences highlight why poverty measurement is not just a technical issue but a policy-critical decision with real-life ramifications. A more consistent, transparent, and representative poverty measure would not only improve the accuracy of poverty statistics but also ensure that policies and budgets are better aligned with the needs of Indonesia's most vulnerable populations.

Considering the arguments to update Indonesia's poverty calculation method and the costs associated with inaction, one is left wondering why the due changes were never implemented. However, as with other policy reforms, the whole process is as much political as it is technical. In fact, problems on the technical side are less of an issue, as various technical recommendations have been offered over time. Choosing when to enact the change, determining which ministry could support the agenda from the legal end, and deciding how Statistics Indonesia could implement the necessary changes with as little pushback as possible is another side of the coin. Yet, blaming "a lack of political will" for the lack of implementation is like saying that one lacks commitment to think of ways to pursue reform—and being an effective policymaker requires one to think about both sides of policy reform.

Measuring Poverty in a Changing Indonesia: Politics and Path Dependency

If Statistics Indonesia were to update its poverty calculation method, it wouldn't be the first time. In fact, it has done so before—first in 1984, when it began using the National Socio-economic Survey to measure poverty, and again in 1999, when it refined its approach to improve the accuracy of the non-food basket. However, these past reforms took place in very different political and economic landscapes. Today, Indonesia operates in a democratic system with new players and shifting power dynamics, making policy changes far more complex.

During Suharto's authoritarian rule, Statistics Indonesia functioned as an extension of the centralized government, with little opposition to changes in methodology. The 1999 reforms, which came in the wake of the Asian financial crisis and the fall of Suharto, were introduced at a critical moment when Indonesia was undergoing major political and economic transformations. The crisis and regime change created an opening for policymakers to introduce new social programs and revise the poverty calculation method. Over time, these changes became embedded in Indonesia's social protection system, shaping the way poverty is measured and addressed. However, under democracy, revising the poverty line is no longer just a technical adjustment but also a political challenge. The rise of decentralization has empowered local governments, shifting the balance of decision making away from Jakarta. As a result, Statistics Indonesia must now navigate a more complex policymaking environment, balancing national priorities with regional interests. On top of this, path dependency, which is the tendency of past policies and institutional practices to persist, makes any reform effort even more difficult. While updating the poverty calculation method remains necessary, it requires careful negotiation with a wider set of actors and a deeper understanding of the political landscape.

During the Asian financial crisis, many factors allowed for the successful enactment of reforms in the poverty line calculation method. At that time, the political vacuum from Suharto's fall opened a space for newly empowered actors, such as Statistics Indonesia and researchers, to influence policy. However, what really empowered these actors rather than others was their newly gained legitimacy. Suharto's military affiliation hurt the credibility of the military's top brass during the democratic transition. Meanwhile, key business owners were hit hard during the financial crisis. Technocrats once close to the government's circle and beyond quickly rallied behind the newly appointed president Bacharuddin Jusuf Habibie. Despite his proximity to Suharto's regime, President Habibie's civilian and technocratic background gave him an air of legitimacy not just among Indonesians seeking political reform, but also among international observers. Part of the technocrats' empowerment came from international institutions, such as the World Bank and International Monetary Fund (IMF), who sought to aid Indonesia in gaining economic and political stability. In the Indonesian government's Letter of Intent, Ginandjar Kartasasmita, the State Coordinating Minister for Economy, Finance, and Industry, described the policies that Indonesia intended to implement in the context of its request for financial support from the IMF. In the letter, the Minister expressed a concern that "accelerating development expenditure is tempered by the importance of ensuring that budgetary resources reach the intended beneficiaries" and a desire to engage various stakeholders to improve "internal government oversight mechanisms, to help identify leakages, and ensure accountability.[8]" This implied a desire to ascertain that social transfers reached the poor.

[8] IMF, 1998. Available from: www.imf.org/external/np/loi/1113a98.htm.

Thus, in cooperation with the World Bank, Statistics Indonesia worked to revise the country's poverty line.

Aside from the power vacuum, the fact that millions fell into poverty during the financial crisis meant that any change to the poverty line would be less consequential as poverty numbers would remain high either way. This situation lessened the pushback against reform. However, after Indonesia's democratic transition and decentralization in particular, Statistics Indonesia was presented with the prospect of pushback from local governments. From the local government's end, a change in poverty numbers might impact their entitlement to development and poverty alleviation-related transfers from the central government. This apprehension was voiced by several provincial governments during informal meetings with regional Statistics Indonesia branches when the latter floated the idea of revising the poverty line in 2007. Recognizing the possible pushback from local governments, Statistics Indonesia became more cautious as they moved forward with the agenda. Thus, Statistics Indonesia sought support from external actors, agencies, and entities to attain their desire to reform the poverty line calculation method.

Since 2007, Statistics Indonesia and BAPPENAS actively engaged external parties in methodological discussions to revise the poverty line. The World Bank, which had been engaged with Statistics Indonesia since the 1998 revision, was among the first to support the initiative. After the TNP2K was established in 2010 with the support of DFAT, the initiative gained broader recognition. With the vice president acting as the head of TNP2K and its authority to coordinate national poverty reduction efforts, the research on reforms of the poverty line calculation method, along with its advocacy, gained further traction. When DFAT launched the Knowledge Sector Initiative in 2012, it became an epistemic space where the best poverty line calculation method was debated among researchers, scholars, and policymakers beyond BAPPENAS and Statistics Indonesia's circle, both at the national and international levels. With various parties bringing valid points into the debate, this discussion would remain heated until 2021, when some methodological agreements were finally reached. As Indonesia was still recovering from the COVID-19 pandemic and Statistics Indonesia's budget was cut, the plan was suspended—at least temporarily.

Between 2007 and 2021, resistance to change also began to emerge from Statistics Indonesia's end. Within the agency itself, practices and norms in collecting data, calculating poverty numbers, and communicating the results had become routinized over time. A change in the poverty calculation method meant not only that Statistics Indonesia would need to deal with external resistance to the reform, but also that it would need to think of how to handle the transition process, as routinized processes would have to be revised. For an agency of its scale, with regional offices in every province as well as municipality and regency offices across Indonesia, this would not be an easy feat.

Throughout the discussions to update the poverty line, other ideas have emerged to supplement or even replace Statistics Indonesia's calculation. Among the most popular approaches were the multidimensional poverty measure and the World Bank's absolute poverty approach.[9] While the former seeks to view poverty from dimensions beyond monetary shortage to fully capture poverty as a complex social phenomenon, the latter takes a monetary approach that puts cross-country and cross-temporal comparison at the forefront. With the support of the United Nations Development Program, the former gained some recognition from BAPPENAS. However, its complexity and data-hungry calculation method made its application limited. The World Bank's calculation method, on the other hand, gained broader recognition as President Joko Widodo set a target to eliminate extreme poverty—calculated using the World Bank's method—by the end of his term in 2024. Although the Bank's method cannot and should not replace Indonesia's approach that seeks to better reflect its own poor population, the method highlights the need for a calculation approach that is consistent and allows for comparability across time and regions in the country.

Moving Beyond the Poverty Line

Over two decades have passed since Indonesia last revised its method for calculating the poverty line in 1999. Since then, numerous attempts have been made to update it, with Statistics Indonesia leading the charge and receiving broad support from experts both within and outside the country. However, these efforts have encountered a dramatically different political landscape. Under Suharto's authoritarian rule, Statistics Indonesia operated as an extension of presidential authority, implementing technical adjustments with minimal resistance. But in the democratic era—especially following decentralization—policy changes now require negotiation with a

[9] Alkire, Kanagaratnam, and Suppa, 2021; World Bank, 2015.

broader set of actors, including local governments. Many local leaders have been wary of any revisions that might alter poverty figures, fearing potential impacts on central government transfers and budget allocations. As a result, what was once a relatively straightforward technical adjustment has become a complex political endeavor.

Since discussions about revising the poverty line began in 2007, the biggest challenge has not been in determining the best technical method but in navigating the politics of reform. Timing has been a crucial concern, but even more delicate has been the task of securing buy-in from various stakeholders—local governments, regional Statistics Indonesia branches, national institutions like TNP2K, and international organizations such as the World Bank. This political balancing act is unlikely to disappear anytime soon. Even if Statistics Indonesia moves forward with reforms, convincing local governments will remain an ongoing challenge.

Ultimately, what matters most is not just the poverty rate at any single point in time, but the broader trends: whether poverty is declining and whether Indonesia's social programs are making a real impact. In this regard, Indonesia is in a strong position—by global standards, absolute poverty has fallen significantly. The country should embrace improvements to its poverty measurement system to ensure it can reliably track and evaluate the performance of its poverty-alleviation efforts.

At the same time, policymakers must not become overly fixated on the poverty line itself and risk losing sight of the bigger picture. A rigid focus on a single threshold often leads to an oversimplified poor/non-poor dichotomy, where eligibility for government assistance depends on whether a household falls just below or just above the line. But poverty is not a binary condition; it is a spectrum of lived experiences shaped by economic insecurity, social exclusion, and limited access to stable income. The poverty line is ultimately just a tool—a metric meant to guide decision making, not to define the entirety of poverty or dictate policy responses. While the poverty line helps governments allocate resources and assess progress, policies should not be constrained by the artificial divide it creates. A household that moves slightly above the poverty line on paper is not necessarily free from hardship, and a measurement system that fails to account for vulnerability risks overlooking those who are in precarious situations. To build effective social policies, Indonesia must recognize that poverty alleviation is not just about shifting people above an arbitrary line but about ensuring long-term economic security and opportunity for all.

Lessons From Indonesia

In exploring Indonesia's social protection system and reform process, we have traced its evolution from minimal social protections under President Suharto's New Order government to a relatively comprehensive system within a democratic setting today that covers nearly 100 million people, or the bottom 40% of the population. This journey has been profoundly shaped by shifts in both political leadership and prevailing political, social, and economic winds, as we have seen in each chapter.

What then can we learn from our exploration of Indonesia's social protection reform over the past 20 years? Drawing on my own experience as a researcher and my extensive policy experience, I outline seven key takeaways that summarize the essential lessons from Indonesia's experiences—lessons which, I believe, are also relevant for researchers and policymakers elsewhere.

Key Takeaway #1: Ask The "Right" Question

The process of giving the right evidence begins with asking the right questions. In the context of evidence-based policymaking, the "right evidence" does not mean evidence that will satisfy the researchers' government counterparts or the donor who funded the research. Rather, it is evidence that has the potential for "buy-in" and can be implemented. It is the kind of evidence that can get adopted into formal policy or be considered in policy debates and decision making. But what is the "right" question?

As researchers, we often begin by identifying gaps in the literature or testing theories in specific settings—questions that advance general knowledge and hold academic value. However, these are not always the questions that matter to politicians and government decision makers, who are more concerned with the practical challenges they encounter daily. For them, empirical evidence tends to be more compelling than theoretical debates. This preference for the empirical may discourage scholars from engaging

Evidence and the Politics of Reform. Sudarno Sumarto, Oxford University Press.
 DOI: 10.1093/9780197831717.003.0011

with policymakers, as they may worry that such work has limited theoretical implications and is unlikely to be published in top journals. Yet researchers must not forget that theories also emerge from observing the world and understanding how things work in practice, including how policies succeed or fail. Bridging the gap between researchers and government officials in evidence-based policymaking is challenging and requires effort. Decision makers, who are often high-ranking bureaucrats, may have little interest in pursuits beyond their immediate governance responsibilities. The real challenge lies in finding a common ground where researchers' intellectual curiosity aligns with policymakers' practical needs. This is the art of identifying the right question, one that both sides agree is worth answering.

Importantly, to get "buy-in," researchers need to think like policymakers, anticipate their concerns, and frame their research in ways that resonate with the interests and priorities of policymakers. For instance, how can we improve as many poor people's food security as possible given a limited government budget? How can we ensure that enough rice reaches the neediest households to actually make a significant impact on their well-being? These were the exact same questions that my research team and our government counterparts were facing, as told in Chapter 4 on reforming Indonesia's rice transfer scheme.

Asking the right question also means realizing that questions around the same issue can change over time. Chapter 5 demonstrates how "improving educational output" means different things in different times, given changes in the policy landscape. Despite spending at least 20% of its budget on education, Indonesia's educational output remains poor. In the past, this might mean looking at how to improve access and enrollment; now, as both situations have improved with both economic growth and policy changes, the question is how money can be better spent to improve quality. This involves exploring how learning can be improved and asking strategic questions, such as why there is a gap between education spending and student learning outcomes, and what reforms are needed to improve teacher quality and student performance.

Instead of just dealing with broad questions of how governments can effectively reduce poverty or improve educational attainment, researchers can craft the right research questions by working closely with policymakers to solve real problems on the ground. By ensuring that research questions are relevant, researchers can improve chances of buy-in. Yet the right questions alone cannot guarantee policy buy-in. Now, let me turn to the next ingredient that fosters evidence buy-in.

Key Takeaway #2: Give The Right Evidence at the Right Time

People say that the flow of time is cruel and spares no one. As a policy researcher, I agree with this. Researchers usually like to let their ideas simmer and plan their work carefully, which could take eons before we have answers. On the other hand, policymakers usually work with a shorter time horizon due to elections, term limits, budgetary cycles, or issues on the ground that call for immediate solutions. Given these time constraints, researchers who seek to engage policymakers should figure out how to provide needed information at the right time. While it is difficult to speed up the process of evidence generation, what we can do is identify the times when our work can be most impactful.

While thinking about when evidence is most likely to influence decision making, we need to put ourselves in the shoes of a decision maker. Understanding how and when these critical windows appear will allow us to position our evidence where it is most likely to be noticed and acted upon—whether it is the right time for the introduction of new policies or the winding down of old ones, or simply time for routine maintenance or changes to existing programs. It does not matter if you have solid evidence if you missed the policymaking window.

The timing of Indonesia's Unified Database, as outlined in Chapter 3, was crucial for securing evidence buy-in. It emerged when budget constraints made optimizing social protection resources essential, and refocusing benefits on those most in need became a priority. Initially, the rice transfer program's "soft targeting" was not a concern, as the 1997–1998 crisis had pushed millions into poverty. However, as the economy recovered, improving targeting became necessary. By then, the government had recognized the value of targeting, particularly during crises, creating an opportunity for researchers to engage policymakers with further evidence.

Key Takeaway #3: Identify What Incentivizes Decision Makers to Act, and Couple It with Evidence

Technical and economic considerations are important in policy planning and implementation. But, in the end, someone in the government needs to champion the idea, see its urgency, or just want to learn the information as they take action. The introduction of this book has described how Indonesia's transition from an authoritarian regime to a democratic government created the political space necessary for extensive social welfare reforms. At the same time, the role of key decision makers was critical in bringing about those significant policy changes that extended social protections to the broader population. These decision makers did not just wake up one morning with a desire to reform the country's social protection system. While some people might already have had an interest in doing so, others might not have thought about it or had any interest in the issue until something drove them to take actions in that direction. The impetus could be some kind of crisis that threatened a lot of people's well-being, or a desire to appeal to their constituency. Whatever the drive is, it not only needs to be identified, it needs to be understood.

Evidence-based policymaking is not a one-off meeting between a researcher and a politician. It is certainly not a passive pursuit, as it demands meaningful engagement from political leaders throughout the policy process. This means more than just their approval or support for a certain reform. Instead, engagement encompasses three key elements: the capacity and willingness to take tough decisions, doing everything possible to mitigate any negative impacts that may arise, and a commitment to explaining new policies effectively both before implementation and while moving forward.

For example, in Chapter 2, the narrative around the reform of fuel subsidies highlights the necessity for political courage and vision. In this case, a politically sensitive reform could be enacted because the drive to act from politicians was met with support from evidence, and the government was able to establish a carefully planned mitigation program instead of ad-hoc means to justify a politically tough decision.

Though such a drive for politicians to act tends to emerge out of crisis and is beyond the researcher's control, it is also possible to create conditions that would allow evidence-based policymaking to flourish and for researchers to quickly respond to emerging opportunity windows. One way is to promote an environment where good practices are encouraged and maintained. Now let me turn to discussing how such an environment is possible.

Key Takeaway #4: Engage Policy Champions and Build a Community of Reformers within Government

When engaging with the government, identifying policy champions—the "reformers"—is a critical strategy to advance evidence-backed policies. These reformers are not just decision makers with the drive to take one-off actions but are those who can actively advocate for policy reform and mobilize support across the government. At the same time, they are also influential leaders who possess the commitment, integrity, and authority to drive policy agendas forward effectively. Policy champions understand the intricacies of the policies they support and can articulate the importance of evidence-based reform in a way that resonates with relevant stakeholders inside the government.

In my experience, effective policy champions are often mid- or upper-level bureaucrats who understand the complexities of rules and regulations, have years of relevant institutional experience, and are adept at identifying resources to support reforms. While this may seem like sidestepping the political process, it's essential to combine the expertise of these technocrats with political figures who can align reforms with constituents' needs and set the direction. We sometimes had the opportunity to collaborate with high-ranking reformers, such as ministers or vice presidents, who could expedite reforms. However, these high-level reformers are rare due to limited time in office and the political nature of their roles. Therefore, it's crucial for researchers to engage a variety of reformers across government levels to ensure the successful implementation and sustainability of reforms. In addition to policy champions, it's essential to cultivate a community of reformers within the government. This involves promoting collaboration between researchers and governmental bodies, enhancing capacity through training and knowledge transfer, and ensuring access to data and analytical tools. By doing so, we build trust in methodologies, enable people to see and understand diverse perspectives, and foster effective teamwork.

What leads to this virtuous cycle of close engagement between researchers, decision makers, and evidence in the first place is the ability for evidence to help deliver political promises or get the government through crises.

Chapter 3 describes how the global oil price shock compelled the government to enact a fuel subsidy cutback. Faced with opposition from the public, economists provided an evidence-based model as a way out of this dilemma through targeted compensation schemes, and eventually policymakers were able to recognize the potential effectiveness of this strategy. Once that initial compensatory scheme succeeded in alleviating popular pushback, researchers were then able to make the case that more could be done to support the most vulnerable by establishing a welfare-ranked targeting instrument for social program beneficiaries. The Unified Database that came out of this became a testament to a forward-looking policy reform driven by a combination of crisis, leadership, and evidence-based policymaking.

If, during the fuel subsidies scale-back, the researchers' suggestions did not lead to improved program targeting, it is hard to imagine that the Unified Database would become a permanent feature of the country's welfare infrastructure, or that in 2012 the government would rely on research evidence when reforming the country's rice transfer policy. Thus, although close engagement is needed to foster trust and collaboration between parties over time, in the end, the quality of evidence is the key to unlock this dynamic. I will now discuss a bit more about trust.

Key Takeaway #5: Converting Evidence into Policy Needs a Trusted Knowledge Broker

Producing rigorous evidence requires significant investment in research, well-maintained knowledge management systems, and current data. As with many other developing countries, the over-reliance on international assistance in Indonesia, coupled with a lack of domestic investment in research, limited our ability to produce relevant, context-specific evidence. This situation highlights the challenge policymakers face when they lack the skills or tools necessary to critically evaluate and differentiate between varying levels of evidence quality. In such an environment, trust becomes a crucial commodity. However, whom should policymakers trust?

Competing studies often present conflicting results, each claiming to be the definitive path to a better world. It is essential to be meticulous about the quality of data, the robustness of research methods, the clarity of any assumptions, and the limitations of the evidence. But policymakers often do not have the time or the capacity to sift through reams of conflicting evidence. They need to be able to trust that the research they rely on is both rigorous and relevant.

Trust is the bridge to making breakthroughs. Apart from the evidence that is produced, who delivers the evidence is an important factor. Policymakers are often more receptive to evidence that is presented by trusted and credible sources—those with whom they have established relationships or those who understand the context within which these policymakers are operating, as well as their problems and constraints. For all that to occur, personal relationships, awareness, external reviews, public discussion, and professionalism all work to build credibility. This is why building long-term relationships with decision makers, understanding the challenges they face and their worldview, and speaking their language are critical factors in influencing policymaking. Our experience in TNP2K shows that establishing credibility, transparency, good networks, and continuously engaging with and adapting to the needs of policymakers are critically important to convert evidence into policy.

My experience at TNP2K highlighted the importance of both personal and institutional trust. Established by presidential regulation, TNP2K had legal standing, a clear mandate, and the authority to advise the vice president while coordinating poverty alleviation across 15 ministries. This gave it bureaucratic legitimacy, but trust is a two-way street—policymakers must be confident that relying on researchers is a sound decision. Supported by development partners, TNP2K maintained independence, upheld research rigor, and built credibility by publishing data, endorsing peer reviews, and correcting errors. Its unique position granted access to key decision makers and primary data while providing the government with high-quality evidence. However, trust was not built on bureaucratic legitimacy alone. A formal mandate helps, but researchers must still prove their credibility beyond titles and degrees.

Key Takeaway #6: Build Knowledge Coalitions Beyond the Government

Building knowledge coalitions and developing policy explainers outside government are crucial for expanding the reach of evidence-based policies and fostering informed public debate. By working with academic institutions, think tanks, NGOs, and media, researchers can break down complex policies, engage stakeholders who might otherwise be excluded, and tap into alternative channels of political influence. These coalitions not only broaden policy discourse but also help shape more adaptive and resilient policies by incorporating diverse perspectives. Equally important are external donors like DFAT, USAID, and the Gates Foundation, whose investments in evidence-gathering and knowledge production—despite uncertain returns—enable organizations like TNP2K to operate effectively. Their flexible, unrestricted funding is essential; without it, independent research efforts would face significant constraints.

The development of the Unified Database in Chapter 3 showcased the power of strategic partnerships with knowledge coalitions. In an early evaluation, TNP2K collaborated with J-PAL and the World Bank to refine beneficiary data collection, demonstrating the critical role of research communities in improving targeting. This collaboration laid the groundwork for the Unified Database, now essential for identifying social assistance beneficiaries. Through multiple evaluations, we combined administrative data from the database with national survey data from Statistics Indonesia, enabling deeper insights into cost-effectiveness, scale, and validity—insights that would have been difficult to achieve using study-specific surveys alone.

Although "collaboration" may sound like a buzzword, our experience shows that adopting a cooperative approach from the start not only enhances the effectiveness of our research but also fosters creativity and relevance in solving complex policy questions. By bringing together diverse perspectives, we learn and grow through the collaborative process. One of our research collaborators from Harvard University once said that their close collaboration with stakeholders on the ground really changed their perspective over time, not only about specific policies but also about the policymaking process.

Beyond partnership with knowledge producers beyond the government, TNP2K also engaged the civil society and tried to democratize data and knowledge. TNP2K was among the more open and transparent government organizations in Indonesia that meaningfully engaged the civil society. For instance, TNP2K engaged universities in policy research and knowledge-sharing forums, shared data and analysis with NGOs, published articles in national media, and actively incorporated input from local communities in many of its policy recommendations.

Although we often see the policy process as something that mainly occurs within the government, in the end, broader engagement is also necessary. This engagement allows researchers and policymakers to gain broader perspectives on planned reforms. Moreover, public outreach can help build up support for reforms.

Key Takeaway #7: Be Patient and Stay Humble

At this point it is clear that in translating research into policy you will be no stranger to challenges that seem impossible to solve, uncertainties, and even setbacks. But it is also a deeply rewarding endeavor for those who want to use evidence to make meaningful policy changes. Research-based evidence, no matter how compelling, can be ignored if it does not fit the current political narrative or priorities. Through this process we need to foster endurance by being patient and staying grounded.

Numerous examples demonstrate the level of persistence required to create and lead reforms. Indonesia's rice transfer reform told in Chapter 4, for instance, was not achieved overnight. In reality it took nearly 18 years to make this change of policy happen, requiring navigation of shifting political landscapes, alignment with changing government priorities, and continuous engagement with local communities to refine our methodology. In the end, policy buy-in requires convincing people at every level—from local government implementers to national decision makers—of the value of evidence-based reforms. This alone takes time and persistence, and it is not enough on its own. At the same time, technical capacities need to be established. At an organizational level, this means ensuring that the relevant ministries have access to the right data, tools, and training. At a personal level, it means equipping policymakers with the skills to understand, appraise, and use evidence. All this takes time.

However, countless hours of policy discussion and stakeholder engagement also does not guarantee policy adoption. For instance, our effort to revise the seemingly consistent poverty measures to get them right has been one of the most intensive and tiring undertakings. I have been involved in this effort since 2006, during my time as SMERU's director, my tenure as head of the FMS, and as a policy adviser at TNP2K. We have held more than 50 meetings and over 25 workshops, met with ministers, written several memos to the vice president's office and BAPPENAS, and reported to the president and the vice president. We have also conducted hundreds of simulations involving local and international experts and engaged with three different heads of BPS, all with no success. In the end, progress is never swift and easy.

At the same time, being patient does not mean being persistent in pushing what we believe to be the truth or the best. It is not enough to be smart; we must be humble as well. As researchers we need to recognize that our insights are just one piece of the larger puzzle. Humility allows us to navigate the complexities of policymaking with sensitivity and awareness of local values. Researchers are not always right, and our ideas can sometimes be too dated for the fast-moving world of policymaking. Commitment to continued learning, being open to feedback, humility, and a willingness to experiment are all essential, especially when gaps in knowledge appear. Resilience that is coupled with flexibility is crucial to maintaining the momentum for reform, especially in a democratic context where political power can be transient and priorities may shift with leadership changes.

When well-researched policy ideas are not immediately implemented, they can still retain value. Often, as noted in lesson #2, it may simply be a matter of premature timing. Through this process, patience and humility can serve as a drive for us to gather more evidence, build understanding, and find new entry points where we can show that better ideas produce better results. Over time, these ideas can help guide future reforms in ways that we might not have thought of before, and influence changes in ways that may not be visible to our eyes today.

Afterword

Reflecting on Indonesia's journey, one thing becomes clear: building a strong social protection system is not a sprint—it's a marathon. As this book has shown, the shift from limited protections under Suharto's centralized rule to a far-reaching safety net under democratic governance was shaped by a blend of economic crises, political upheaval, and deliberate policymaking. Democratic transitions opened the door to reform, but they also brought uncertainty and competing interests. Each administration faced its own mix of challenges—from economic shocks to political instability to resistance from entrenched power structures. And yet, progress was made. Indonesia's experience offers valuable lessons for other developing countries navigating similar terrain.

This book is more than a collection of policy stories. It is a reflection on how meaningful change happens when collective action is guided by evidence. Moving forward, adapting to a shifting political, economic, and social landscape is a given. Grounding decisions in data and analysis not only strengthens policy design but also upholds democratic values. But we must aim even higher. Evidence-based policymaking should go beyond fixing individual problems; it should also confront deeper structural and global issues. In this, scholars and researchers have a crucial role to generate insights that illuminate root causes and to advocate for transformative solutions. It is then up to policymakers to translate that knowledge into action that truly supports those who need it most.

The future of social protection, both in Indonesia and around the world, rests on a shared commitment to progress. The lessons from Indonesia's reform journey as explored in this book offer valuable insights for building more equitable and resilient societies. But the work doesn't stop here. To meet the complex challenges of the 21st century, we must not only improve what already exists but also design bold, innovative solutions that anticipate future needs. This means moving beyond reactive policies and embracing forward-looking approaches: ones that not only catch people when they fall but also help them rise. With collaboration, creativity, and a steadfast focus on inclusion, we can build systems that empower individuals and strengthen the social fabric for generations to come.

As the new Indonesian government administration took office at the end of 2024, I found myself at a turning point. After years immersed in the day-to-day work of shaping social policy, I needed to recalibrate and better understand the shifting landscape of institutions and actors. This led me to take a sabbatical at the Harvard Kennedy School as an opportunity to not only write and consolidate the lessons of the past, but also to observe, from a distance, how the new political dynamics are unfolding back home. It was not an easy decision to make, but it felt necessary. The work I had done, alongside my dedicated colleagues, government partners, and policymakers, was deeply rewarding. Yet I came to realize that my role had evolved. I was no longer just a participant in the policy process; I had become a witness to the broader system, one that requires constant adaptation, negotiation, and perspective.

From this vantage point, the horizon looks both challenging and full of possibility—not just for Indonesia but for the world. Globally, social policy is being tested. While Indonesia continues its journey, broader geopolitical shifts are reshaping the very foundations of international cooperation. The United States, long a key architect of global norms and development leadership, has signaled a retreat from this role. The closure of USAID missions and withdrawal from commitments like the United Nations' Sustainable Development Goals have created real gaps in support—gaps that directly impact the work of scholars, practitioners, and communities striving for evidence-based solutions. Compounding this, the Trump administration's abrupt budget cuts to academic and development programs have curtailed the kind of rigorous research and cross-border learning that this book champions.

Equally consequential are the trade disruptions triggered by policy decisions such as the tariffs imposed by the United States in the Spring of 2025, which rattled financial markets and signaled a deeper unraveling of globalization. These moves have profound consequences for least-developed countries, many of which are deeply integrated into global value chains. As these systems are restructured, the risk of deepening poverty and inequality grows.

And yet, moments of disruption can also spark transformation. They remind us that progress is never guaranteed, and that the pursuit of justice and inclusion must be constantly renewed. For Indonesia and beyond, this is a chance to reimagine the future: to build more resilient systems, strengthen cooperation, and ensure that knowledge continues to serve the public good. The road ahead is demanding but filled with possibilities if we are willing to meet it with imagination, solidarity, and a commitment to truth.

Indonesia stands at a pivotal moment that is poised for transformative growth, yet mindful of the lessons that history offers. The stories in this book reveal a country that has long wrestled with complex challenges, navigating its way through crises, reforms, and renewal. As President Prabowo Subianto begins his term, his administration brings forward an ambitious policy agenda that signals a bold, expansive vision for Indonesia's future. Among his flagship initiatives, the Free Nutritious Meal Program (*Makan Bergizi Gratis*) is designed to combat child malnutrition, reduce learning deficits, boost school attendance, and stimulate local agricultural production, goals that, if realized, could produce ripple effects across generations.

Beyond this, the administration has proposed revitalizing village cooperatives and strengthening food security through local production and procurement schemes. These efforts aim to empower rural communities, reduce dependence on imports, and reinvigorate grassroots economic development. This proposal reflects a state-led, interventionist approach that seeks to accelerate economic transformation and build national resilience.

But bold policies are only as effective as their implementation. Indonesia's past teaches us that without transparency, community engagement, and rigorous monitoring, even the best-designed programs can fall short or be co-opted by vested interests. For these new initiatives to deliver real, lasting change, they must be informed by data, guided by public accountability, and continuously adapted based on evidence. As Indonesia writes this next chapter, it has an opportunity not only to pursue growth—but to do so with integrity, inclusion, and care for those most often left behind.

Nonetheless, I remain optimistic about the future. While the political landscape continues to shift, the seeds we planted—data-driven policies, collaborative partnerships, and targeted social assistance—are resilient. However, they require careful nurturing to flourish. Power may ebb and flow, but knowledge endures, and even if these ideas are not embraced today, their value will be recognized in time. Though my work has taken me away from Indonesia physically, my heart and mind remain deeply committed to its development. Years of collaboration with brilliant minds, both locally and internationally, have forged enduring relationships that will continue to inspire and guide the work ahead.

As you reach the final page of this book, a new step awaits. It is one that is fraught with challenges yet also brimming with possibility. The lessons and stories of resilience and innovation shared here serve as guiding lights in an unpredictable world. Reflect with determination and hope on how these insights can strengthen the foundations of social protection. Whether you are a policymaker, a student of development, an activist, or a concerned citizen, the journey ahead is demanding but not without promise. By engaging with the evidence, understanding the political landscape, and championing the needs of the most vulnerable, there is an opportunity to navigate a course toward meaningful change. The journey of social protection reform remains a critical endeavor, and your role in shaping its trajectory offers a glimmer of hope in uncertain times.

Glossary

ASEAN Association of Southeast Asian Nations

ASKESKIN *Asuransi Kesehatan untuk Rakyat Miskin* (Health Insurance for the Poor)

ASLUT *Asistensi Sosial Lanjut Usia Telantar* (Social Assistance for Abandoned Elderly Persons)

BAPPENAS *Kementerian Perencanaan Pembangunan Nasional/Badan Perencanaan Pembangunan Nasional Republik Indonesia* (Ministry of National Development Planning of the Republic of Indonesia)

BKKBN *Badan Kependudukan dan Keluarga Berencana Nasional* (National Population and Family Planning Agency)

BPDPK *Badan Penyelenggara Dana Pemeliharaan Kesehatan* (Executing Agency of Health Maintenance Funds)

BP Taskin *Badan Percepatan Pengentasan Kemiskinan* (Task Force for Poverty Alleviation)

BPJS Kesehatan Badan Penyelenggara Jaminan Sosial Kesehatan (Social Security Administrator for Health)

BPJS-TK Badan Penyelenggara Jaminan Sosial Ketenagakerjaan (Social Security Administrator for Employment)

BPNT *Bantuan Pangan Non-Tunai* (Non-Cash Food Assistance)

BSM *Bantuan Siswa Miskin* (Cash Transfers for Poor Students)

BULOG *Badan Urusan Logistik* (Logistics Affairs Agency)

COVID-19 Coronavirus Disease 2019

CPIS Center for Policy and Implementation Studies

DFAT The Australian Department of Foreign Affairs and Trade

DJSN Dewan Jaminan Sosial Nasional (The National Social Security Board)

DTKS *Data Terpadu Kesejahteraan Sosial* (Integrated Social Welfare Data)

FMS *Forum Masyarakat Statistik* (Indonesian Statistical Community)

GDP Gross Domestic Product

IDR Indonesian Rupiah

IISD International Institute for Sustainable Development

IMF International Monetary Fund

JAMKESDA *Jaminan Kesehatan Daerah* (Regional Public Health Insurance)

JAMKESMAS *Jaminan Kesehatan Masyarakat* (Public Health Insurance)

JKN *Jaminan Kesehatan Nasional* (National Health Insurance)

JPS *Jaring Pengaman Sosial* (Social Safety Net)

KAJS *Komite Aksi Jaminan Sosial* (The Action Committee on Social Security)

KDP Kecamatan Development Project

KSP *Kantor Staf Presiden* (Executive Office of the President of the Republic of Indonesia)

TNP2K *Tim Nasional Percepatan Penanggulangan Kemiskinan* (The National Team for the Acceleration of Poverty Reduction)

Raskin *Beras Miskin* (Rice for the Poor)

Rastra *Beras Sejahtera* (Rice for Prosperity)

RISE Programme Research on Improving Systems of Education Programme

OECD Organization for Economic Co-operation and Development

OPEC Organization of the Petroleum Exporting Countries

OPK *Operasi Pasar Khusus* (Special Market Operation)

PBDT 2015 *Pemutakhiran Basis Data Terpadu 2015* (The 2015 Unified Database Updating)

PISA Program for International Students Assessment

PKH *Program Keluarga Harapan* (Family Hope Programme)

PNPM Mandiri *Program Nasional Pemberdayaan Masyarakat Mandiri* (National Independent Community Empowerment Program)

PPLS 2008 *Pendataan Program Perlindungan Sosial 2008* (The 2008 Data Collection for Social Protection Programs)

PPLS 2011 *Pendataan Program Perlindungan Sosial 2011* (The 2011 Data Collection for Social Protection Programs)

PSE 2005 *Pendataan Sosioekonomi 2005* (The 2005 Socioeconomic Data Collection)

Perum ASTEK *Perusahaan Umum Asuransi Tenaga Kerja* (Public Corporation for Manpower Insurance)

PDI-P *Partai Demokrasi Indonesia – Perjuangan* (Democratic Party of Struggle)

PT ASKES *Perseroan Terbatas Asuransi Kesehatan* (Health Insurance Incorporated)

PT JAMSOSTEK *Perusahaan Terbatas Jaminan Sosial Tenaga Kerja* (Manpower Social Insurance Incorporated)

Posyandu *Pos Pelayanan Terpadu* (Integrated Healthcare Provider)

Puskesmas *Pusat Kesehatan Masyarakat* (Healthcare Center)

USD United States Dollar

WHO World Health Organization

Bibliography

Acosta, P.A., and R. Velarde. 2015. "Sa Pantawid, Malapit Nang Makatawid!: An Update of the Philippine Conditional Cash Transfer's Implementation Performance." *Philippine Social Protection Note* 8:12.

Adji, Ardi, Taufik Hidayat, Hendratno Tuhiman, Sandra Kurniawati, and Achmad Maulana. 2020. "Pengukuran Garis Kemiskinan Di Indonesia: Tinjauan Teoretis Dan Usulan Perbaikan." 48. TNP2K Working PaperKertas Kerja TNP2K. Jakarta, Indonesia: TNP2K.

Afkar, Rythia, Joppe de Ree, and Noviandri Khairina. 2018. "Who Learns What in Basic Education? Evidence from Indonesia." World Bank, Washington, DC.

Agustina, Rina, Teguh Dartanto, Ratna Sitompul, Kun A. Susiloretni, Null Suparmi, Endang L. Achadi, Akmal Taher, et al. 2019. "Universal Health Coverage in Indonesia: Concept, Progress, and Challenges." *Lancet (London, England)* 393 (10166): 75–102.

Alatas, V., A. Banerjee, R. Hanna, B.A. Olken, and J. Tobias. 2012. "Targeting the Poor: Evidence from a Field Experiment in Indonesia." *American Economic Review* 102 (4): 1206–1240.

Alderman, Harold. 2002. "Subsidies as Social Safety Nets: Effectiveness and Challenges." In *Social Protection Discussion Paper*. World Bank.

Alifia, Ulfah, Rezanti Putri Pramana, and Shintia Revina. 2022. "A Policy Lens on Becoming a Teacher: A Longitudinal Diary Study of Novice Teacher Professional Identity Formation in Indonesia." Research on Improving Systems of Education (RISE).

Alkire, Sabina, Usha Kanagaratnam, and Nicolai Suppa. 2021. "The Global Multidimensional Poverty Index (MPI) 2021." 51. Oxford: Oxford Poverty and Human Development Initiative (OPHI).

Alm, James, Jorge Martinez-Vazquez, and Sri Mulyani Indrawati. 2005. *Reforming Intergovernmental Fiscal Relations and the Rebuilding of Indonesia: The Big Bang Program and Its Economic Consequences*. Edward Elgar Publishing.

Antlöv, Hans. 2002. *Negara Dalam Desa: Patronase Kepemimpinan Lokal*. Yogyakarta: Lappera Pustaka Utama.

Antlöv, Hans. 2003. "Village Government and Rural Development in Indonesia: The New Democratic Framework." *Bulletin of Indonesian Economic Studies* 39 (2): 193–214. doi:10.1080/00074910302013.

Arends, Helge. 2020. "The Dangers of Fiscal Decentralization and Public Service Delivery: A Review of Arguments." *Politische Vierteljahresschrift* 61 (3): 599–622.

Arifianto, Alex. 2004. "Social Security Reform in Indonesia: An Analysis of the National Social Security Bill (RUU Jamsosnas)." SMERU Working Paper. Jakarta: The SMERU Research Institute.

Arnold, Chris. 2019. "Ecuador Reaches Fuel Subsidy Deal to End Violent Protests : NPR." National Public Radio, October 14, 2019.

Asian Development Bank. 2015. *Fossil Fuel Subsidies in Indonesia - Trends, Impacts, and Reforms*. Mandaluyong City: Asian Development Bank.

Asian Development Bank. 2020. *Report and Recommendation of the President to the Board of Directors: Proposed Countercyclical Support Facility Loans to the Republic of Indonesia for the COVID-19 Active Response and Expenditure Support Program.* Manila: Asian Development Bank.

Aslaksen, Silje. 2010. "Oil and Democracy: More than a Cross-Country Correlation?" *Journal of Peace Research* 47 (4): 421–431.

Asmanto, Priadi, Siti Nurfitriah Farah Dewi, Imelda Leiwakabessy, Mohammad Maulana, and Sutikno. 2020. "Utilization of Village-Owned Enterprises in Economic Recovery After the COVID-19 Outbreak." Policy Brief. Jakarta: National Team for the Acceleration of Poverty Reduction (TNP2K).

Asmanto, Priadi, Taufik Hidayat, Ardi Adji, and Gracia Hadiwidjaja. 2020. "Kecukupan Dan Cakupan Manfaat Bantuan Sosial Pada Masa Pandemi COVID-19." Jakarta: National Team for the Acceleration of Poverty Reduction (TNP2K).

Asmanto, Priadi, Taufik Hidayat, Mohammad Maulana, G. Irwan Suryanto, and Ardi Adji. 2020. "Prioritising Cash Transfers from the Village Fund for COVID-19 Response." Policy Brief. Jakarta: National Team for the Acceleration of Poverty Reduction (TNP2K).

Asmanto, Priadi, Mohammad Maulana, and Bagus Jutarto. 2020. "Prioritising Village Fund Utilisation: Cash-for-Work to Prevent COVID-19." Jakarta: National Team for the Acceleration of Poverty Reduction (TNP2K).

Aspinall, Edward. 2010. "Indonesia: The Irony of Success." *Journal of Democracy* 21 (2): 20–34.

Aspinall, Edward. 2014a. "Health Care and Democratization in Indonesia." *Democratization* 21 (5): 803–823.

Aspinall, Edward. 2014b. "Indonesia's 2014 Elections: Parliament and Patronage." *Journal of Democracy* 25 (4): 96–110.

Assariy, Afif. 2020. "Program Prakerja Tak Efektif Di Tengah Pandemi." *DetikNews*, April 27, 2020.

Bacon, Robert, and Masami Kojima. 2006. "Coping with Higher Oil Prices." 323/06. Washington, DC: World Bank.

Bacon, Robert, and Masami Kojima. 2006. "Phasing Out Subsidies." 37199. Public Policy for the Private Sector. Washington, DC: World Bank.

Bah, A., S. Bazzi, S. Sumarto, and J. Tobias. 2014. "Finding the Poor vs. Measuring Their Poverty: Exploring the Drivers of Targeting Effectiveness in Indonesia." *TNP2K Working Paper 20.*

Baidowi, Sodikin, Irdam Ahmad, Budiasih, Ahmad Avenzora, Dyah Retno P, Kartiana Siregar, and Astri Kartikasari. 1999. *Penyempurnaan Metodologi Penghitungan Penduduk Miskin Dan Profil Kemiskinan 1999.* Jakarta: Statistics Indonesia.

Banerjee, A., R. Hanna, B.A. Olken, E. Satriawan, and S. Sumarto. 2023. "Electronic Food Vouchers: Evidence from an At-Scale Experiment in Indonesia." *American Economic Review* 113 (2): 514–547.

Banerjee, Abhijit, Amy Finkelstein, Rema Hanna, Benjamin A. Olken, Arianna Ornaghi, and Sudarno Sumarto. 2021. "The Challenges of Universal Health Insurance in Developing Countries: Experimental Evidence from Indonesia's National Health Insurance." *American Economic Review* 111 (9): 3035–3063.

Banerjee, Abhijit, Rema Hanna, Jordan Kyle, Benjamin A. Olken, and Sudarno Sumarto. 2019. "Private Outsourcing and Competition: Subsidized Food Distribution in Indonesia." *Journal of Political Economy* 127 (1): 101–137.

Banerjee, Abhijit, Rema Hanna, Benjamin A. Olken, and Sudarno Sumarto. 2020. "The (Lack of) Distortionary Effects of Proxy-Means Tests: Results from a Nationwide Experiment in Indonesia." *Journal of Public Economics Plus* 1 (January): 100001.

Banerjee, Abhijit, Rema Hanna, Jordan Kyle, Benjamin A. Olken, and Sudarno Sumarto. 2018 "Tangible Information and Citizen Empowerment: Identification Cards and Food Subsidy Programs in Indonesia." *Journal of Political Economy* 126 (2): 451–491.

Barca, V. 2017. "Integrating Data and Information Management for Social Protection: Social Registries and Integrated Beneficiary Registries." Canberra: Australian Aid.

Barca, V., and M. Hebbar. 2020. "On Demand and Up-to-Date? Dynamic Inclusion and Data Updating for Social Assistance." Bonn: Deutsche Gesellschaft für Internationale Zusammenarbeit.

Barrientos, Armando, and David Hulme. 2009. "Social Protection for the Poor and Poorest in Developing Countries: Reflections on a Quiet Revolution." *Oxford Development Studies* 37 (4): 439–456.

Barro, Robert J. 2013. "Education and Economic Growth." *Annals of Economics and Finance* 14 (2): 301–328.

Basri, M. Chatib, and Hal Hill. 2004. "Ideas, Interests and Oil Prices: The Political Economy of Trade Reform During Soeharto's Indonesia." *The World Economy* 27 (5): 633–655.

Basri, M. Chatib, and Sjamsu Rahardja. 2011. "Should Indonesia Say Goodbye to Its Strategy of Facilitating Exports?." In Managing Openness: Trade and Outward Oriented Growth After the Crisis, edited by Mona Haddad and Ben Shepherd, 217-32. Washington, DC: World Bank.

Basri, M. Chatib, and Sjamsu Rahardja. 2011a. "Mild Crisis, Half Hearted Fiscal Stimulus: Indonesia during the GFC." In Ito, T. and F. Parulian (eds.), *Assessment on the Impact of Stimulus, Fiscal Transparency and Fiscal Risk*, 169–211. Jakarta: Economic Research Institute for ASEAN and East Asia.

Bazzi, Samuel, Sudarno Sumarto, and Asep Suryahadi. 2015. "It's All in the Timing: Cash Transfers and Consumption Smoothing in a Developing Country." *Journal of Economic Behavior & Organization* 119 (November): 267–288.

BBC News. 2022. "Kazakhstan Unrest: Government Restores Fuel Price Cap after Bloodshed." *BBC News*, January 6, 2022, sec. Asia.

Beaton, C., and L. Lontoh. 2010. "Lessons Learned from Indonesia's Attempts to Reform Fossil-Fuel Subsidies." Trade, Investment and Climate Change Series. Winnipeg: International Institute for Sustainable Development.

Beaton, Christopher, and Lucky Lontoh. 2010. *Lessons Learned from Indonesia's Attempts to Reform Fossil-Fuel Subsidies*. Winnipeg: International Institute for Sustainable Development.

Beatty, Amanda, Emilie Berkhout, Luhur Bima, Menno Pradhan, and Daniel Suryadarma. 2021. "Schooling Progress, Learning Reversal: Indonesia's Learning Profiles Between 2000 and 2014." *International Journal of Educational Development* 85 (September): 102436.

Beatty, A., E. Berkhout, L. Bima, T. Coen, M. Pradhan, and D. Suryadarma. 2018. '15 years of education in Indonesia: rising enrolment and flat learning profiles.' Paper Presented at RISE Conference July 2018.

Berenschot, Ward. 2018. "The Political Economy of Clientelism: A Comparative Study of Indonesia's Patronage Democracy." *Comparative Political Studies* 51 (12): 1563–1593.

Berkhout, Emilie, Menno Pradhan, Rahmawati, Daniel Suryadarma, and Arya Swarnata. 2020. "From Cheating to Learning: An Evaluation of Fraud Prevention on National Exams in Indonesia." 20/046. *RISE Working Paper*. Jakarta.

Berkhout, Emilie, and Florischa Ayu Tresnatri. 2020a. "How Indonesia Attempts to Address Inequity in Access to Quality Education: The Case of Junior Secondary Schools in Yogyakarta." *RISE Programme in Indonesia*. September 2, 2020. https://rise.smeru.or.id/en/blog/how-indonesia-attempts-address-inequity-access-quality-education-case-junior-secondary-schools.

Berkhout, Emilie, and Florischa Ayu Tresnatri. 2020b. "Why Low-Performing and Poor Students in Yogyakarta Do Not Go to High-Quality Junior Secondary Schools, Even If They Could." *RISE Programme in Indonesia*. September 7, 2020. https://rise.smeru.or.id/en/blog/how-indonesia-attempts-address-inequity-access-quality-education-case-junior-secondary-schools.

Besley, Timothy, and Ravi Kanbur. 1988. "Food Subsidies and Poverty Alleviation." *The Economic Journal* 98 (392): 701–719.

Bhatnagar, Deepti, Ankita Dewan, Magui Moreno Torres, and Parameeta Kanungo. 2003. "Kecamatan Development Project." 51462. Empowerment Case Studies. Washington, DC.

Blunt, Peter, Mark Turner, and Henrik Lindroth. 2012. "Patronage's Progress in Post-Soeharto Indonesia." *Public Administration and Development* 32 (1): 64–81.

Brodjonegoro, Bambang. 2009. "Fiscal Decentralization and Its Impact on Regional Economic Development and Fiscal Sustainability." In Holtzappel, J. G. and Ramstedt, M. (eds.), *Decentralization and Regional Autonomy in Indonesia: Implementation and Challenges*, 196–221. Berlin: De Gruyter Brill.

Brodjonegoro, Bambang, and Shinji Asanuma. 2000. "Regional Autonomy and Fiscal Decentralization in Democratic Indonesia." *Hitotsubashi Journal of Economics* 41 (2): 111–122.

Brown, Taylor, Emily Rudland, and Peter Bazeley. 2012. "Providing the Environment for Evidence-Based Policy Making in Indonesia: A Case Study of AusAID's Support to The National Team for Accelerating Poverty Reduction." *Office of Development Effectiveness*. Canberra: AusAID.

Cahyadi, Nur, Rema Hanna, Benjamin A. Olken, Rizal Adi Prima, Elan Satriawan, and Ekki Syamsulhakim. 2020. "Cumulative Impacts of Conditional Cash Transfer Programs: Experimental Evidence from Indonesia." *American Economic Journal: Economic Policy* 12 (4): 88–110.

Cameron, Lisa. 1999. "Survey of Recent Developments." *Bulletin of Indonesian Economic Studies* 35 (1): 3–41.

Casier, Liesbeth, and Christopher Beaton. 2015. "Fossil-Fuel Subsidy Reform and Higher Fuel Prices in Indonesia: Impacts and Expectations." Geneva: International Institute for Sustainable Development.

Chelminski, Kathryn. 2018. "Fossil Fuel Subsidy Reform in Indonesia." In Skovgaard, Jakob and Harro van Asselt (eds.), *The Politics of Fossil Fuel Subsidies and Their Reform*, 193–211. Cambridge University Press.

Coordinating Ministry for Human Development and Cultural Affairs. 2020. "Penyaluran Bantuan Langsung Tunai Dana Desa (BLT-DD) Tahun 2020 Hampir Rampung." Kementerian Koordinator Bidang Pembangunan Manusia dan Kebudayaan. December 1, 2020. https://www.kemenkopmk.go.id/penyaluran-bantuan-langsung-tunai-dana-desa-blt-dd-tahun-2020-hampir-rampung.

Dartanto, Teguh, M. Halley Yudhistira, Chaikal Nuryakin, Nurlatifah C. Hanum Siregar, Andhika Putra Pratama, Fadhila Maulida, et al. 2021. "Melihat Indonesia dari Angkasa: COVID-19 dan pemulihan ekonomi di desa." Jakarta, Indonesia, January.

De La O, Ana L. 2015. *Crafting Policies to End Poverty in Latin America.* Cambridge University Press.

Dharmawan, Goldy Fariz. 2022. "Membedah Tiga Tujuan Utama RUU Sisdiknas: Payung Hukum Baru Yang Akan Merombak Sistem Pendidikan Indonesia." The Conversation. Available at: http://theconversation.com/membedah-tiga-tujuan-utama-ruu-sisdiknas-payung-hukum-baru-yang-akan-merombak-sistem-pendidikan-indonesia-190538.

Dharmawan, Goldy Fariz, and Daniel Suryadarma. 2021. "Education Quality across Indonesia's Districts: Estimations from a Policy Experiment." *Journal of Southeast Asian Economies* 38 (3): 401–425.

Drazen, Allan, and Vittorio Grilli. 1993. "The Benefit of Crises for Economic Reforms." *The American Economic Review* 83 (3): 598–607.

Duflo, Esther. 2001. "Schooling and Labor Market Consequences of School Construction in Indonesia: Evidence from an Unusual Policy Experiment." *American Economic Review* 91 (4): 795–813.

Dunning, Thad. 2008. *Crude Democracy: Natural Resource Wealth and Political Regimes.* Cambridge: Cambridge University Press.

Erlangga, Darius, and Lizheng Shi. 2014. "Comparing Health Care Financing in Indonesia and Thailand from 1995–2010: What Lessons Could Be Learned?" *Journal of Health Economics and Outcomes Research* 1 (3): 224–238.

Faguet, Jean-Paul. 2014. "Decentralization and Governance." *World Development*, Decentralization and Governance, 53 (January): 2–13.

G20. 2019. "Indonesia's Effort to Phase Out and Rationalise Its Fossil-Fuel Subsidies." Osaka: G20.

Gaduh, Arya, Menno Pradhan, Jan Priebe, and Dewi Susanti. 2020. "Scores, Camera, Action? Incentivizing Teachers in Remote Areas." Research on Improving Systems of Education (RISE).

Galasso, E., and M. Ravallion. 2005. "Decentralized Targeting of an Antipoverty Program." *Journal of Public Economics*, Cornell - ISPE Conference on Public Finance and Development, 89 (4): 705–727.

Gibilisco, Michael. 2021. "Decentralization, Repression, and Gambling for Unity." *The Journal of Politics*, 83 (4): 1353–1369.

Haber, Stephen, and Victor Menaldo. 2011. "Do Natural Resources Fuel Authoritarianism? A Reappraisal of the Resource Curse." *The American Political Science Review* 105 (1): 1–26.

Hanna, R., and B.A. Olken. 2018. "Universal Basic Incomes versus Targeted Transfers: Anti-Poverty Programs in Developing Countries." *Journal of Economic Perspectives* 32 (4): 201–226.

Hanushek, Eric A, and Ludger Woessmann. 2008. "The Role of Cognitive Skills in Economic Development." *Journal of Economic Literature* 46 (3): 607–668.

Harimurti, Pandu, Eko Pambudi, Anna Pigazzini, and Ajay Tandon. 2013. "The Nuts and Bolts of Jamkesmas: Indonesia's Government-Financed Health Coverage Program." 74996. Universal Health Coverage Studies Series (UNICO). Washington, DC: World Bank.

Hastuti, Bambang Sulaksono, and Sulton Mawardi. 2012. "Tinjauan Efektivitas Pelaksanaan Raskin Dalam Mencapai Enam Tepat." Jakarta: SMERU Research Institute.

Hastuti, Nina Toyamah, Syaikhu Usman, Bambang Sulaksono, Sri Budiyati, Wenefrida Dwi Widyanti, Meuthia Rosfadhila, et al. 2006. "A Rapid Appraisal of the Implementation of the 2005 Direct Cash Transfer Program in Indonesia: A Case Study in Five Kabupaten/Kota." Jakarta: SMERU Research Institute.

Hastuti, S. S., Asep Suryahadi, Sulton Mawardi, Bambang Sulaksono, Akhmadi, Silvia Devina, Rima Prama Artha, Ratna Dewi, Joni Saputra, Heri Rubianto, Laode Udin, Kate Weatherley, and Joan Hardjono. 2008. *The Effectiveness of the Raskin Program.* Jakarta: The SMERU Research Institute.

Hastuti, S. Usman, B. Sulaksono, R.J. Sodo, A. Yusrina, Rahmitha, G. Hadiwidjaja, and P. Sambodho. 2016. "*Kajian Cepat Terhadap Pendataan Program Perlindungan Sosial* (PPLS) 2011." Jakarta: SMERU Research Institute.

Heywood, Peter, and Yoonjoung Choi. 2010. "Health System Performance at the District Level in Indonesia After Decentralization." *BMC International Health and Human Rights* 10 (1): 3.

Hill, Hal. 2013. "The Political Economy of Policy Reform: Insights from Southeast Asia." *Asian Development Review* 30 (1): 108–130.

Hook, Walter, and Michael Replogle. 1996. "Motorization and Non-Motorized Transport in Asia: Transport System Evolution in China, Japan and Indonesia." *Land Use Policy* 13 (1): 69–84.

Houtenville, Andrew J., and Karen Smith Conway. 2008. "Parental Effort, School Resources, and Student Achievement." *Journal of Human Resources* 43 (2): 437–453.

Howes, Stephen, and Robin Davies. 2014. "Survey of Recent Developments." *Bulletin of Indonesian Economic Studies* 50 (2): 157–183.

Huang, Aris R., Shintia Revina, Rizki Fillaili, and Akhmadi. 2020. "The Struggle to Recruit Good Teachers in Indonesia: Institutional and Social Dysfunctions." Research on Improving Systems of Education (RISE).

Hults, David R. 2011. "Petróleos de Venezuela, S.A. (PDVSA): From Independence to Subservience." In *Oil and Governance: State-Owned Enterprises and the World Energy Supply*, edited by David G. Victor, David R. Hults, and Mark C. Thurber, 418–477. Cambridge: Cambridge University Press.

Inchauste, Gabriela, and David G. Victor. 2017. *The Political Economy of Energy Subsidy Reform.* World Bank Publications.

Indonesia Statistics. 2020. "Booklet Survei Angkatan Kerja Nasional Februari 2020." Jakarta.

Indonesia Statistics. 2021. "Booklet Survei Angkatan Kerja Nasional Februari 2021." Jakarta.

International Energy Agency, Organisation for Economic Co-Operation and Development, and World Bank. 2010. "The Scope of Fossil-Fuel Subsidies in 2009 and a Roadmap for Phasing Out Fossil-Fuel Subsidies." G-20 Summit Joint Report.

International Labour Organization. 2002. *Social Security in Indonesia: Advancing the Development Agenda.* Geneva: International Labour Organization. Accessed March 6, 2026. https://www.ilo.org/media/296861/download

International Labour Organization. 2022. "World Social Protection Data." 2022. www.social-protection.org.

International Monetary Fund. 1998. "Indonesia Letter of Intent, November 13, 1998."1998. https://www.imf.org/external/np/loi/1113a98.htm.

International Monetary Fund. 2020. "World Economic Outlook Update: January 2020." Washington, DC: International Monetary Fund.

Isdijoso, Widjajanti, A. Suryahadi, and Akhmadi. 2016. "*Penetapan Kriteria Dan Variabel Pendataan Penduduk Miskin Yang Komprehensif Dalam Rangka Perlindungan Penduduk Miskin Di Kabupaten/Kota.*" SMERU Working Paper. Jakarta: SMERU Research Institute.

Johar, Meliyanni, Retno Pujisubekti, Prastuti Soewondo, Harsa Kunthara Satrio, and Ardi Adji. 2018. "Access Inequity, Health Insurance and the Role of Supply Factors." *Social Science & Medicine* 213: 134–145.

Jung, Eunsook. 2016. "Campaigning for All Indonesians: The Politics of Healthcare in Indonesia." *Contemporary Southeast Asia* 38 (3): 476–494.

Kacaribu, Febrio. 2020. "Social Protection Programs to Respond COVID-19 Pandemic." Jakarta, Indonesia, September 22.

Kementerian Pendidikan Dasar dan Menengah. "Data Pokok Pendidikan (DAPODIK) – Data Sekolah." https://dapo.kemendikdasmen.go.id/sp

Komite Pemberantasan Korupsi. 2020. "KPK Minta Pemerintah Tunda Program Kartu Prakerja." Press Release. Jakarta. www.kpk.go.id/id/berita/siaran-pers/1700-kpk-minta-pemerintah-tunda-program-kartu-prakerja.

Kurniawan, Asep. 2020. "Bantual Langsung Tunai Dana Desa Untuk Menangani Dampak Pandemi COVID-19: Cerita Dari Desa." 04/2020. Catatan Penelitian SMERU. Jakarta: SMERU Research Institute.

Kurniawati, Sandra, Daniel Suryadarma, Luhur Bima, and Asri Yusrina. 2019. "Education in Indonesia: A White Elephant?" In *The Indonesian Economy in Transition*, edited by Hal Hill and Siwage Dharma Negara, 185–199. Singapore: ISEAS–Yusof Ishak Institute.

Laan, Tara, and Neil McCulloch. 2019. "Energy Transition in Support of the Low-Carbon Development Initiative in Indonesia: Transport Sector." Geneva: International Institute for Sustainable Development.

Lal, Deepak, and Hla Myint. 1996. *The Political Economy of Poverty, Equity, and Growth.* Oxford: Oxford University Press.

Leite, P., T.G. Karippacheril, C. Sun, T. Jones, and K. Lindert. 2017. "Social Registries for Social Assistance and Beyond: A Guidance Note & Assessment Tool." https://openknowledge.worldbank.org/entities/publication/fa0d1270-2511-5f30-80fd-90b3feb5b03d

Leite, P. G., P. George, T. George, C. Sun, T. Jones, and K. A. Lindert. *Social Registries for Social Assistance and Beyond: A Guidance Note and Assessment Tool.* Social Protection and Labor Discussion Paper No. 1704. Washington, DC: World Bank Group. http://documents.worldbank.org/curated/en/698441502095248081

Lee, Jong-Wha and Ruth Francisco. 2012. "Human Capital Accumulation in Emerging Asia, 1970–2030." *Japan and the World Economy* 24 (2): 76–86.

Lindert, K., C. Andrews, C. Msowoya, B.V. Paul, E. Chirwa, and A. Mittal. 2018. "Rapid Social Registry Assessment: Malawi's Unified Beneficiary Registry (UBR)." 1803. Social Protection & Jobs Discussion Paper. Washington, DC: World Bank.

Lockley, A., J. Tobias, and A. Bah. 2013. "*Hasil Kajian Gender Dari Basis Data Terpadu.*" Jakarta: TNP2K.

Lockley, A., J. Tobias, and A. Bah. 2021. "SIKS-NG | *Data Terpadu Kesejahteraan Sosial.*" *Data Terpadu Kesejahteraan Sosial.* 2021. https://dtks.kemensos.go.id/Profil%20DTKS/topic/333.

Manning, Chris. 2000. "Labour Market Adjustment to Indonesia's Economic Crisis: Context, Trends and Implications." *Bulletin of Indonesian Economic Studies* 36 (1): 105–136.

Marzoeki, Puti, Ajay Tandon, Xiaolu Bi, and Eko Setyo Pambudi. 2014. "Universal Health Coverage for Inclusive and Sustainable Development: Country Summary Report for Indonesia." 91217. Japan–World Bank Partnership Program for Universal Health Coverage. Jakarta.

Maulana, Nirwan, Prastuti Soewondo, Nadhila Adani, Paulina Limasalle, and Anooj Pattnaik. 2022. "How Jaminan Kesehatan Nasional (JKN) Coverage Influences out-of-Pocket (OOP) Payments by Vulnerable Populations in Indonesia." *PLOS Global Public Health* 2 (7): e0000203.

Mboi, Nafsiah. 2015. "Indonesia: On the Way to Universal Health Care." *Health Systems & Reform* 1 (2): 91–97.

McAuley. 2018. "France Suspends Fuel Tax after Weeks of Unrest." *The Washington Post*, December 4, 2018.

McCawley, Peter. 2014. "The Sum Is Greater Than the Parts: Doubling Shared Prosperity in Indonesia through Local and Global Integration." *Bulletin of Indonesian Economic Studies* 50 (2): 300–302.

McKenzie, Phillip, Dita Nugroho, Clare Ozolins, Julie McMillan, Sudarno Sumarto, Nina Toyamah, et al. 2014. "Teacher Absenteeism in Indonesia: Policy Brief." Education Sector Analytical and Capacity Development Partnership.

Miller, Gary J. 2005. "The Political Evolution of Principal-Agent Models." *Annual Review of Political Science* 8 (1): 203–225.

Ministry of Co-operatives and SMEs. 2018. "Perkembangan Data Usaha Mikro, Kecil, Menengah (UMKM) dan Usaha Besar (UB 2017–2018)." Jakarta, Indonesia: Kementerian Koperasi dan UKM.

Ministry of Finance. 2006. "Laporan Keuangan Pemerintah Pusat Tahun 2005." Jakarta: Kementerian Keuangan Republik Indonesia.

Ministry of Finance. 2016. *Nota Keuangan dan Anggaran Pendapatan dan Belanja Negara Tahun Anggaran 2016*. Jakarta: Ministry of Finance. https://anggaran.kemenkeu.go.id/assets/FTPPortal/Peraturan/NK%20UU%20APBN%20Lapsem/NK%20APBN%202016.pdf

Ministry of Finance. 2020. "*UMKM Bangkit Ekonomi Indonesia Terungkit*." Jakarta: Ministry of Finance. https://www.djkn.kemenkeu.go.id/artikel/baca/13317/UMKM-Bangkit-Ekonomi-Indonesia-Terungkit.html.

Ministry of Finance. 2021a. "Laporan Monev PEN s/d Jumat 24 Desember 2021." Jakarta: Ministry of Finance.

Ministry of Finance. 2021b. "Laporan Monev PEN s/d Senin 4 Januari 2021." Jakarta: Ministry of Finance.

Ministry of Finance. 2021c. "Pemulihan Ekonomi Nasional 2021." Jakarta.

Ministry of Manpower. 2020. "Menaker: Badai Pasti Berlalu, Panggil Kembali Pekerja yang ter-PHK Nanti." Kementerian Ketenagakerjaan Republik Indonesia. April 22, 2020. https://www.kemnaker.go.id/news/detail/menaker-badai-pasti-berlalu-panggil-kembali-pekerja-yang-ter-phk-nanti.

Ministry of Social Affairs. 2020. "*Kebangkitan (Data) Nasional*." Jakarta: Ministry of Social Affairs. https://kemensos.go.id/kebangkitan-data-nasional.

National Social Security Council. 2024. "Sistem Monitoring Dan Evaluasi Jaminan Sosial." https://sismonev.djsn.go.id/.

Nehru, Vikram. 2013. "Manufacturing in India and Indonesia: Performance and Policies." *Bulletin of Indonesian Economic Studies* 49 (1): 35–60. doi:10.1080/00074918.2013.772938.

Nichols, Albert L., and Richard J. Zeckhauser. 1982. "Targeting Transfers through Restrictions on Recipients." *The American Economic Review* 72 (2): 372–377.

Nielsen, H. Dean. 1998. "Reforms to Teacher Education in Indonesia: Does More Mean Better?" *Asia Pacific Journal of Education* 18 (2): 9–25. Organisation for Economic Co-Operation and Development. 2023. "Country Notes: Indonesia."

Nikijuluw, Ruth. 2021. "The Impact of Female Leadership on Public Spending and Service Access: Causal Evidence from Indonesia." Presented at the ASE Session at ASSA National Meeting 2021, Canberra. https://www.aeaweb.org/conference/2021/preliminary/powerpoint/h39HdhaQ.

OECD. 2019. "Indonesia's Effort to Phase Out and Rationalise Its Fossil-Fuel Subsidies." Osaka: Organisation for Economic Co-operation and Development.

Olken, Benjamin A. 2006. "Corruption and the Costs of Redistribution: Micro Evidence from Indonesia." *Journal of Public Economics* 90 (4): 853–870.

Olken, Benjamin A. 2007. "Monitoring Corruption: Evidence from a Field Experiment in Indonesia." *Journal of Political Economy* 115 (2): 200–249.

Olken, Benjamin A., Musriyadi Nabiu, Nina Toyamah, and Daniel Perwira. 2001. "Sharing the Wealth: How Villages Decide to Distribute OPK Rice." SMERU Working Papers. Jakarta.

Organisation for Economic Co-Operation and Development. 2023. "Country Notes: Indonesia." PISA 2022 Results (Volume I and II). Paris: Organisation for Economic Co-operation and Development. https://www.oecd.org/en/publications/2023/11/pisa-2022-results-volume-i-and-ii-country-notes_2fca04b9/indonesia_0e09c072.html.

Perdana, Ari A. 2014. "The Future of Social Welfare Programs in Indonesia: From Fossil-Fuel Subsidies to Better Social Protection." Geneva: International Institute for Sustainable Development.

Perhimpunan Rumah Sakit Seluruh Indonesia. 2024. "Jelang Implementasi KRIS, Inilah Tantangan Yang Dihadapi RS Swasta." 2024. https://www.persi.or.id/jelang-implementasi-kris-inilah-tantangan-yang-dihadapi-rs-swasta/.

Pierskalla, Jan H., and Audrey Sacks. 2020. "Personnel Politics: Elections, Clientelistic Competition and Teacher Hiring in Indonesia." *British Journal of Political Science* 50 (4): 1283–1305.

Pisani, Elizabeth, Maarten Olivier Kok, and Kharisma Nugroho. 2017. "Indonesia's Road to Universal Health Coverage: A Political Journey." *Health Policy and Planning* 32 (2): 267–76.

Pradhan, Menno, Asep Suryahadi, Sudarno Sumarto, and Lant Pritchett. 2001. "Eating like Which 'Joneses?' An Iterative Solution to the Choice of a Poverty Line 'Reference Group.'" *Review of Income and Wealth* 47 (4): 473–487.

Pratiwi, Indah. 2019. "Efek Program PISA terhadap Kurikulum di Indonesia." *Journal Pendidikan dan Kebudayaan* 4 (1): 51–71.

Presiden Republik Indonesia. 2014. *Peraturan Presiden Republik Indonesia Nomor 191 Tahun 2014 Tentang Penyediaan, Pendistribusian, Dan Harga Jual Eceran Bahan Bakar Minyak.*

Priebe, Jan. 2014. "Official Poverty Measurement in Indonesia since 1984: A Methodological Review." *Bulletin of Indonesian Economic Studies* 50 (2): 185–205.

Pritchett, Lant, Sudarno Sumarto, and Asep Suryahadi. 2001. "Targeted Programs in an Economic Crisis: Empirical Findings from Indonesia's Experience." *MPRA Paper*, no. 58727: 1–53.

Pritchett, Lant, Sudarno Sumarto, and Asep Suryahadi. 2002. "Targeted Programs in an Economic Crisis: Empirical Findings from the Experience of Indonesia." *SMERU Research Institute Working Paper.*

de Ree, Joppe, Karthik Muralidharan, Menno Pradhan, and Halsey Rogers. 2018. "Double for Nothing? Experimental Evidence on an Unconditional Teacher Salary Increase in Indonesia." *The Quarterly Journal of Economics* 133 (2): 993–1039.

Rentschler, Jun, and Morgan Bazilian. 2017. "Policy Monitor—Principles for Designing Effective Fossil Fuel Subsidy Reforms." *Review of Environmental Economics and Policy* 11 (1): 138–155.

Revina, Shintia. 2019. "Rapor Kompetensi Guru SD Indonesia Merah, dan Upaya Pemerintah untuk Meningkatkannya Belum Tepat." *The Conversation Indonesia*, July 20. https://theconversation.com/rapor-kompetensi-guru-sd-indonesia-merah-dan-upaya-pemerintah-untuk-meningkatkannya-belum-tepat-120287

Revina, Shintia. 2022. "Rapor Kompetensi Guru SD Indonesia Merah, Dan Upaya Pemerintah Untuk Meningkatkannya Belum Tepat." The Conversation. Accessed November 2, 2022. http://theconversation.com/rapor-kompetensi-guru-sd-indonesia-merah-dan-upaya-pemerintah-untuk-meningkatkannya-belum-tepat-120287.

Revina, Shintia, Rezanti Putri Pramana, Rizki Fillaili, and Daniel Suryadarma. 2020. "Systemic Constraints Facing Teacher Professional Development in a Middle-Income Country: Indonesia's Experience Over Four Decades." *RISE Working Paper.* Jakarta: SMERU Research Institute.

Rizal, Jawahir Gustav. 2020. "Kritik Kartu Prakerja, Muncul Prakerja.Org Yang Berikan Pelatihan Daring Gratis." *KOMPAS.Com*, May 17, 2020. https://www.kompas.com/tren/read/2020/05/17/080034465/kritik-kartu-prakerja-muncul-prakerjaorg-yang-berikan-pelatihan-daring?page=all.

Rokx, Claudia, George Schieber, Pandu Harimurti, Ajay Tandon, and Aparnaa Somanathan. 2009. "Health Financing in Indonesia: A Reform Road Map." Washington, DC: World Bank.

Ross, Michael L. 2012. *The Oil Curse: How Petroleum Wealth Shapes the Development of Nations.* Princeton University Press.

Rosser, Andrew, and Mohamad Fahmi. 2018. "The Political Economy of Teacher Management Reform in Indonesia." *International Journal of Educational Development* 61 (July): 72–81.

Saputri, Nurmala Selly, Arif Budi Darmawan, Nina Toyamah, and Rizki Fillaili. 2024. "Political Economy Analysis of Health Financing Reforms in Times of Crisis: Identifying Windows of Opportunity for Countries in the SEA Region; Indonesia Case Study Report." SMERU Research Report. The SMERU Research Institute.

Satriawan, Elan, Ari A. Perdana, and Rizal Adi Prima. 2015. "Pembelajaran Dari Uji Coba Desain Baru Raskin 2012: Temuan Dari Studi Penantauan TNP2K." TNP2K Working Paper. Jakarta.

Satriawan, Elan, and Ranjan Shrestha. 2018. "Mistargeting and Regressive Take Up of the Indonesian Rice Subsidy Program." *Asian Economic Journal* 32 (4): 387–415.

Sátyro, N.G.D., and J. Mostafa. 2014. "Cadastro Único: A Registry Supported by a National Public Bank." *International Policy Centre for Inclusive Growth (IPC-IG) Working Paper* 126: 18.

Scott, J.C. 1998. *Seeing Like a State: How Certain Schemes to Improve the Human Condition Have Failed.* Yale University Press.

Sdralevich, Carlo, Randa Sab, Younes Zouhar, and Giorgia Albertin, eds. 2014. *Subsidy Reform in the Middle East and North Africa: Recent Progress and Challenges Ahead.* Washington, DC: International Monetary Fund, Middle East and Central Asia Dep.

Sen, A. 1976. "Poverty: An Ordinal Approach to Measurement." *Econometrica* 44 (2): 219–231.

Seymour, Richard, and Sarah Turner. 2002. "Otonomi Daerah: Indonesia's Decentralisation Experiment." *New Zealand Journal of Asian Studies* 4 (2): 33–51.

Shrestha, Ranjan. 2021. "Health Insurance for the Poor, Healthcare Use and Health Outcomes in Indonesia." *Bulletin of Indonesian Economic Studies* 57 (1): 85–110. https://doi.org/10.1080/00074918.2020.1753655.

Siddig, Khalid, Angel Aguiar, Harald Grethe, Peter Minor, and Terrie Walmsley. 2014. "Impacts of Removing Fuel Import Subsidies in Nigeria on Poverty." *Energy Policy* 69 (June): 165–178.

SMERU Research Institute, UNDP, and UNICEF. 2020. "The Social and Economic Impacts of COVID-19 on Households and Strategic Policy Recommendations for Indonesia." Jakarta, Indonesia.

Sparrow, Robert. 2007. "Protecting Education for the Poor in Times of Crisis: An Evaluation of a Scholarship Programme in Indonesia." *Oxford Bulletin of Economics and Statistics* 69 (1): 99–122.

Statistics Indonesia. 2011. "*Rumah Tangga Sasaran (RTS) Provinsi Jawa Tengah: Hasil Pendataan Program Perlindungan Sosial 2008* (PPLS08)." Jakarta: Statistics Indonesia.

Statistics Indonesia. 2021. "*Pendataan Program Perlindungan Sosial* (PPLS) 2011 (Indonesian Version)." Jakarta: Badan Pusat Statistik. https://www.bps.go.id/news/2011/07/11/4/pendataan-program-perlindungan-sosial--ppls--2011–indonesian-version-.html.

Statistics Indonesia. 2020a. "Profil Kemiskinan di Indonesia Maret 2020." Berita Resmi Statistik. Jakarta, Indonesia: Indonesia Statistics.

Statistics Indonesia. 2020b. "Keadaan Ketenagakerjaan Indonesia Agustus 2020." Berita Resmi Statistik. Jakarta, Indonesia: Indonesia Statistics.

Statistics Indonesia. 2021a. "Pertumbuhan Ekonomi Indonesia Triwulan I –2021." Berita Resmi Statistik. Jakarta, Indonesia: Statistics Indonesia.

Statistics Indonesia. 2021b. "Pertumbuhan Ekonomi Indonesia Triwulan II –2021." Berita Resmi Statistik. Jakarta, Indonesia: Statistics Indonesia.

Statistics Indonesia. 2024. "Statistik Keuangan Pemerintah Desa 2022 dan 2023." Jakarta: Badan Pusat Statistik.

Sumarto, S. 2024. "Promoting Better Targeting to Achieve Indonesia with Zero Extreme Poverty in 2024." Presented at the South-South Learning J-PAL, Jakarta, Indonesia.

Sumarto, S, E. Satriawan, B.A. Olken, A. Banerjee, A. Tohari, V. Alatas, and R. Hanna. 2025. "Community Targeting at Scale." *NBER Working Paper Series*, 33322. Cambridge, MA: National Bureau of Economic Research.

Sumarto, S., A. Suryahadi, and W. Widyanti. 2002. "Designs and Implementation of Indonesian Social Safety Net Programs." *The Developing Economies* 40 (1): 3–31.

Sumarto, Sudarno, Asep Suryahadi, and Lant Pritchett. 2000. "Safety Nets and Safety Ropes: Comparing the Dynamic Benefit Incidence of Two Indonesian 'JPS' Programs." Jakarta: SMERU Research Institute.

Sumarto, Sudarno, Asep Suryahadi, and Wenefrida Widyanti. 2001. "Designs and Implementation of the Indonesian Safety Programs: Evidence from the JPS Module in the 1999 SUSENAS." Jakarta: SMERU Research Institute.

Sumarto, Sudarno, Asep Suryahadi, and Wenefrida Widyanti. 2010. "Design and Implementation of the Indonesian Social Safety Net Programs." In Hardjono, Joan, Nuning Akhmadi, and Sudarno Sumarto (eds.), *Poverty and Social Protection in Indonesia*, 111–148. Singapore: Institute of Southeast Asian Studies.

Suryahadi, Asep, Gracia Hadiwidjaja, and Sudarno Sumarto. 2012. "Economic Growth and Poverty Reduction in Indonesia before and after the Asian Financial Crisis." *Bulletin of Indonesian Economic Studies* 48 (2): 209–227.

Suryahadi, Asep, Ridho Al Izzati, and Daniel Suryadarma. 2020. "The Impact of COVID-19 Outbreak on Poverty: An Estimation for Indonesia." *SMERU Research Institute Working Paper.*

Suryahadi, Asep, Ridho Al Izzati, and Athia Yumna. 2021. "The Impact of Covid-19 and Social Protection Programs on Poverty in Indonesia." *Bulletin of Indonesian Economic Studies* 57 (3): 175–192.

Suryahadi, Asep, Yusuf Suharso, and Sudarno Sumarto. 2001. "Coverage and Targeting in the Indonesian Social Safety Net Programmes." *ASEAN Economic Bulletin* 18 (2): 161–175.

Suryahadi, Asep, Sudarno Sumarto, and Lant Pritchett. 2003. "Evolution of Poverty During the Crisis in Indonesia." *Asian Economic Journal* 17 (3): 221–241.

Suryahadi, Asep, Athia Yumna, and Deswanto Marbun. n.d. "Review of Government's Poverty Reduction Strategies, Policies, and Programs in Indonesia." https://smeru.or.id/sites/default/files/publication/povertyreductionreview.pdf

Sutanto, Agus, and Ahmad Avenzora. 1999. *Pengukuran tingkat kemiskinan di Indonesia 1976–1999: Metode BPS.* Jakarta: BPS.

Syarifah, Zahra A. 2022. "Women's Role in Family Survival Amidst the COVID-19 Pandemic." Policy Brief. Jakarta: National Team for the Acceleration of Poverty Reduction (TNP2K).

Syukri, Muhammad, Palmira Permata Bachtiar, Asep Kurniawan, Gema Satria Mayang Sedyadi, Kartawijaya, Rendy Adriyan Diningrat, and Ulfah Alifia. 2018. "Studi Implementasi Undang-Undang No. 6 Tahun 2014 Tentang Desa Laporan Baseline." Laporan Penelitian SMERU. Jakarta: SMERU Research Institute.

Tabor, Steven R., and M. Husein Sawit. 2001. "Social Protection Via Rice: The Opk Rice Subsidy Program in Indonesia." *The Developing Economies* 39 (3): 267–294.

Thabrany, Hasbullah. 2008. *Politics of National Health Insurance of Indonesia.* Jakarta: Center for Health Economic and Policy Studies.

TNP2K. 2015. "Indonesia's Unified Database for Social Protection Programmes: Management Standards." Jakarta: TNP2K.

TNP2K. 2015. "Raskin: The Challenge of Improving Programme Effectiveness." Jakarta: TNP2K.

TNP2K. 2015. "The Road to National Health Insurance (JKN)." Jakarta: TNP2K.

TNP2K. 2017. "Basis Data Terpadu 2015." Jakarta: TNP2K.

TNP2K. 2018. "Monitoring of the Rastra Social Assistance (Bansos Rastra) Implementation January–February, 2018." Jakarta, April.

TNP2K. 2018. "The Future of the Social Protection System in Indonesia: Social Protection for All." Jakarta: National Team for the Acceleration of Poverty Reduction (TNP2K).

TNP2K. 2019. "*Menanggulangi Kemiskinan Dan Mengurangi Kesenjangan Melalui Peningkatan Efektivitas Kebijakan Dan Program: Laporan Pelaksanaan Tugas Sekretariat* TNP2K 2015–2019." Jakarta: TNP2K.

TNP2K. 2020. "Memo Internal Kemiskinan Maret 2020." Memo Internal. Jakarta, Indonesia: TNP2K.

TNP2K. 2020. "Policy Note: Maximising the Benefits of Program Sembako During the COVID-19 Pandemic." Jakarta.

TNP2K. 2021. "*Data Terpadu Kesejahteraan Sosial.*" Presented at the Internal Meeting, Jakarta.

Todd, Petra E., and Kenneth I. Wolpin. 2007. "The Production of Cognitive Achievement in Children: Home, School, and Racial Test Score Gaps." *Journal of Human Capital* 1 (1): 91–136.

Tohari, A., C. Parsons, and A. Rammohan. 2019. "Targeting Poverty under Complementarities: Evidence from Indonesia's Unified Targeting System." *Journal of Development Economics* 140 (September): 127–144.

Torani, Kiran, Gordon Rausser, and David Zilberman. 2016. "Innovation Subsidies versus Consumer Subsidies: A Real Options Analysis of Solar Energy." *Energy Policy* 92 (May): 255–269.

Torrens, Anthony. 2005. "Economic Impact Analysis of Kecamatan Development Program Infrastructure Projects." 93698. Jakarta: World Bank.

Tresnatri, Florischa Ayu, Asep Kurniawan, Daniel Suryadarma, Shintia Revina, and Niken Rarasati. 2020. "Human Capital Index." Text/HTML. World Bank. 2020. https://www.worldbank.org/en/publication/human-capital.

Tresnatri, Florischa Ayu, Asep Kurniawan, Daniel Suryadarma, Shintia Revina, and Niken Rarasati. 2022. "Does Higher Parental Involvement Lead to Learning Gains? Experimental Evidence from Indonesia." Research on Improving Systems of Education (RISE).

UNICEF. 2020. "Situasi Anak Di Indonesia: Tren, Peluang, Dan Tantangan Dalam Memenuhi Hak-Hak Anak." Jakarta: UNICEF Indonesia.

Vagliasindi, Maria. 2013. "Implementing Energy Subsidy Reforms : Evidence from Developing Countries." Washington, DC.

Widianto, B. 2012. "*Pengelolaan Dan Pemanfaatan Basis Data Terpadu Untuk Program Perlindungan Sosial.*" Jakarta: TNP2K.

Wie, Thee Kian. 2002. "The Soeharto Era and after: Stability, Development and Crisis, 1966–2000." In, Houben, V.J.H and J.Th.Lindblad (eds,), *The Emergence of a National Economy*, 194–243. Crows Nest: Allen and Unwin.

Wisnu, Dinna. 2007. "Governing Social Security: Economic Crisis and Reform in Indonesia, the Philippines and Singapore." PhD Dissertation, Colombus: Ohio State University.

Wisnu, Dinna, Faisal Basri, and Gatot Arya Putra. 2017. "Ambitious but Inadequate: Social Welfare Policies under Yudhoyono." In Aspinall, Edward, Marcus Mietzner, and Dirk Tomsa (eds.), *The Yudhoyono Presidency: Indonesia's Decade of Stability and Stagnation*, 325–344. Singapore: ISEAS–Yusof Ishak Institute.

World Bank. 2004. "Making a Pro-Poor Budget Reallocation: A Strategy to Help the Poor While Reducing Fuel Subsidies." World Bank Office Jakarta, October 18.

World Bank. 2015. *Purchasing Power Parities and the Real Size of World Economies: A Comprehensive Report of the 2011 International Comparison Program.* The World Bank.

World Bank. 2018. "Indonesia Economic Quarterly, June 2018: Learning More, Growing Faster." *Economic Updates and Modeling*. https://elibrary.worldbank.org/doi/epdf/10.1596/29921.

World Bank. 2020. "The Long Road to Recovery." Indonesia Economic Prospects. Jakarta, Indonesia: World Bank.

World Bank. 2022. "Fact Sheet: An Adjustment to Global Poverty Lines." The World Bank. 2022. https://www.worldbank.org/en/news/factsheet/2022/05/02/fact-sheet-an-adjustment-to-global-poverty-lines#6.

World Bank. 2024. "Mortality Rate, Infant (per 1000 Live Births) - Indonesia." World Bank Open Data. 2024. https://data.worldbank.org.

World Bank. n.d. "World Bank Open Data." World Bank Open Data. Accessed May 2, 2024. https://data.worldbank.org.

World Health Organization. 2022. "Global Spending on Health: Rising to the Pandemic's Challenges." Geneva: World Health Organization. https://iris.who.int/bitstream/handle/10665/365133/9789240064911-eng.pdf.

World Health Organization. 2023. "Global Health Workforce Statistics." https://www.who.int/data/gho/data/themes/topics/health-workforce.

World Health Organization. 2024. "The Global Health Observatory." https://www.who.int/data/gho/data/indicators.

World Health Organization. 2026. *Global Health Observatory Data: Indicators*. https://www.who.int/data/gho/data/indicator

Wright, G., M. Noble, H. Barnes, A. Moechtar, D. McLennan, A. Anshory Yusuf, K. Gasior, and R. Muyanto. 2021. "Estimating the Distributional Impacts of the COVID-19 Pandemic and the Remedial Tax and Benefit Policies in Indonesia." *International Journal of Microsimulation* 14(2): 50–80.

Xie, Yihao, and Marietta Harjono. 2020. "The Retail Fuels Market in Indonesia." 2020–2023. International Council on Clean Transportation Working Paper. Washington, DC: International Council on Clean Transportation.

Yemtsov, Ruslan, and Amr Moubarak. 2018. *Energy Subsidy Reform Assessment Framework*. ESMAP Papers. World Bank.

Yusrina, Asri, Ulfah Alifia, Shintia Revina, Rezanti Putri Pramana, and Luhur Bima. 2022. "Is the Game Worth the Candle? Examining the Effectiveness of Initial Teacher Education in Indonesia." Research on Improving Systems of Education (RISE).

Yusrina, Asri, Luhur Bima, Emilie Berkhout, and Daniel Suryadarma. 2022. "Selecting Teachers in Indonesia: Predicting Teacher Performance Using Pre-Employment Information." Research on Improving Systems of Education (RISE).

Yusuf, Arief Anshory. 2020. "Economic Impact of the COVID-19 Pandemic." Jakarta, Indonesia.

Yusuf, Arief A., Arianto A. Patunru, and Budy P. Resosudarmo. 2017. "Reducing Petroleum Subsidy in Indonesia: An Interregional General Equilibrium Analysis." In *Regional Growth and Sustainable Development in Asia*, edited by Amitrajeet A. Batabyal and Peter Nijkamp, 91–112. New Frontiers in Regional Science: Asian Perspectives. Cham: Springer International Publishing.

Sen, Kunal, and Steer, Liesbet (2005). "Survey of Recent Developments." *Bulletin of Indonesian Economic Studies*, 42(3): 279–304.

Index

For the benefit of digital users, indexed terms that span two pages (e.g., 52–53) may, on occasion, appear on only one of those pages.

Tables, figures, and boxes are indicated by an italic *t*, *f*, or *b*.